In *Transforming English Through Drama*, Jane Coles and Maggie Pitfield have presented an overwhelmingly forceful argument for the enactment of the 'drama-in-English' pedagogy formulated in their earlier work, *Drama at the Heart of English*. This collection of international classroom-based case studies offers powerfully persuasive accounts of the ways in which 'drama-in-English' approaches can foster enjoyment and motivation, stimulate creativity and create rich and meaningful learning for students. Coles and Pitfield rightly argue that English is in need of transformation; for all those involved in the subject who share this view, and who believe in the centrality of effective learning and teaching of English for young people's development *Transforming English Through Drama* should be essential reading.

Simon Gibbons, *Reader in English Education, King's College London*

Maggie Pitfield and Jane Coles are to be warmly congratulated on their new edited book, *Transforming English Through Drama: Case Studies in Classroom Practice*. This wide-ranging collection promises to be an invaluable handbook for English, Language Arts, English as Additional Language teachers and the broader drama-in-education community. Each chapter makes a strong case for embedding drama-rich strategies and experiences in fostering deep and critical literacy learning. An experienced group of researchers and practitioners demonstrate how these inherently inquiry-based approaches motivate and engage learners, nurturing their creativity and imagination while drawing on their own identities and cultural understandings. A very welcome and very timely addition to the field.

Robyn Ewing AM, *Professor Emerita, Co-Director, The CREATE Centre, Faculty of Arts and Social Sciences, University of Sydney*

The push to bring in the 'knowledge-rich curriculum' has swept aside much of the arts curriculum in schools and one victim of this has been drama. Maggie Pitfield and Jane Coles have done a superb job here of building on their previous work by drawing in other practitioners to the cause. *Transforming English Through Drama: Case Studies in Classroom Practice* is a timely and much-needed book which lays out both the 'what' and the 'why' of collaborative drama work in schools, specifically in subject English.

Michael Rosen, *Professor of Children's Literature, Goldsmiths, University of London; poet and children's author*

Transforming English Through Drama

This unique collection promotes and develops 'drama-in-English', a hybrid pedagogy combining reader response theory with literacy research and educational drama. Drawing on experienced practitioners' classroom insights, the authors show how embedded drama approaches can be used to revitalise the English/Language Arts curriculum and motivate young people to make personal and critical connections with their learning.

Readers will find eight reader-friendly accounts exploring how drama-inflected approaches support diverse learners across all aspects of English teaching. Contributors discuss engaging with literary texts through spoken, written, and multimodal responses; digital storytelling; embodied approaches to creative and informative writing; developing language competency; and preparation for formal examinations. The research-informed content, rooted in real classroom practice, demonstrates sustainable and fully integrated creative approaches applicable to UK and international contexts.

This essential resource benefits all those working in English/Language Arts education: secondary teachers, teacher educators, trainee teachers, and teachers of English as an additional language.

Maggie Pitfield, an experienced English and Drama teacher, is currently a Research and Knowledge Exchange Fellow at Goldsmiths, University of London.

Jane Coles, a former Head of English and Deputy Headteacher, is also an experienced teacher educator and educational researcher, most recently at UCL's Institute of Education.

Maggie and Jane are joint recipients of the NATE Outstanding Contribution to Research award (2024).

Transforming English Through Drama

Case Studies in Classroom Practice

Edited by Maggie Pitfield and Jane Coles

LONDON AND NEW YORK

Designed cover image: © Getty Images

First published 2026
by Routledge
4 Park Square, Milton Park, Abingdon, Oxon OX14 4RN

and by Routledge
605 Third Avenue, New York, NY 10158

Routledge is an imprint of the Taylor & Francis Group, an Informa business

© 2026 selection and editorial matter, Maggie Pitfield and Jane Coles; individual chapters, the contributors

The right of Maggie Pitfield and Jane Coles to be identified as the authors of the editorial material, and of the authors for their individual chapters, has been asserted in accordance with sections 77 and 78 of the Copyright, Designs and Patents Act 1988.

All rights reserved. No part of this book may be reprinted or reproduced, or utilised in any form or by any electronic, mechanical, or other means, now known or hereafter invented, including photocopying and recording, or in any information storage or retrieval system, without permission in writing from the publishers.

For Product Safety Concerns and Information please contact our EU representative GPSR@taylorandfrancis.com. Taylor & Francis Verlag GmbH, Kaufingerstraße 24, 80331 München, Germany.

Trademark notice: Product or corporate names may be trademarks or registered trademarks and are used only for identification and explanation without intent to infringe.

British Library Cataloguing-in-Publication Data
A catalogue record for this book is available from the British Library

ISBN: 978-1-041-10553-4 (hbk)
ISBN: 978-1-041-10540-4 (pbk)
ISBN: 978-1-003-65567-1 (ebk)

DOI: 10.4324/9781003655664

Typeset in Times New Roman
by SPi Technologies India Pvt Ltd (Straive)

Contents

List of Contributors   ix
Acknowledgements   xi

1 **Introduction**   1
JANE COLES AND MAGGIE PITFIELD

2 **Adapting Texts, Adapting Practice: Applying Rehearsal Room Methodology to the Study of Novels**   18
SUSIE FERGUSON

3 **Drama in English: A Decolonial Strategy**   33
KATHERINE BARBER

4 **Shakespeare on Zoom!**   49
ERIN WOODFORD

5 **Writing-in-Role: The Significance of Visualising Fictional Worlds Through Drama**   62
THEO BRYER

6 **Drama-Rich Translanguaging for Multilingual Meaning-Making**   76
RAFAELA CLEEVE GERKENS AND JULIE CHOI

7 **Embodied Approaches to English 'Exam Prep' in an Attainment-Driven Climate: 'Coming in through the pleasurable route'**   95
CAMILLA STANGER

8 **Multilingual Digital Storytelling: Enhancing the Learning of English Through Drama** 111
VICKY MACLEROY

9 **Teaching English Under Occupation: Classroom Fictions and the World Outside** 131
RAJA' FARAH, GHOSON OROUQ AND MAGGIE HULSON

Index *146*

Contributors

Katherine Barber is currently a doctoral student at King's College, University of London, following a ten-year teaching career in schools in the UK and China. Her research interests focus on transformative pedagogies, critical literacy, and decolonising the English classroom.

Theo Bryer leads the PGCE English with Drama course at UCL's Institute of Education, London. She has many years of experience teaching Drama in schools and leading Drama/Media projects with bilingual learners. Her research and publication interests are in cross-curricular drama, creative literacies, and the relationship between English, Media, and Drama.

Julie Choi leads the Master of TESOL and Modern Languages courses in the Faculty of Education, University of Melbourne. She is co-editor and author of multiple books on language, culture, identity, autoethnography, plurilingualism, and academic writing.

Jane Coles a former Head of English and Deputy Headteacher, is also an experienced teacher educator and educational researcher. Until recently, she led the MA English Education programme at UCL's Institute of Education, London. Research and publication interests include creative literacies, the teaching of Shakespeare, and the relationship between drama and English.

Raja' Farah has taught English language in secondary schools in Ramallah, Palestine, for 23 years. She has worked with the A.M. Qattan Foundation in Ramallah since 2020 and has a particular interest in applying 'Mantle of the Expert' to the teaching of English.

Susie Ferguson works as a freelance creative learning practitioner while a PhD candidate at the University of Sheffield. She has taught English and Drama in comprehensive schools for over 20 years. She writes about drama-inflected approaches to the teaching of novels and is the author of several National Theatre learning guides.

Rafaela Cleeve Gerkens coordinates subjects for pre-service primary and early childhood teachers across literacy and the arts at the Faculty of Education, University of Melbourne. Her research areas include drama-rich pedagogy for learning across the curriculum and arts-rich experiences to support the development of children's critical language awareness.

Maggie Hulson is an experienced drama-in-education practitioner. A former Head of Expressive Arts in a London comprehensive, she is a long-standing member of the National Association for the Teaching of Drama, editor of *The Journal for Drama in Education*, and author of *Schemes for Classroom Drama* (2006).

Vicky Macleroy is Director of the Centre for Language, Culture and Learning and Head of MA Children's Literature at Goldsmiths, University of London. She has led numerous research projects and published widely in the area of multilingual digital storytelling.

Ghoson Orouq is an English language teacher working in Jenin, Palestine, with an MA in TEFL and seven years' teaching experience. She joined the A.M. Qattan Foundation's training programme for teaching drama in 2022.

Maggie Pitfield taught English and Drama in London secondary schools for 24 years. Formerly the Head of Educational Studies and currently a Research and Knowledge Exchange Fellow at Goldsmiths, University of London, her research and publication interests include the contribution that educational drama practices make to the reading of literary texts.

Camilla Stanger is an experienced English teacher, teacher-educator, researcher, and youth arts project manager, working across secondary and higher education sectors within the UK. Her research and publication interests focus on transformative, critical pedagogies and social justice.

Erin Woodford until recently Dean and Head of English at a Singaporean Junior College, received the 2018 'Inspiring Teacher of English (Leadership)' prize awarded by the *Straits Times*/Singapore Government. She has researched and written about inclusive and dialogic approaches to Literature.

Acknowledgements

Much work in education, whether teaching or researching, is collaborative. We pay tribute to the teachers and learners we have benefited from working alongside over our many years in education, all of whom have shaped our thinking immeasurably.

This current volume is the result of our latest collaboration, and it has been a privilege to bring together the invaluable knowledge, expertise, and practical skills of the various contributors whose thought-provoking chapters make up this collection MP & JC.

Chapter 1

Introduction

Jane Coles and Maggie Pitfield

One of the great joys we have derived over many years from our work as teachers and as teacher-educators has been working collaboratively with colleagues to develop rich and fulfilling learning experiences for school students and student-teachers alike. This unique collection of essays continues that tradition: an international collaboration that brings together teachers and researchers who, in their various ways, are committed to advocating for drama's potential to revitalise English/Language Arts as a school subject. Each chapter serves to illustrate the capacity of drama-inflected approaches to facilitate creative – yet rigorously critical – responses to different aspects of the English/Language Arts curriculum in a range of international contexts. Examples of classroom practice documented across the following eight chapters include reading and critically responding to literary texts; developing spoken language; writing creative and non-fiction texts; multimodal storytelling; digital media production; translanguaging; and even English Language examination preparation. While our principal focus is on the secondary phase of schooling, we include two examples of innovative primary practice with the intention of encouraging productive cross-phase conversations.

The breadth of the work represented in this volume demonstrates both the strong disciplinary base of English and its capacity to look beyond narrow definitions of the subject, crucial factors in ensuring that it is responsive to future innovations and challenges. Taken together, the chapters serve to locate English as a creative, imaginative and fundamentally humane subject within which students are very clearly motivated to learn.

'Drama-in-English': learning, not acting

Each individual chapter has been carefully selected to build on the drama-influenced pedagogical approach we developed in our earlier book *Drama at the Heart of English* (2024, also published by Routledge), co-authored with Theo Bryer. In that publication we define 'drama-in-English' as a concept by synthesising three core theoretical perspectives: reader response theory, in particular the work of Louise Rosenblatt (1994); 'process drama' influenced by the work of renowned drama in education specialist Dorothy Heathcote (see O'Neill 2015); and a social constructivist approach to literacy such as that developed by Myra Barrs (for example, 1987; Barrs and Cork 2001). Crucially, we argue that drama-in-English is about *learning*, not acting. By combining a fuller range of communicative modes than routinely feature in English lessons (principally, gesture, gaze and embodiment alongside speaking, listening, reading and writing), it represents an inherently inclusive pedagogy, encouraging all learners to make sense of their lives and their worlds as part of the English curriculum. Although we maintain that there exists a natural affinity between English and Drama on both a disciplinary and a pedagogical level, one of our guiding principles in *Drama at the Heart of English* is that, if it is to be widely adopted by classroom teachers, any innovative pedagogy needs to be practical, rooted in the day-to-day business of the English classroom and sustainable over a period of time. Hence, our emphasis on embedded, small-scale, even fleeting moments of in-role activity (both spoken and written) and other drama-associated strategies, which may involve students in some physical movement or which might easily be accomplished seated at a classroom desk. As the contributors to this volume amply demonstrate, English teachers – whether in London, Singapore or Ramallah – naturally possess the professional skills and knowledge to work in this way and are creatively adept at opening up pedagogical space even when operating within highly constrained institutional or political contexts. Indeed, from our own research over many years in British classrooms, we have been struck by learners' readiness to enter these physical and intellectual spaces, to slip in and out of role in a way that accords with Raymond Williams' assertion as to the everyday attributes of role-play in today's 'dramatized society' (1983).

While the various chapters in this volume are reflective of classroom practice situated in a range of contrasting contexts, there are a number of common threads. The contributors are all experienced teachers and researchers. Each has developed, often as part of a collaborative team, drama-inflected forms of transformative pedagogy with the shared aim of enhancing the learning experience for their students. Encouraging learners to ask the question 'what if?' serves to foreground the importance of creativity and imagination, both on the part of the learners and the teacher. This is not to say, however, that the contributors in this volume interpret 'drama-in-English' in identical ways. It is, after all, a concept that we have always envisaged as existing on a broad spectrum encompassing, for example, writing in role (what Barrs would call 'drama on paper') at one end, and at the other physically active workshop-style lessons potentially taking place in a drama studio. Two examples of practice serve to illustrate the pedagogical breadth specifically in this volume: while Susie Ferguson's starting point is 'rehearsal room' pedagogy with its roots in the practices of professional theatre companies (Chapter 2), Camilla Stanger

(Chapter 7) draws inspiration from bell hooks' 'engaged pedagogy' (hooks 1994), which promotes almost visceral understandings of feelings and lived experiences in the mind of a reader.

Contributors also testify to the immense adaptability of active, drama-inflected approaches, which are shown to be successfully applicable within a wide range of contexts and levels of resourcing. So, in Chapter 4 Erin Woodford begins with questioning whether she and her Singaporean high school colleagues can find a way to continue teaching Shakespeare 'actively' even under stringent Covid-related restrictions (the answer is an emphatic yes); in Chapter 6 Rafaela Cleeve Gerkens and Julie Choi reflect on mime's potential to support multilingual children writing about a scientific process in a Melbourne primary classroom; in Chapter 9 Palestinian teachers of English, Raja' Farah and Ghoson Orouq, describe their experiments with 'Mantle of the Expert', a very specific form of drama pedagogy that has a liberatory effect on their respective students even in the extreme circumstances in which they live, learn and work.

Each chapter documents ways in which various practitioners exploit their considerable professional resources in the interests of their learners, and in doing so, they are pushing at the boundaries of what we mean by drama-in-English. This volume stands as a tribute to the inherent creativity of the international community of English teachers.

Why do we say that English needs transforming?

English teaching, wherever it happens in the world, does not exist in a vacuum. The global market-based 'neoliberal turn in education' (Reay 2025, p. 23) is characterised by top-down regimes of measurement and accountability concerned with the competitive ranking of schools and learners. Centralised curricula, largely dismissive of learners' own knowledge and experiences, are frequently reinforced by means of pre-packaged formulaic scripted lesson templates – a practice commonly adopted by US charter schools and, increasingly, Multi-Academy Trusts (MATs) in England, even at the level of the micro-management of classroom discourse (see Cushing 2021). As indicated by Traianou et al.'s (2025, p. 2) wide-ranging research for the UK's largest teachers' union, such a mechanistic approach to matters of curriculum and pedagogy places severe limits not only on teachers' professional autonomy but also on learners' agency. Implications for a social, creative subject like English are profound.

At the time of writing, a major government-commissioned Curriculum and Assessment Review (Department for Education 2024, 2025) is taking place in England against a growing chorus of professional concern over a constrained, monolithic curriculum, a narrowing of pedagogic approaches to learning (Perryman et al. 2011), and a worrying decline in students expressing enjoyment in their learning (see, for example, APPG 2025; Jerrim 2025). According to the Common English Forum (n.d.), a recently assembled umbrella group of highly respected UK-based subject associations, over the last decade English as a curriculum subject in England:

> has suffered significant damage, at every level, and in multiple ways…leading to children not enjoying the subject, not learning to read, write, speak and listen as well as they might, not choosing to study it at A Level, not choosing degrees in the subject….

Recruitment onto postgraduate teacher training courses in the UK has suffered as a consequence, and as the Common English Forum notes: 'For those who do enter the profession, a delivery model and excessive accountability mean that job satisfaction is low and retention is poor'.

The current iteration of curricular English in England is the product of a series of increasingly utilitarian government policies filtered through inspection frameworks, institutional imposition and formal assessment requirements. In official documentation, learning has been defined as the acquisition of an abstracted form of canonical 'knowledge' (often referred to as a 'knowledge-rich' curriculum. See, for instance, Ofsted 2022). Furthermore, English has suffered particularly acutely from this regime as a 'core' subject, with its key role in government accountability protocols for measuring student progress and school performance. As an inherently 'political' subject, it has been the target of direct ideological interference from successive governments, even, at times, a victim of the so-called culture wars (Coles 2013; Elliott 2014; Wheale 2022).

In hyper-accountable systems, test and examination preparation has a tendency to distort the curriculum as it is manifested in classroom practice. Since 2014, the literature curriculum in England, as dictated by formal GCSE[1] examination requirements, has promoted a myopic focus on pre-20th-century canonical texts. Memorisation of quotations, feature-spotting and facts to be learnt take precedence over meaning-making and the exploration of ideas. Research for the Runnymead Trust (Elliott et al. 2021) estimates that fewer than 1% of all 14–16-year-olds in England study a book by a writer of colour – leaving many young people without the chance to see themselves reflected in the literature curriculum (an issue addressed by Katherine Barber as part of her broader proposals for decolonising the teaching of literature in Chapter 3 of this volume). The pernicious effects of this regime can be felt rippling downwards, similarly distorting the curriculum for 11–14-year-olds (Smith 2020). Not surprisingly, reading enjoyment amongst school-age young people in the UK has fallen to its lowest level in two decades, according to the latest survey of reading habits conducted by the National Literacy Trust (Clark et al. 2025). This echoes research published by the Progress in International Reading Literacy Study (PIRLS 2021)[2], which indicates that young people in England are more likely to hold negative attitudes to reading in comparison with other OECD countries. Broader evidence collated in a recent UK parliamentary report (APPG 2025) makes it clear that levels of learner engagement are closely linked to curriculum content and delivery. As we indicate in more detail below, one of the key features of the practices described in the following chapters is the high level of student engagement right across the range of ages and contexts.

The benefits of role: creativity *and* criticality

The breadth of drama-inflected activities employed by our contributors speaks to their strongly held belief in the importance of role as a way to involve students in their learning. The roots of these types of engagements are to be found in dramatic play. Barrs (2022, p. 130) draws the links between play and educational in-role activities, citing 'Vygotsky's marvellous metaphor' that in role-play a child 'can become "a head taller" than in his [sic] ordinary life'. Even the briefest moments of in-role activity can have a significant impact on learning, as we see in Theo Bryer's account (Chapter 5).

Role-play, like other strategies such as still image (freeze frame), embodiment, and hot-seating, is associated with a process drama approach, the underpinning principle of which is inquiry-based learning. In process drama, as defined by Drama specialists, roles within an authentic but imagined context are developed and sustained over time. Drama-in-English, however, *borrows* from process drama methodology rather than adopting it in its fullest form. For example, role-play in the Critical Connections project (Chapter 8) is central to students' personal storytelling and experimentation with languages, which they share using digital technologies. Cleeve Gerkens and Choi in Chapter 6 focus on the 'bodiliness' of role-play (Franks et al. 2014, p. 172). They demonstrate that, by physicalising a chemical reaction so that it is 'felt' in the body, young multilingual learners can develop both their understanding of a scientific concept and the language they use to describe it.

In Chapter 9, Farah and Orouq draw more explicitly on process drama than other contributors. Benefiting from an international collaboration with Drama specialists, including Maggie Hulson, they explore the possibilities offered by Mantle of the Expert (MoE). This is an inquiry-based pedagogy designed to support learners' agency through a complex, structured form of collaborative in-role learning, during which the students don a mantle of expertise. The authors demonstrate the value of this approach in realising the aim of Communicative Language Teaching to develop learners' communicative competence 'in a meaningful, purposeful and learner-centred context' (To et al. 2011, p. 519). Although their Arabic-speaking students are learning English as a second language, in one respect they are already 'experts' in that they have first-hand knowledge of the real-world background to the imaginative scenarios that they create in collaboration with their teachers. Crucially, they expand their expertise by adopting key roles that enable them to be 'a head taller' in terms of their language use and understanding of their characters' motivations and actions, both of which are enhanced by out-of-role research. Raja' Farah's example in particular demonstrates how the in-role work lends a necessary distancing effect as learners explore some very challenging issues.

Being in role serves to develop both creativity and criticality on the part of the learners. The key Drama concept of 'metaxis' is relevant here, whereby students are participating in the fictional world they have created whilst simultaneously reflecting on and making judgements about their actions within it (see pages 78-79, Chapter 9 and pages 136-137, Chapter 6 for a more detailed explanation). Cleeve Gerkens and Choi, however, innovatively apply the term 'metaxis' to the translanguaging context. They argue that multilingual learners inhabit two worlds at the same time on a daily basis, constantly navigating between different languages, cultures, and identities. Thus, in Cleeve Gerkens and Choi's classroom-based example, the learners are both within their mime as molecules and observing it from the outside, the teacher's narration serving as the link between their embodiment and their language learning.

It is sometimes appropriate for role-play to 'shift into script' (Hulse & Owens 2019, p. 19) and from there into performance, as Woodford and her fellow English teachers demonstrate (see Chapter 4). As their students work towards Readers' Theatre-style presentations based on *The Merchant of Venice*, they develop an in-depth understanding not only of characters and events but also of the theatricality of the piece. The final performances serve to validate the students' authority as co-creators of meaning and interpreters of the play.

Reading, writing, speaking and listening

Although drama-based activities have traditionally been most closely associated with the development of talk and the 'active' teaching of Shakespeare, it has long been our contention that an embedded drama-inflected classroom approach has the potential to enrich learning much more broadly across subject English, including all three key strands: reading, writing, and speaking/listening. It is worth adding that we also advocate for an English/Language Arts curriculum that is fit for the 21st century, one that attends to the prevalence and importance of digital media – an argument which we develop further below.

i Reading

Several of our authors attest to both the enjoyment and cognitive challenge derived from interactive and collaborative reading approaches (in particular, see Chapters 2, 3, 5 and 7). Their focus is variously on role-play, enactment and embodiment in the English/Language Arts classroom, and the practices they describe build upon the notion that the reading of literary texts is an essentially playful activity (see Iser 1989; Mackey 2007; Burn 2022). Importantly, and what drama-in-English takes full account of, is that children's dramatic play, educational role-play and the reading of literature all require immersion in a 'what if' world as filtered through the experiences and insights that learners bring from their real-world contexts. Thus, employing such approaches enables learners to make sense of and engage creatively and critically with the texts they are studying.

The pleasure to be gained in reading 'from the inside out' (see Coles and Pitfield 2022) is relevant in light of key findings from the latest PIRLS report: 'that pupils who enjoy reading have higher average reading achievement' (Lindorff et al. 2023, p. 10), and that 'there appears to be a positive relationship between self-reported engagement in reading lessons and liking of reading' (Lindorff and Stiff 2024, p. 56). Cremin and Scholes (2024) propose that the reasons behind these findings are many and complex. However, what happens in the classroom is undeniably significant in the formation of habits that potentially engender lifelong enthusiasm and – yes – joy in reading. This begs a number of questions which the authors of Chapters 2, 3, 5 and 7 seek to address. A range of pedagogical approaches to classroom reading and assessment of reading are explored in all the chapters mentioned, as are ways to motivate and engage learners with the texts read in English.

How texts are selected or mandated for study is interrogated by more than one contributor. As noted by Camilla Stanger in Chapter 7, the curriculum for English in England has for many years tended to centre around an Anglocentric and canonical understanding of 'what counts as worthy literature', producing 'experiences of disengagement and disenfranchisement' for many learners in an increasingly diverse school population (p. 95). Indeed, this is a phenomenon common to the US and other Anglophone jurisdictions (e.g., Dyches et al. 2024). Stanger is not alone in taking up the challenge of engaging young people with canonical literature in personally meaningful and intellectually worthwhile ways. Susie Ferguson (Chapter 2) draws on her familiarity with stage adaptations of classic prose texts such as *Great Expectations*. She develops a form of rehearsal room pedagogy appropriate for a classroom context, involving the range of creative-expressive activities, roles and artistic decisions that a theatre company might employ. In Chapter 3, Katherine Barber utilises embodied enactment to spark an in-depth engagement with *The Strange Case of Dr Jekyll and Mr Hyde*. Her pedagogical approach offers a powerful strategy through which to address colonialist legacies in the English Literature curriculum and to highlight diverse ways of knowing and learning.

For Theo Bryer (Chapter 5), drama-in-English 'offers opportunities for students to engage with texts in creative ways by bringing characters, incidents, atmosphere and metaphor into a physical and visual dimension' (p. 62). She demonstrates how in-role 'what if' moments during the study of *Beowulf* and *Frankenstein* enable learners to move seamlessly from 'drama in the head' (i.e., reading) into physical enactment from inside the narrative to 'drama on paper' (i.e., writing-in-role). Bryer focuses attention on the affordances of in-role activities and how they support the development of students' critical awareness and insights. She argues that not only does this way of working enable students to take ownership of what might be regarded as an archaic and alien text, but also that their visual sense of the text is heightened through moments of classroom drama.

Working within the comparatively open and progressive policy context of Singapore,[3] Erin Woodford and her high school colleagues have for many years embedded interactive, collaborative and dialogic practices into the day-to-day work of their department. Faced with particular challenges involved in engaging their ethnically and linguistically diverse 14-year-olds in *The Merchant of Venice*, they recognised in Gibson's 'active Shakespeare' approach (Gibson 1998) a powerful vehicle for 'leverag[ing] our students' multi-cultural backgrounds as a strength' (Chapter 4, p. 51). After all, as Shakespeare scholar Farah Karim-Cooper (2024) points out, while the antisemitic tropes of *The Merchant of Venice* are undoubtedly problematic, it is also a play which explicitly interrogates lives that have been 'othered'. Woodford's account demonstrates how an active, learner-centred pedagogy is still very possible in the online context. It enables her students to explore critically issues of unequal power in the play, with one group, for example, expressing their ideas symbolically by imaginatively exploiting the available technology.

ii Writing

Developing students' writing is a key aspect of English/Language Arts curricula, but in jurisdictions where the curriculum is test-driven, an overly instrumental and formulaic pedagogy can too easily predominate. International research highlights the adverse effects on student attitudes associated with this approach to writing (see, for instance, Kiger Lee et al. 2017, in the context of elementary schools in the USA). In *Drama at the Heart of English* (2024), we argue that the relationship between role-play, enactment and writing for a range of purposes deserves greater attention, and we explore how the processes that are integral to both mirror and support each other. An essential playfulness underpins in-role engagements with literature, and this can be utilised in order to immerse students in their learning and facilitate their move into critical writing mode (see also Coles & Pitfield 2022).

In this volume, several authors take such ideas into new territory. Cleeve-Gerkens and Choi explore how playful, purposeful embodiment helps learners expand their conceptual and linguistic understanding of a scientific phenomenon, which in turn provides the starting point for written explanation. Through physically embodying the reactions of molecules, then sharing their understandings orally, in labelled drawings, and in writing, they are engaged in a comprehensive 'languaging' process. The social semiotic activity of the classroom (see Yandell 2008), in which the body is a key communicative resource, is integral to the learning that takes place. It enables these multilingual learners to participate, communicate and feel supported towards developing their target language use in scientific writing. Importantly, it acknowledges their proficiency in English as emergent rather than (linguistically and intellectually) deficient.

Aspects of the extracurricular 'Empowered English' session described by Stanger in Chapter 7 have a playful, indeed fun, quality, even though she is preparing a group of GCSE students from a London comprehensive school to write critically about 'unseen' literary extracts in the examination situation. Her drama-motivated approaches are designed to address what two otherwise high-attaining, outspoken students independently refer to as the blankness they routinely experience when faced with such demands. Stanger questions the frequent use of supposedly supportive 'writing frames' and instead offers a drama-inflected alternative which unleashes her students' potential and confidence, eliciting positive and more insightful responses than has previously been the case. Drawing on Barrs' view of reading characterised as drama in the head, Stanger combines this with the affective engagement that is so important in reading (see Rosenblatt 1994) and which we have described previously as drama in the heart (see Coles & Pitfield 2024).

The synergies between role and writing have long been highlighted, as for example by the literacy specialist Margaret Meek Spencer in her 'Preface' to a report on important research with primary school learners (Meek Spencer 2001). She is attentive to the ways in which 'features of dramatic role-play appeared in [the children's] writing' and notes that 'To write as someone else is to accomplish a kind of reflexivity, "me, yet not me", peculiar to authors' (p. 12). There is, though, a similarity here with the reflexive stance taken by participants during physical role play: they are inside and immersed in the action yet simultaneously detached from it, as they observe and make mental judgements about their moment-by-moment, in-role decision-making. Therefore, writing that is produced 'in-the-moment' during the role-play itself (see Cremin et al. 2006) can fruitfully draw on this 'me, yet not me' quality. In such an iteration of writing-in-role, the drama continues inside the learners' heads as they write and provides a very immediate impetus for their responses. This spontaneous act of writing serves to deepen the learners' thinking about a character's situation and the language they might use at that time, in that place.

Bryer (Chapter 5) provides an example of teacher-in-role that stimulates creative writing in response to the reading of *Beowulf*. The writing occurs following the dramatic event and has a more crafted feel than in-the-moment writing-in-role. Bryer focuses on the ways in which the visual dimension of the drama inflects the genre aspects of the writing, as well as reflecting the moments of tension on which the in-role activities are based.

During Bryer's second project, her student-teachers embody the 'monster' created by Dr Frankenstein at the moment when he comes to life, opening his eyes for the first time. Again, the visual dimension proves to be very important in their writing-in-role. In Bryer's words, they are 'envisaging the world through the creature's eyes and then speculating about what the future holds for him' (pp. 72-73), whilst adopting an appropriately gothic tone to do so. Although each of these dramatic moments is very brief and is part of a wider range of active approaches to reading the *Beowulf* and *Frankenstein* texts, they have a powerful impact on the in-role writing that they inspire.

iii Speaking and listening/dialogic pedagogy

For the last decade in England, the requirements of formal assessment have disproportionately shifted teacherly attention onto the composition of timed, formulaic written answers, with the result that speaking and listening have become relegated to the curricular margins of subject English. Yet the value of carefully structured classroom talk and its relationship to learning is well-documented (see, for example, Mercer 2000; Oracy Commission 2024), just as drama pedagogy's part in specifically developing a talk-rich English curriculum has been long recognised. To quote Dorothy Heathcote from a pamphlet written for English teachers over 40 years ago: 'One of the most valuable uses of the dramatic mode is the way it can provide context and purpose for talk, because talk arises out of the nature of situations' (Heathcote 1980, p. 22). In Chapter 5, Bryer (p. 64) alludes to what has become known as Heathcote's constant 'press for language', referring to the way, often in role herself alongside her students, she exploited opportunities for learners to extend their use of language (vocabulary, register, etc.) beyond their everyday range.

In varying ways, all contributors to this volume attest to the inherently dialogic properties of drama-based pedagogy. By this, we denote learning that emerges out of meaningful classroom dialogue, where a range of perspectives and ideas are exchanged and explored, thereby deepening learning and leading to the co-construction of new knowledge. In her development of a decolonial pedagogy, Barber (Chapter 3) combines moments of role-play with longer chains of exploratory classroom discussion. The professional theatre roots of the 'rehearsal room' strategies adapted by Ferguson (Chapter 2) are themselves in essence dialogic – in that they are characterised by working together as an 'ensemble' engaged in 'participation, collaboration, trust and mutual respect' (Neelands & O'Hanlon 2011, p. 246). Woodford's proposals for the teaching of *The Merchant of Venice* (see Chapter 4) echo Karim-Cooper's advice to regard any Shakespeare play as 'a conversation, an invitation to imagine and interrogate' (2024, p. 6).

A growing body of international research points to significant benefits in employing drama strategies to develop learners' language competence, including English as an additional or second language (see, for instance, Bundy et al. 2016; Dutton & Rushton 2022; Ntelioglou 2011; Stinson & Piazzoli 2013). Three chapters in this volume illustrate how an embedded drama-based pedagogy draws on, develops and challenges learners' existing language repertoires in an inclusive and culturally responsive way. In Chapter 6, Cleeve Gerkens and Choi describe the way in which children learn to use specific terminology through a combination of mime and collaborative talk. Allowed to experiment with language and movement in playful and creative ways, the learners are able to develop confidence without fear of judgement. Working with multilingual students as part of a global literacy project, Vicky Macleroy explores how the learning of English and other languages can be enhanced by combining drama and the process of multilingual digital storytelling (Chapter 8). Her research indicates that learners become more agentive and imaginative in their use of language when provided with the space to improvise and experiment in the telling of stories dealing with 'difficult truths and complex, contradictory realities' (p. 113).

Operating within the immensely challenging constraints of occupation and the political instability that brings, Palestinian teachers of English, Farah and Orouq, describe ways in which they have liberated their classroom practice as a result of an international collaboration (Chapter 9). Resisting institutional pressure to adhere to the narrowly instructional pedagogy and colonially inflected curriculum underpinning their core English Language Teaching (ELT) textbooks, Farah and Orouq explore ways of incorporating authentic uses of language in their classroom practice. By linking age-appropriate ELT topics (such as celebrating a birthday) with the pupils' own worlds outside the classroom, Farah and Orouq's pedagogy serves to enhance engagement and reduce their learners' understandable resistance to learning and speaking English.

iv   Digital media/multimodal approaches to learning

The assessment and curriculum system in England is certainly not unique in its outdated reliance on the written word (e.g., Burnett et al. 2014). Yet it seems obvious that the curricular exclusion of digital media, including moving image texts, is hardly a fitting preparation for adult life in the 21st century. We share with several of our contributors a commitment to developing a literacy curriculum that equips the next generation with the necessary skills and knowledge to navigate the evolving digital landscape – at the very least, to understand how stories are told and different 'truths' produced in a range of media and on a range of platforms.

Macleroy makes the point in Chapter 8 that filmmaking, like drama, is a communal art form requiring participation and co-operation. Her research indicates ways in which students move from talk to movement and performance, and from there to filmmaking. Macleroy argues that when students are invited to author the stories of their own lives through this process, spaces are opened up, facilitating the potential for 'activist citizenship' (p. 112). Moreover, digital technology represents both a medium for learning and, subsequently, a platform for sharing the fruits of that learning with international partners.

For Woodford, the unexpectedly generative affordances of online technology only become apparent when she and her colleagues experiment with the transfer of drama-rich forms of learning into virtual spaces. Echoing Whipday's (2023) findings, Woodford notes that the pandemic-enforced shift challenges learners to dig deep into their creative and imaginative resources. Her group of students became 'more imaginative, playful and non-literal in how they introduced performative elements into their work – for example, through disappearing Zoom boxes, witty soundtracks, memes, and symbolic props' (p. 59).

More broadly, whenever drama-inflected approaches are combined with different forms of media, learners are afforded particularly rich opportunities to make meaning using multiple modes of representation. Cleeve Gerkens and Choi reflect on the ways in which young learners engage with complex academic content by drawing simultaneously on a combination of resources (e.g., cultural, physical, cognitive and linguistic). The sequence of learning they describe combines warm-up games, information in video format, the construction of a word wall, mime, drawing and writing – all embedded within a framework of collaborative talk. They conclude that 'the visual nature of diagrams in combination with the visual element of embodiment essentially creates a scaffold that supports meaning-making while students continue developing their academic language skills' (p. 88).

Learner-centred pedagogy

We have argued elsewhere (Bryer et al. 2024) that a learner-centred approach in English is both 'attentive to the social and cultural lives of learners' (p. 10) and inextricably bound up with a pedagogy we identify as 'creative-critical'. The contributors to this volume likewise demonstrate the power of bringing students' identities and experiences to bear on their learning of English in a range of settings, highlighting the unique opportunities that drama-rich activity affords in this respect.

Camilla Stanger's practice (Chapter 7) challenges any notion of a lack of rigour in student-centred learning. She demonstrates how embodied approaches prepare GCSE students to respond to examination questions confidently, with skill and authenticity. A learner-centred, drama-inflected pedagogy enables the students to draw on 'head' and 'heart' engagements with literature, the benefits of which are reflected in both their analytical and creative writing and in their newfound confidence when facing a previously daunting examination task.

The work of the highly regarded Critical Connections global literacy project (Chapter 8) is also a testament to the importance of a student-centred approach, as it enables young people to express their identities, creativity and technical prowess through digital filmmaking and sharing. As Macleroy highlights, drama in the context of Project-Based Language Learning (PBLL) is a transformative pedagogy precisely because it involves a high degree of student agency and voice. The young participants explore texts, ideas, narrative and language(s) in order to tell their (multilingual) stories, and they prove themselves to be both critical and hopeful interpreters and presenters of their worlds. The global reach of the project highlights how this type of artistic, creative endeavour is of benefit, not just to the well-being of the individual in society, but to society itself, and therefore, as the influential Soviet psychologist Vygotsky (1971) argues, fulfils what should be one of the main objectives of education.

The importance of collaborative ways of working, whether in the classroom or between teams of professionals at local and international level, is a thread that runs throughout this volume. Teachers working creatively together to develop their curriculum is a key feature of Chapters 4, 6 and 7. International collaborative endeavours are crucial to the projects described in Chapters 8 and 9, inspiring students and teachers alike and creating exciting learning opportunities both in and beyond the classroom. Chapters 5 and 9 suggest ways in which closer learner-teacher relationships might be developed through teachers working alongside students in role.

We note that collaborative learning and small-group collaborative talk have been linked to raised academic outcomes in a number of studies (see, for instance, Burgess et al. 2022; EEF 2021; Kyndt et al. 2013). As we argued earlier, drama-in-English pedagogies lend themselves to the development of talk-rich environments for learning, and across many chapters in this volume we see the power of co-operative student-to-student group work for engaging participants and moving their learning forward.

The importance of motivation and enjoyment

Crucially, drama-in-English represents a motivating form of pedagogy – and the accounts of classroom practice collated in this volume lend weight to that claim. Arising out of our own decades of classroom experience, it is our belief that playfulness and pleasure are important elements in learning, a personal conviction that is increasingly supported by published research, including large-scale survey data linking a loss of enjoyment and engagement with absenteeism and diminished academic outcomes (e.g., Jerrim 2025). A lack of pupil agency and of enjoyment in learning appear to be consistent elements behind the research (Parentkind 2024; TIMSS 2023), which Reay (2025) argues amounts to a matter of social justice (see also Hargreaves, Quick & Buchanan 2025).

How English teachers might best counter dispiriting levels of learner disengagement is a question that is of central interest to us and to the authors contributing to this volume. In reviewing available research into the successful development of reading and writing for pleasure with primary-aged learners, renowned literacy specialist Teresa Cremin and her colleagues (2023) recommend the adoption of social approaches, where attention is paid to learners' own experiences, interests and preferences. They emphasise the importance of providing playful activities within a framework of interactive peer support. Coincidentally, we note, these are all elements to be found in a drama-in-English methodology.

Ultimately, in asking 'what if?' we are encouraging learners to make sense of their lives and imagine new futures as engaged citizens and fulfilled social beings.

This could not be better illustrated than by Ghoson Orouq's seven-year-olds' impatience to get back to school after a forced closure, excited by the prospect of meaningful engagement in a whole-class role-play which enables them to take back a semblance of control over their lives in the proposed fictional context (see Chapter 9). Or by Erin Woodford's Singaporean adolescents who respond on a properly critical level to the serious business of studying a play as dark as *The Merchant of Venice* (Chapter 4); at the same time, their drama-based responses are laced with a good deal of wit alongside a large degree of playful creativity in the way they manipulate the available technology to support their readings. We should note that their playfulness is mirrored by their teachers in the form of a collective end-of-unit celebration, complete with a mock awards ceremony.

Finally, Woodford's example acts as a reminder to us of the importance of *teacher* enjoyment and enthusiasm, neither of which is likely to be cultivated through the routine 'delivery' of pre-packaged PowerPoint slides or adherence to a textbook (see Bleiman 2020). The practitioners who have contributed chapters to *Transforming English Through Drama* stand testament to what a former colleague of ours refers to as 'the intellectual creativity of English teaching' (Daly 2004, p. 196), not least in the processes by which they apply professional curiosity to the ways meanings are made, contested and remade in the dynamic social arena of the English/Language Arts classroom.

Notes

1 General Certificate of Secondary Education (GCSE) is a set of qualifications in a range of separate subjects typically taken by students who are in their final year of compulsory schooling, aged 15–16 years old.
2 The Progress in International Reading Literacy Study is an international comparison of children's reading literacy at the end of their fourth year of formal schooling (around age 10).
3 Principles underpinning the Singapore Ministry of Education curriculum policy include: 'nurturing the joy of learning' and the aim to 'cultivate in our students qualities such as creativity, collaboration and compassion.' (See: https://www.moe.gov.sg/-/media/files/about-us/overview_of_singapore_education_system.pdf).

References

All-Party Parliamentary Group (APPG) (2025). *Inquiry into 'The Loss of the Love of Learning'*. Retrieved from: https://educationappg.org.uk/wp-content/uploads/2025/07/APPG-LoL-Report.pdf

Barrs, M. (1987). Voice and role in reading and writing. *Language Arts*, 64(2), 8–11.

Barrs, M. (2022). *Vygotsky the Teacher: A Companion to his Psychology for Teachers and Other Practitioners*, London and New York: Routledge.

Barrs, M., & Cork, V. (2001). *The Reader in the Writer: The Links Between the Study of Literature and Writing Development at Key Stage 2*, London: Centre for Language in Primary Education.

Bleiman, B. (2020). What matters in English? Retrieved from https://www.englishandmedia.co.uk/blog/what-matters-in-english/

Bryer, T., Pitfield, M. & Coles, J. (2024). *Drama at the Heart of English: Transforming Practice in the Secondary Classroom*. London: Routledge.

Bundy, P., Piazzoli, E., & Dunn, J. (2016). Sociocultural theory, process drama and second language learning. In S. Davis, B. Ferholt, H. Grainger-Clemson, S.-M. Jansson, & A. Marjanovic-Shane, eds., *Dramatic Interactions in Education: Vygotskian and Sociocultural Approaches to Drama, Education and Research*, London and New York: Bloomsbury, pp. 153–170.

Burgess, S., Rawal, S., & Taylor, E. (2022). *Characterising Effective Teaching*, London: The Nuffield Foundation. Retrieved from www.nuffieldfoundation.org/project/characterising-effective-teaching-2

Burn, A. (2022). *Literature, Videogames and Learning*, Abingdon: Routledge.

Burnett, C., Davies, J., Merchant, G., & Rowsell, J. (eds.) (2014). *New Literacies Around the Globe: Policy and Pedagogy*, Abingdon and New York: Routledge.

Clark, C., Picton, I., & Cole, A. (2025). *Children and Young People's Reading in 2025*, National Literacy Trust. Retrieved from: https://nlt.cdn.ngo/media/documents/Children_and_young_peoples_reading_in_2025_bqtGfIs.pdf

Coles, J. (2013). 'Every child's birthright'? Democratic entitlement and the role of canonical literature in the English National Curriculum. *Curriculum Journal*, 24(1), 50–66.

Coles, J., & Pitfield, M. (2022). Reading Shakespeare from the inside out. *Teaching English*, 29, 22–26.

Coles, J., & Pitfield, M. (2024). Editorial. Drama-in-English: A transformative pedagogy. *Teaching English* (Special Issue: Drama-in-English), 35, 17–18.

Common English Forum (n.d.). *Manifesto for English*. Retrieved from: https://commonenglishforum.org/a-manifesto-for-english/

Cremin, T., Goouch, K., Blakemore, L., Goff, E., & Macdonald, R. (2006). Connecting drama and writing: Seizing the moment to write. *Research in Drama Education: The Journal of Applied Theatre and Performance*, 11(3), 273–291.

Cremin, T., Hendry, H., Chamberlain, L., & Hulston, S. (2023). *Reading and Writing for Pleasure: A Framework for Practice*. Mercers' Company/Open University. Retrieved from https://cdn.ourfp.org/wp-content/uploads/20231201185032/Reading-and-Writing-for-Pleasure_FRAMEWORK-DIGITAL-FINAL-30.11.23.pdf

Cremin, T., & Scholes, L. (2024). Reading for pleasure: scrutinising the evidence. *Language and Education*, 38(4), 537–559.

Cushing, I. (2021). Language, discipline and 'teaching like a champion'. *British Educational Research Journal*, 47(1), 23–41.

Daly, C. (2004). Trainee English teachers and the struggle for subject knowledge. *Changing English: An International Journal of English Teaching*, 11(1), 189–204.

Department for Education. (2024). *Curriculum and Assessment Review: Review Aims, Terms of Reference and Working Principles*. Retrieved from https://assets.publishing.service.gov.uk/media/6699698f49b9c0597fdb0010/Curriculum_and_assessment_review_-_aims_terms_of_reference_and_working_principles.pdf

Department for Education. (2025). *Curriculum and Assessment Review: Interim Report*. Retrieved from: https://assets.publishing.service.gov.uk/media/67e6b43596745eff958ca022/Curriculum_and_Assessment_Review_interim_report.pdf

Dutton, J., & Rushton, K. (2022). Drama pedagogy: subverting and remaking learning in the third space. *The Australian Journal of Language and Literacy*, 45, 159–181.

Dyches, J., Howell, E., Thomas, D., & Updegraff, A. (2024). Multimodality and critical race theory as tools of canonical subversion. *English in Education* 58(3), 222–239.

EEF (Education Endowment Foundation) (2021). Collaborative learning approaches. Retrieved from: https://educationendowmentfoundation.org.uk/education-evidence/teaching-learning-toolkit/collaborative-learning-approaches

Elliott, V. (2014). The treasure house of a nation? Literary heritage, curriculum and devolution in Scotland and England in the twenty-first century. *Curriculum Journal*, 25(2), 282–300.

Elliott, V., Nelson-Addy, L., Chantiluke, R., & Courtney, M. (2021). Lit in colour. *Diversity in Literature in English Schools*. Penguin Books/Runnymede Trust. Retrieved from: https://litincolour.penguin.co.uk/assets/Lit-in-Colour-research-report.pdf

Franks, A., Thomson, P., Hall, C., & Jones, K. (2014). Teachers, arts practice and pedagogy. *Changing English: Studies in Culture and Education*, 21(2), 171–181.

Gibson, R. (1998). *Teaching Shakespeare*, Cambridge: Cambridge University Press.

Hargreaves, E., Quick, L. & Buchanan, D. (2025). 'This is *too* boring': A life-history approach to primary pupils' distress and lack of motivation for school-work. *Pastoral Care in Education*, 1–19. https://doi.org/10.1080/02643944.2025.2454650

Heathcote, D. (1980). Drama as context for talking and writing: The Ozymandias saga at Broadwood Junior School. In M. Barrs, ed., *Drama as Context: NATE Papers in Education*, Aberdeen: NATE in association with Aberdeen University Press, pp. 4–24.

hooks, b. (1994). *Teaching to Transgress*, London: Routledge.

Hulse, B., & Owens, A. (2019). Process drama as a tool for teaching modern languages: supporting the development of creativity and innovation in early professional practice. *Innovation in Language Learning and Teaching*, 13(1), 17–30.

Iser, W. (1989). *Prospecting: From Reader Response to Literary Anthropology*, Baltimore, MD and London: The John Hopkins University Press.

Jerrim, J. (2025). *Mind the Engagement Gap: A National Study of Pupils Engagement in England's Schools*. Retrieved from: https://www.impactedgroup.uk/resources/report-mind-the-engagement-gap

Karim-Cooper, F. (2024). *The Great White Bard: How to Love Shakespeare While Talking About Race*, London: Bloomsbury.

Kyndt, E., Raes, E., Lismont, B., Timmers, F., Cascallar, E. & Dochy F. (2013). A meta-analysis of the effects of face-to-face cooperative learning. Do recent studies falsify or verify earlier findings? *Educational Research Review*, 10, 133–149.

Lee, B. K., Enciso, P., & Alliance, Austin Theatre. (2017). The Big Glamorous Monster (or Lady Gaga's Adventures at Sea): Improving student writing through dramatic approaches in schools. *Journal of Literacy Research*, 49(2), 157–180.

Lindorff, A., & Stiff, J. (2024). *Additional Findings from PIRLS 2021: Research Report*, London: Department for Education.

Lindorff, A., Stiff, J., & Kayton, H. (2023). *PIRLS 2021: National Report for England: Research Report*, London: Department for Education.

Mackey, M. (2007). *Literacies across Media: Playing the Text*, 2nd edn, London: Routledge.

Meek Spencer, M. (2001). Preface. In M. Barrs and V. Cork, eds., *The Reader in the Writer*, London: Centre for Language in Primary Education, pp. 9–20.

Mercer, N. (2000). *Words and Minds: How We Use Language to Talk Together*, London & New York: Routledge.

Neelands, J., & O'Hanlon, J. (2011). 'There is some soul of good': An action-centred approach to teaching Shakespeare in Schools. *Shakespeare Survey*, 64, 240–250.

Ntelioglou, B. Y. (2011). 'But why do I have to take this class?' The mandatory drama-ESL class and multiliteracies pedagogy. *Research in Drama Education*, 16(4), 595–616.

O'Neill, C. (ed.) (2015). *Dorothy Heathcote on Education and Drama: Essential Writings*, Abingdon: Routledge.

Ofsted. (2022). Research Review Series: English, 23 May 2022. Retrieved from: https://www.gov.uk/government/publications/curriculum-research-review-series-english/curriculum-research-review-series-english

Oracy Education Commission (2024). *We Need to Talk: The Report of the Commission on the Future of Oracy Education in England*. Retrieved from https://oracyeducationcommission.co.uk/wp-content/uploads/2024/10/Future-of-Oracy-v23-web-13.pdf

Parentkind (2024). *The National Parent Survey 2024*. Retrieved from https://nationalparentsurvey.parentkind.org/the-national-parent-survey-2024/0434338001728294862

Perryman, J., Ball, S., Maguire, M., & Braun, A. (2011). Life in the pressure cooker: School league tables and English and Mathematics teachers' responses to accountability in a results-driven era. *British Journal of Educational Studies*, 59(2), 179

PIRLS (2021). *International Results in Reading*. Retrieved from https://pirls2021.org/results/

Reay, D. (2025). *Miseducation: Inequality, Education and the Working Class* (2nd edn), Bristol: Policy Press.

Rosenblatt, L. (1994). *The Reader, the Text, the Poem: The Transactional Theory of the Literary Work*, Carbondale: Southern Illinois University Press.

Smith, L. (2020). Top ten texts: A survey of commonly-taught KS3 class readers. *Teaching English*, 23, 30–33.

Stinson, M., & Piazzoli, E. (2013). Drama for additional language learning: Drama contexts and pedagogical possibilities. In M. Anderson & J. Dunn, eds., *How Drama Activates Learning: Contemporary Research and Practice*, London and New York: Bloomsbury, pp. 208–225.

TIMSS (2023). *International Results in Mathematics and Science: Student Experiences and Attitudes*. Retrieved from https://timss2023.org/results/school-belonging/#:~:text=In%20the%20fourth%20grade%2C%20students,mathematics%20and%20493%20in%20science

To, L. D., Chan, Y. P., Lam, Y. K., & Tsang, S. Y. (2011). Reflections on a primary school teacher professional development programme on learning English through Process Drama. *Research in Drama Education, The Journal of Applied Theatre and Performance*, 16(4), 517–539.

Traianou, A., Stevenson, H., Pearce, S., & Brady, J. (2025). *Are you on slide 8 yet? The Impact of Standardised Curricula on Teacher Professionalism*, National Education Union. Retrieved from: https://neu.org.uk/sites/default/files/2025-03/NEU3679%20Are%20you%20on%20slide%208%20yet-%20Full%20Report%20%28Digital%29%20v3.pdf

Vygotsky, L. S. (1971). *The Psychology of Art*, Cambridge, MA: MIT Press.

Wheale, S. (2022). UK's 'strictest headmistress' fears schools will stop teaching Shakespeare. *The Guardian*, 22 May. Retrieved from: https://amp.theguardian.com/education/2022/may/22/uks-strictest-headmistress-fears-schools-will-stop-teaching-shakespeare

Whipday, E. (2023). *Teaching Shakespeare and his Sisters: An Embodied Approach. Cambridge Elements Series*, Cambridge: Cambridge University Press.

Williams, R. (1983). Drama in a dramatized society. In *Writing in Society*, London: Verso, pp. 11–21.

Yandell, J. (2008). Embodied readings: Exploring the multimodal social semiotic resources of the English classroom. *English Teaching: Practice and Critique*, 7(1), 36–56.

Chapter 2

Adapting Texts, Adapting Practice
Applying Rehearsal Room Methodology to the Study of Novels

Susie Ferguson

Introduction

A survey of theatrical offerings in London's West End at the time of writing demonstrates the popularity of literary adaptation in the theatre repertoire, with thirteen literature-inspired productions amongst the most popular choices of plays and musicals. A brief exploration of regional touring productions across the UK paints a similar picture: audiences are keen to engage with theatrical interpretations of their favourite novels, curious to see how characters and narratives are presented through a visual medium, and attendance is often inspired by nostalgia for the stories that inspired them in the past. The presence of literary adaptations within both the English Literature and Drama curricula in the UK signifies their acceptance as a literary form in their own right. Teachers often expose students to adaptations of novels as part of a scheme of work within the secondary phase (11–18 year olds) of English Literature study, but students tend to be positioned as passive audience members, requiring little contribution beyond their attention in the moment. However, I suggest that classroom activities which invite students to explore novels through theatre rehearsal room techniques can move students away from a passive assumption that the adaptation they are watching is the definitive one, towards a deeper and more enriched position of understanding writers' choices and intentions and a development of their own creative skills. By employing drama-based tasks, and some of those used in the creation of theatre productions, teachers can inspire students to develop their identities as consumers and creators of artistic and creative content.

In August 2024, I visited rehearsals for the National Theatre's touring adaptation of Michael Morpurgo's 1984 novel *War Horse* (2007–present). I was struck by the similarity between the activities within the rehearsal room and discussions that I have had in my own classroom. Directors Tom Morris and Katie Henry were not solely interested in directing the actors to move from A to B or in instructing an actor on the delivery of a particular line of dialogue. Instead, the rehearsal resembled a description by Mercer (2008, n.p, cited by

Elliot 2021) of the ideal environment for exploratory classroom talk in which 'people ask questions; people share relevant information; ideas may be challenged; reasons are given for challenges; contributions build on what has gone before; everyone is encouraged to contribute ideas, and opinions treated with respect'. This is particularly significant because the rehearsal was for a revival of a play which had already been seen by over eight million people worldwide. Despite its success, Morris (who was also editing the script) and his team were still exploring new alternatives and additional nuance, rather than simply recreating what had gone before. At its simplest level, 'what else might we do?' is a question that could be applied to an adaptation that students watch, inviting a debate about what students consider to be the most important elements of a narrative and how they might do things differently.

In selecting *My Name Is Leon* by Kit de Waal (2016) and Dickens' *Great Expectations* (1996), originally published in 1860–1861, for this chapter, I have identified two texts which share thematic and character-based attributes. Both centre on a boy who questions his place in society and seeks acceptance. Both involve benevolent and malevolent secondary characters whose impact on the protagonists' lives is, hyperbole aside, life-changing. Most importantly, both offer myriad choices of how they might be adapted for performance and provide a range of opportunities to explore challenging yet important issues such as race, class, belonging and identity. The suggestions and activities offered here are based on 23 years of classroom teaching and my work as a creative learning consultant, in which I have written about and discussed adaptation with professional playwrights, directors, designers and actors.

Context

In March 2025, the initial findings of the UK government's Curriculum and Assessment Review were published in its Interim Report. It outlines the decline in the study of the arts, with Drama being one of the most significantly impacted subjects (p. 14), as well as reporting that the review 'heard compelling arguments that the curriculum needs to do more in ensuring that all young people feel represented' (p. 28). The full report is scheduled for publication in autumn 2025; however, numerous concerns raised in the initial findings are also evidenced in the 'Striking the Balance' report (2024) commissioned by the UK examination board OCR, in which Jo Johnson, Chair of the Lords Education for 11–16-year-olds Committee, is quoted as saying:

> The evidence we have received is compelling. Change to the education system for 11–16 year olds is urgently needed, to address an overloaded curriculum, a disproportionate exam burden and declining opportunities to study creative and technical subjects.
>
> (p. 13)

Whilst English teachers should not be tasked with compensating for the decline in provision of Drama as a discrete subject, I argue that they can embrace opportunities for students to learn creatively in their own classrooms. The National Literacy Trust's most recent Annual Report (2025) warns of 'a steady erosion of reading enjoyment across generations, with implications for literacy, wellbeing, and personal development that cannot be ignored' (p. 1).[1] It is not possible to identify one clear reason why this might be, but it is vital that teachers of literature contribute to the solution of the problem. If solely teacher-led and/or exam-focused teaching is not sufficient, then perhaps a participatory rehearsal room methodology might be applied as part of a wider repertoire of teaching approaches.

Defining rehearsal room methodology

Much of the writing about rehearsal room pedagogy and its application in the classroom has, to date, centred on the Royal Shakespeare Company's (RSC) education work, which includes the influences of Cicely Berry and Rex Gibson, and projects such as the Learning Performance Network (LPN). Joe Winston (2015) also extols the benefits of applying active rehearsal methods – those that are used in rehearsals with professional actors for productions of Shakespeare plays – to the academic study of Shakespeare's work in schools. The RSC's 'Time To Act' report (2024) and their 'Learning Performance Network: Final Impact Evaluation Report' (2016) demonstrate a positive correlation between the application of rehearsal room methods and students' improvement in literacy and oracy. In this form of rehearsal room pedagogy, teachers facilitate a series of exercises and discussions based on playscripts. The focus is on practical exploration, including group work, acting, creative discussion or 'making' tasks that go beyond more traditional activities such as reading aloud, reading silently or engaging through written tasks. It is perhaps this practical element which can seem intimidating to English teachers who often have received little drama-specific input during training. However, as my visit to the *War Horse* rehearsal room demonstrates, the scope of a rehearsal room-based practice can be much wider and just as productive, and some activities can still be desk-based where necessary. Having worked alongside creative teams from high-profile literary adaptations such as *War Horse*, *The Ocean at the End of the Lane*, *The Curious Incident of the Dog in the Nighttime* and *Life of Pi*, I propose a definition of rehearsal room pedagogy which includes all of the roles that exist in the rehearsal room – from performers to creative practitioners and writers. By expanding the definition, this form of drama pedagogy can justifiably encompass tasks from songwriting to costume design, from creating a prop list to acting and directing. This should help to allay concerns about teachers' ability to deliver drama-informed activities in the English classroom. Fiona Banks (2013) explains that every session of the Creative Shakespeare pedagogy adopted by Shakespeare's Globe (on London's Southbank) 'relies on the interaction between teacher, students and play' (p. 1). The concept of play and playfulness is vital when adopting any form of rehearsal room praxis: there is more than one way in which to interpret and present a text, and it is through exploration and experimentation, ownership and agency that students are likely to be most engaged. Banks quotes Rex Gibson's definition of his active methods, which 'comprise a wide range of expressive, creative and physical activities' (p. 4). In my own application of the term 'rehearsal-room pedagogy', therefore, I include tasks that do not rely only on acting or script writing but instead reveal the array of creative decisions that form a theatrical adaptation. In that *War Horse* rehearsal room, the directors and actors were joined by composer Adrian Sutton, movement director Toby Sedgwick and various technical experts involved in the staging of the novel. The democratic process of transferring a story from one form to another combined skills and embraced the range of expressive activities encouraged by Gibson in his practice.

Gibson's *Teaching Shakespeare* (1998) suggests teaching activities which are mostly designed with classrooms in mind. In contrast, activities advocated by the RSC and Shakespeare's Globe (London) often require large spaces or involve visiting a specific theatre or other off-site location to participate in one-off workshops or events. Gibson's activities are described by Coles and Pitfield (2022) as 'demanding a high level of intellectual challenge, imaginative participation and emotional engagement on the part of the learners' (p. 25). In my application of rehearsal room pedagogy, I identify the classroom teacher as the skilled facilitator and leader of drama-based and theatre-informed activities, fully equipped to lead the intellectually rigorous discussion and exploration as described by Mercer and applied to interpreting a novel. During rehearsals for the National Theatre's *Small Island* (2019, 2022), director Rufus Norris worked with the actors playing the adult and child Hortense, placing them both on stage together. The *Rehearsal Diaries* (written by Staff Director Anna Himali Howard, 2019, p. 6) tell us this was

> an interesting process, to see how simply placing Hortense and Little Hortense together creates a really poignant image and allows us access into Hortense's memory – especially into her close relationship with her grandmother, Miss Jewel, and her fear of Mr Phillips. The young actors are so adept at …using their physicality to tell the story of Michael and Hortense.

This technique could be applied in a classroom to demonstrate the influences – past and present – in Pip and Leon's lives (in *Great Expectations* and *My Name Is Leon*, respectively). Both boys are haunted by memories of people who have played transient roles in their childhood but who remain a strong influence. During that discussion of how to portray Hortense's memory, the *Small Island* creative team will have taken note of sensory details in Andrea Levy's novel, such as sound and sight, to develop ways to evoke a deeper response from an audience.

Working with adaptation

Mike Alfreds, founder of theatre company Shared Experience, discusses the challenges and rewards of working with novels in his book *What Happens Next? Storytelling and Adapting for the Theatre* (2013). He says:

> Each story, whatever its source...requires a unique treatment of its own. It is the particular needs of a particular story, the individual dramatic choices it demands, that will light the fuse of your imagination.
>
> (p. xxiv)

This 'spark' is perhaps one way of engaging students and revealing what reading for pleasure might look like: not a passive, solo activity (unless by choice) but one which challenges a reader to ask questions and engage with issues and worlds different from their own experience. Detractors may argue that creating a dramatic rendering of an existing novel is merely a distraction or displacement activity, perhaps only dealing with the superficial details of plot and character. However, Bryer et al. (2024, p. 98) suggest that:

> rather than deploy drama techniques in a way that may serve to mask awkward questions about literary knowledge and cultural authority, it is our contention that a truly drama-in-English classroom has the capacity to meet – and illuminate – these challenges.

Year 9 students (13–14 year olds) in my mixed attainment class who were asked to create a dream cast list for an imagined adaptation of *Lord of the Flies* (Golding 1954) quickly noticed the lack of female characters and considered how an all-female play version might differ from a more faithful adaptation, considering current issues around female stereotypes and toxic masculinity – an observation which may not emerge so easily in a more straightforward reading of the novel alone. It encourages an enquiry-based approach where teachers are fellow curators, rather than an authority that seeks to remain unchallenged. As Banks explains, the Globe's 'Creative approaches are active, physically and/or intellectually. They require students to engage fully with the moment they are exploring' (p. 5). Students need to develop a curiosity about, and engagement with, the artistic products that teachers place before them and to understand how their own responses to an adaptation have been elicited by creative choices, with an opportunity to explore those techniques for themselves. The adaptation approach also insists that the adapters (and therefore students) know the novel well. Alfreds espouses the same view:

> The intention is to create something more fluid and flexible, true as far as possible to both spirit and world of the story we're telling, closer to its original forms and structures. To make this transposition, we have to know

precisely what we're transforming – which means deconstructing a story, breaking it down into its component parts to study how each of them functions, so that we can reassemble them with a fuller understanding of how they interrelate.

(p. 57)

Deconstructing novels is the quotidian activity for teachers of English Literature, but too often this is purely for the purpose of meeting the requirements of formal assessments. It is my contention that deconstructing a novel as a group project and as a creative endeavour can be highly rewarding, whilst still enabling students to meet assessment demands.

Kneehigh Theatre Company often presented existing stories and novels, ranging from traditional Cornish folktales to novels such as *Rebecca* (2015), *Nights at the Circus* (2005) and *Hansel and Gretel* (2009). A common methodology in all their productions was itself inspired by a UK primary school teacher named Miss Hibbs in the 1980s. In her work with primary school children (aged 5–11), she would ask students to identify an odd number of sentences (for example, seven) which would summarise the entire story. Each sentence would identify a vital point in the story – which could be articulated as headlines – to define the narrative arc. Then, within those seven sentences, individual scenes could emerge. In this approach, students are not confined to writing traditional scripted scenes: Kneehigh's work is characterised by playfulness, mischief and non-naturalistic devices such as song and dance. This, therefore, invites a much wider range of creative tasks that students might include in their adaptation. Former Artistic Director of Kneehigh, Emma Rice (cited in Ferguson 2025, n.p.), explains that:

> With the writer or writers, we talk and dream, we map out the structure and the overall shape of the piece. They go away and write collections of poems or lyrics or ideas. Each writer works in a different way but what none of them do is to write a script or a scene in isolation.

This focus on collaboration and rejection of isolated pockets of effort or input foregrounds accountability within the creative classroom. In *Great Expectations*, students might find a poem or song a perfect interlude in which to describe Herbert Pocket's chaotic family, whilst a scene in Magwitch's Newgate cell might invite a more traditional response. Either way, students are being asked to engage with content and to synthesise it in a way that speaks clearly to them and their own intended audience. There will be some students who are keen to perform their work, whilst others may express a preference not to. When we apply rehearsal room methodology here, we return to the definition of a democratic and collaborative process evoked by Mercer in his description of oracy and Morris in his rehearsal room. Performance is not necessarily the only possible outcome. Such an approach can also help develop a positive class dynamic, particularly when using Banks' football analogy: 'As footballers, actors involved in ensemble playing work as a team, playing together at all times, but all have individual roles to play in the scene' (2013, p. 193). Banks' description advocates a collective responsibility and might reduce disengagement. Students do not need to become actors in the literal sense, but they will take a role within the creative process.

Alfreds also describes the potential that adaptation provides for the creation of ensemble – the antithesis of the fears of isolation or exposure that teachers may anticipate. He says that:

> in story-theatre four disciplines converge: storytelling, theatrical performance, the adaptation of material from non-dramatic sources and the development of an ensemble with the necessary skills to fulfil its special demands.
>
> (p. xxiv)

This development of ensemble creates a sense of a combined effort to solve a common problem: how best to stage a text about which students will convey a variety of different ideas, opinions and experiences. For classroom practitioners who might consider group work as counter-intuitive when studying novels (i.e., texts are surely intended to be read as a solitary activity), we might remember RSC actor Geoffrey Streatfield, quoted by Winston (2015), who identifies that 'this ensemble is a secure environment without ever being a comfort zone. All of us are continually challenging ourselves and being inspired by those around us to reach new levels in all aspects of our work' (p. 98). Collaboration is both challenging and reassuring.

I suggest that approaching the study of a novel through the lens of literary adaptation also helps reduce the potential reverence for those canonical texts which have been on the examination curriculum for a long time. Their presence (including that of Shakespeare) can suggest to students that these texts must not be challenged but instead accepted without question in the quest to find the 'right' answer for exam-style questions. As Gibson (1998, p. xii) says, 'Shakespeare is not a museum exhibit with a large Do Not Touch label, but a living force inviting active, imaginative creation…'. The same is true for any text in the English (exam) curriculum, including novels and poetry. Dramatic exploration of the text diminishes any hagiographic tendency. Texts should be challenged, subverted and recreated: the ability to do so demonstrates a greater depth of understanding than the recollection of even the most impressive list of quotations which have been taken out of context. Ambiguities in text and changing attitudes towards themes they contain can be explored through imaginative creation and recreation. As Winston (p. 90) suggests, although there is a 'general ambivalence toward the value of play that permeates all culture', students generally delight in finding alternatives which better suit their own personal outlook and experience. In practice, the ending of *Great Expectations* invites the reader to imagine just what Pip means when he 'saw the shadow of no parting' from Estella (p. 484). Discussions surrounding the level of satisfaction a reader or audience may or may not achieve at the end of the narrative could include imagined scenes. Additionally, hot seating exercises in which students pose an agreed list of questions to one volunteer (or the teacher) who answers in role as either Pip or Estella can interrogate the possible meanings behind the final paragraph and the conclusion of their narrative journey. In rehearsal, two actors might undertake this hot seating activity – both answering the same set of questions – and any discrepancies between the answers might provide material for actor, director and playwright alike. Given that *Great Expectations* was adapted for theatre performance from 1861 onwards (shortly after the final chapter was published in Dickens's *All the Year Round* magazine), this also offers students the opportunity to discuss potential changes in audience demands and dramatic taste since 1861 and why it continues to enthral audiences in both novel and literary adaptation forms.

In my suggestion that drama and theatre techniques be used to explore novels, I also seek to dismantle a potential hierarchisation of professional theatre practices. Bryer et al. (2024, p.92) raise concerns about the ways in which theatre practitioners, on occasion, engage in 'a rhetoric of professional deficit on the part of regular English teachers'. For instance, Jonathan Neelands and Jacqui O'Hanlon, both directly involved in RSC Education projects, comment that teachers 'tended to lack confidence in key pedagogical skills…such as the use of sophisticated questioning skills, group work and setting tasks that encourage higher order thinking' (2011, p. 246). It is therefore unsurprising that teachers might be reluctant to experiment with unfamiliar approaches, particularly with the perpetual pressure of assessment, inspection and curriculum content noted by several respondents to the 'Striking the Balance' inquiry. However, purposeful questioning forms a considerable part of an English teacher's skill set and may only need minor adjustment to make those questions drama-focused. For example, having taught Priestley's *An Inspector Calls* (1992; first performed in 1945), and examined the substantial stage directions in the opening pages, a teacher can explore the power of stage directions with their students to then apply to an adaptation. Making connections between text types and genres helps students develop a wider understanding of the relationships between texts (moving towards the historicist approach favoured in courses for 16–18-year-olds, such as A levels) rather than considering them in isolation from each other.

Writers and directors are not the sole authorities in a rehearsal room, and this offers even more potential to exploit students' individual skills and interests. One example is the way in which a writer and a stage manager might work together to identify important props that a production might need.

My Name Is Leon and *Great Expectations* feature food very heavily: In the former, food is at first a nourishing necessity, as Leon and his brother are malnourished. However, it becomes a compensatory or placatory offering when Leon suffers distress, rejection or frustration. The contents of Maureen's biscuit tin, the food planned for the Royal Wedding street party or the food and drink offered by adults on the allotment all create a picture of how food sustains Leon physically and emotionally. Food in *Great Expectations* is significant from the very beginning: Pip's theft of 'wittles' (p. 5) for Magwitch in Chapter 1 is the inciting incident for the entire novel, and the semiotics of decaying food on Miss Havisham's table convey character, plot and theme without the need for lengthy dialogue in a play adaptation. Of course, a teacher might simply tell their students about the significance of the food motif to expedite instruction, but the process of investigating, mapping, and looking for patterns or repetition for a practical purpose is ultimately more rewarding for students and teachers alike. The identification of patterns is the foundation on which greater analysis can be built with increasing complexity and sophistication. In the same way that Mathematics builds ability and skill through the practice of problem solving, a drama-based approach achieves the same outcome without the associated rote learning identified by students and teachers as damaging to their enjoyment of reading and of English Literature in general.[2]

My approach to adapting novels within the classroom was inspired by the challenges of teaching *To Kill a Mockingbird* (Lee 1960). As a newly qualified teacher in the early 2000s, with a high-attaining, energetic class of GCSE students, I was daunted by the task of harnessing their enthusiasm for the long-awaited and complex court scene. By allocating small groups a short section from each of the four chapters (comprising forty pages of dense text), my instructions simply asked students to perform what was written on the page – speaking characters' words with the prose providing stage directions. This simple act of mining the text and 'putting it on its feet' mimics initial professional rehearsals in which directors and adapters might explore the dramatic potential of a scene from a novel. From this, we could analyse Lee's allocation of dialogue – who spoke and who did not – and note interruptions, silences and courtroom reactions. These workshop sessions naturally led to discussions surrounding representation and authority. In the 2022 production (London and Broadway) of *To Kill a Mockingbird*, similar observations were made in Aaron Sorkin's adaptation, in which Calpurnia and Tom are given much more agency, and Calpurnia actively challenges some of Atticus Finch's comments and actions (Ferguson 2022). By bringing the prose to life, students are highly astute in identifying injustice and questioning how and why some characters are silenced. Likewise, in *My Name Is Leon*, students can be invited to create simple tableaux or short scenes of all the moments in which Leon is physically surrounded by adults or abandoned by them. Examining Chapter 1, in which Leon is left looking after his newborn brother, Chapter 6, when Leon is taken to Maureen's house, and Chapter 21, when Sylvia is called in to see the headteacher, can be a simple way in which to demonstrate Leon's lack of agency and status. Everyone is taller, older and louder than him, and very few people consider approaching Leon on his level, rather than vice versa. Leon's outburst in Chapter 37, in which he shouts, 'No one cares about me … Everyone steals things from me' (de Waal 2016, p. 229), is also an ideal opportunity for students to script an alternative speech or missing scene in which Leon can express himself at different moments. Noting the importance of classroom oracy, striking evidence given by the Office of the Children's Commissioner to the All-Party Parliamentary Group Inquiry[3] (2021, p. 24), 'Speak for Change', states:

> One child said to us that she just felt like a parcel being passed around in care. Oracy can be powerful for those children to help them, to empower them to speak for themselves and make it harder to overlook them and have things done to them.

Scripting, or improvising, a scene in which Leon does express himself verbally, rather than stealing money or running away, offers students an opportunity to dig deeper into a character's experience in the same way that an actor might do something similar as a rehearsal technique. Linking the above evidence with Leon's predicament amplifies the need for students to develop not only oracy but also the ability to consider other people's experience and perspective. It might never be intended to be part of a final performance or production, but an active task which encourages students to synthesise information that is (and, in some cases, is not) provided promises to have both academic and personal impact for young people. Banks (2013) identifies the way in which Shakespeare's plays can resonate with the young people we are teaching. These plays, she says,

> Are simultaneously distant from our world, yet relevant to our humanity. … Students feel 'safe' discussing a character's situation and exploring their feelings because they belong to the specific world of the play, yet in doing so they are enabled to reflect on their own feelings and response to such a situation.
>
> (p. 205)

It is, however, not just Shakespeare's plays that have this potential. Approaching the novel through the lens of plays and play*ing* can achieve the same for the sensitive topics covered in *My Name Is Leon*.

When leading practical activities, a teacher's acceptance of a facilitator role (rather than instructor or expert) can support teachers in building their confidence in providing support in a slightly different way. Neelands and O'Hanlon (2011) explain that the use of rehearsal room pedagogy

> …places an emphasis on negotiated learning, teacher as facilitator rather than as instructor and the use of questioning and higher order thinking skills in enacted and embodied fictional situations that refer in content to real world issues and dilemmas.
>
> (p. 243)

English teachers already possess the ability to deconstruct and analyse texts and evaluate the use of particular techniques in extant plays. They are certainly fluent in the use of questioning and developing their students' higher order thinking skills. Within this shift to facilitator, teachers can offer ideas and alternatives for students to try out in activities which are low stakes but potentially high impact. Franks, Thomson, Hall and Jones (2014, p.171) raise the notion that it is a shift in perception for teachers about their role in the classroom that might also be a notable result of working with a drama-based pedagogy. Within my definition of rehearsal room pedagogy, perhaps English teachers will find reassurance that not every task must end with an enactment or performance. Instead, the creative 'product' might be an item of costume (drawn or constructed), a series of monologues and/or duologues, or the simple retelling of a chapter from different characters' points of view. All these activities have the same intellectual rigour and engagement that would take place in the professional rehearsal room, sometimes practically and physically, and at other times seated at a desk.

Examining the various roles performed by people in the rehearsal room demonstrates just how diverse and dynamic such an environment can be.

Within the roles listed in Figure 2.1, most teachers will identify opportunities for their students to thrive and apply their own individual skills to interpreting a text. Whilst these roles denote the traditional roles of director, choreographer, etc., the other creative practitioners also contribute to the discussion of creating a production concept from the beginning of the process. For example, a composer might watch rehearsals and improvise or create a soundtrack in the room as the actors rehearse. Moving beyond the RSC's narrower range of acting-based methodologies can make the classroom a more inclusive environment in which individual skills are recognised, and students are given voice and agency in collaborating in a group project. In a 2024 workshop for teachers on the National Theatre's *Small Island*, the revival's Associate Director Denzel Westley-Sanderson suggested asking group members to clearly state the skills and talents they bring to any drama task. By identifying skills, interests and lived experience that students already possess, the level of engagement is likely to be considerably higher than in groups where roles are arbitrarily assigned.

Adapting Texts, Adapting Practice 29

> **Director**: leads and facilitates discussions, responsible for production concept and overview.
>
> **Choreographer/movement director**: works with the director on physical movement from large dance numbers to smaller scale, individual character movement work.
>
> **Set designer**: responsible for designing the set(s) for the production according to the overall theme, structure and content of the play, and the director's interpretation.
>
> **Costume designer**: designs the clothes worn by the characters.
>
> **Lighting designer**: responsible for creating lighting 'states' which not only ensure the audience can see, but also create setting, mood and atmosphere.
>
> **Sound designer**: responsible for the audience's aural experience which can include sound effects (live and/or recorded), music and soundscapes.
>
> **Composer**: creates new and original music which can convey characterisation, mood, atmosphere, setting, progression of plot. Can be instrumental or include song lyrics as appropriate.
>
> **Stage manager**: responsible for the smooth running of a performance and production. Often responsible for obtaining and maintaining props.

Figure 2.1 Definitions of theatre roles and responsibilities.

Opportunities for oracy

An important aspect of oracy is the 'empowering' concept of voice (see the UK's All-Party Parliamentary Group Inquiry 2021, p. 31), enabling young people to 'express their thoughts, share ideas with the world and be heard.' Working with drama techniques to tackle the content of a novel significantly increases the potential to achieve this outcome. Drama activities such as role play, set design, elevator pitches[4] for sound design, and hot seating all exploit students' use of voice: expressing ideas and opinions, justifying comments and approaches, and playful exploration of embodying a character are considerably more relevant than the often-criticised GCSE spoken language presentations.[5]

One of the challenges of *Great Expectations* for adolescent students is the vast range of dialogue, which varies from Jaggers' legal and formal register to

Mrs Joe's severe admonishments followed by her absence of speech after Orlick's vicious attack. A playwright or adapter would explore this in a rehearsal room, as Pip struggles to find his own identity in the world into which he has been thrown. Jaggers instructs Pip in Chapter 18 (p. 139) that:

> you are to distinctly understand that you are most positively prohibited from making any inquiry on this head, or any allusion or reference, however, distant, to any individual whomsoever as the individual, in all communications you may have with me.

A teacher might invite students to speak these lines out loud, in a way that befits Jaggers' status and profession. This could be within the students' usual classroom layout without the need to move furniture or within the context of a staged dramatic improvisation. In either situation, the teacher can then ask what effect such a register might suggest about Jaggers' posture, gait, and facial expression and ask students to model how Pip might respond physically as he stammers his brief reply. The syntax of Jaggers' speech is complex, and students may struggle to comprehend it upon first and, indeed, second reading. However, much can be gleaned by reading out loud about the effect of the sentence structure and punctuation used in Jaggers' speech – this is likely to emphasise his status and aloofness for the young people who might see large swathes of heavily punctuated text as intimidating and incomprehensible. Physically enacting the scene allows them to empathise with Pip, who also struggles to interpret Jaggers' speech. Ideas surrounding register and code-switching can often emerge by 'trying on words for size', understanding the power of language on self-identity and others' perception. I therefore advocate the provision of opportunities to experiment with different forms of language provided in novels rather than simply in plays. There are also several play scripts of *Great Expectations* available commercially, and discussions might focus on the choices made for a particular scene, which can then be compared to the original novel.

Speaking in role is not confined to speaking as a particular character in my definition of rehearsal room pedagogy. Students can speak in the role of a costume designer, for example, or as a contextual expert (many professional theatre companies seek external experts to educate the company on historical or political events, for example). A student fulfilling the role of sound designer for an adaptation of *My Name Is Leon* might present their ideas for a soundscape based on 1980s chart music and influences from the TV programme *The Dukes of Hazzard*, the TV show that Leon watches religiously. Rehearsal rooms often have visual references such as photographs, sketches and artworks displayed on the walls to inspire and inform rehearsal. Classrooms already adopt this practice, suggesting that the difference between rehearsal room and classroom may not be as significant as one might think.

Conclusion

Theatre companies such as the National Theatre and the RSC have staged numerous high-profile and commercially successful adaptations, some of which have made their way into the UK's Drama and English Literature curricula in their own right – evidence that adaptation is considered a legitimate form of artistic practice. Whilst the RSC's published rehearsal room pedagogy has always been based on their Shakespeare plays as opposed to their literary adaptations (which have included *Matilda* in 2011, *Wolf Hall* in 2015 and *Hamnet* in 2024), the artistic and creative processes involved in staging them are very similar to those prescribed in their Shakespeare education offerings. Teachers and students will find their exploration of these techniques engaging and rewarding when applied to novels. Although previous definitions of rehearsal room pedagogy have perhaps suggested a hierarchisation of the skills of theatre practitioners over classroom teachers, I advocate for an exploratory approach in which teachers join students in asking, 'how would *we* adapt it?' and 'how can we apply our own skills and experiences to *our* interpretation of a novel?' The ensemble approach of working on a literary interpretation is a potential panacea to the solitary, isolating experience of reading a novel that may initially appear to offer little engagement for an adolescent who does not immediately see themselves represented in a text. The discursive approach witnessed in the *War Horse* rehearsal room between a variety of experts and practitioners presents ways of increasing opportunities for oracy and for students to consider themselves an expert. This emphasis on creativity offers students a gateway to future enjoyment and appreciation of a range of literary forms beyond the confines of assessment and examination.

Notes

1. The Trust's research states that 'Just 1 in 3 (32.7%) children and young people aged 8–18 reported enjoying reading 'very much' or 'quite a lot' in 2025 and that 'Enjoyment levels dropped slightly (by 1.9 percentage points) from the previous year. (p. 1) Reading enjoyment is now at its lowest level for two decades'.
2. OCR's 'Striking the Balance' report represents the views of more than 1000 students who were surveyed during the consultation. Responses included comments that 'Exams are just questions on content memorised instead of allowing students to delve deeper into a subject they enjoy' and 'some bits are memory tests – such as learning quotes for GCSE English Literature from a play, a book and lots of poems' (p. 17).
3. The role of Children's Commissioner promotes and advocates for the rights of children. Their office regularly contributes to All-Party Parliamentary Group (APPG) inquiries by providing evidence. APPGs are groups of Members of Parliament from across the various political parties who work together to investigate specific issues.
4. An elevator pitch is an explanation of a concept or idea, intended to pique interest from potential supporters or investors. It should be short and pithy enough to deliver within the time it takes to travel in an elevator.

5 These individual presentations are given by students on a topic of their choice. Presentations frequently centre on topics such as knife crime, gender pay gaps, and the climate emergency. Students apply rhetorical devices when writing their own speeches. The Spoken Language Assessment does not contribute to the GCSE English Language or Literature grades: it is an assessment in its own right.

References

Alfreds, M. (2013). *Then What Happens? Storytelling and Adapting for the Theatre*. London: Nick Hern Books.
APPG (2021). Speak for Change: Final Report and Recommendations from the Oracy All-Party Parliamentary Group Inquiry. Retrieved from https://www.education-uk.org/documents/pdfs/2021-appg-oracy.pdf
Banks, F. (2013). *Creative Shakespeare: The Globe Education Guide to Practical Shakespeare*. London: Bloomsbury.
Bryer, T., Pitfield, M., & Coles, J. (2024). *Drama at the Heart of English: Transforming Practice in the Secondary Classroom*. London: Routledge.
Coles, J., & Pitfield, M. (2022). *Reading Shakespeare Through Drama*. Cambridge: Cambridge University Press.
Curriculum and Assessment Review (2025). Interim Report. Retrieved from https://assets.publishing.service.gov.uk/media/6821d69eced319d02c9060e3/Curriculum_and_Assessment_Review_interim_report.pdf
De Waal, K. (2016). *My Name Is Leon*. London: Penguin.
Dickens, C. (1996). *Great Expectations*. London: Penguin.
Elliot, V. (2021). *Knowledge in English: Canon, Curriculum and Cultural Literacy*. London: Routledge.
Ferguson, S. (2022). *To Kill a Mockingbird Education Guide*. Retrieved from https://golivetheatre.org.uk/wp-content/uploads/To-Kill-a-Mockingbird.pdf
Ferguson, S. (2025). Interview with Emma Rice. (Unpublished).
Franks, A., Thomson, P., Hall, C., & Jones, K. (2014). Teachers, arts practice and pedagogy. *Changing English: Studies in Culture and Education*, 21(2), 171–181.
Gibson, R. (1998). *Teaching Shakespeare*. Cambridge: Cambridge University Press.
Golding, W. (1954, 1996). *Lord of the Flies*. London: Faber and Faber.
Himali Howard, A. (2019). *Small Island Rehearsal Diaries*. National Theatre. Retrieved from https://images.nationaltheatre.org.uk/uploads/2023/06/small-island-rehearsaldiaries.pdf#_gl=1*1nl3f3x*_gcl_au*MjEzNjY2NzU4LjE3NDk2NDk3MTM.
Lee, H. (1960, 1989). *To Kill A Mockingbird*. London: Heinemann.
Mercer, N. (2008). *Three Types of Talk*. Cambridge: Faculty of Education, University of Cambridge. Retrieved from https://thinkingtogether.educ.cam.ac.uk/resources/5_examples_of_talk_in_groups.pdf
National Literacy Trust. (2025). *Children and Young People's Reading, 2025*. Retrieved from https://nlt.cdn.ngo/media/documents/Children_and_young_peoples_reading_in_2025_bqtGfIs.pdf
Neelands, J., & O'Hanlon, J. (2011). There is Some Soul of Good: An action-centred approach to teaching Shakespeare in Schools. *Shakespeare Survey*, 64, Cambridge: Cambridge University Press, pp. 240–250.
OCR. (2024). *Striking the Balance: A Review of 11–16 Curriculum and Assessment in England*. Cambridge: Cambridge University Press and Assessment.
Priestley, J. B. (1992). *An Inspector Calls*. Harlow/Oxford: Heinemann.
Winston, J. (2015). *Transforming the Teaching of Shakespeare with the Royal Shakespeare Company*. London: Bloomsbury.

Chapter 3

Drama in English
A Decolonial Strategy

Katherine Barber

Introduction

Visiting the theatre last year to see a performance of Hansberry's *A Raisin in the Sun*, I was pleased to note that a group associated with *Lit in Colour*[1] was giving away copies of Black British novels to audience members as they waited in the auditorium. The *Lit in Colour* report (Elliott et al. 2021), which has inspired my own research, reveals the lack of diversity in UK classrooms, citing that whilst 34.4% of students are of Black, Asian or other minority ethnic heritage, less than 1% of 14–16-year-olds study an author of colour at GCSE. The report exposes a clear disjunct between the curriculum we teach and the students we serve. It reveals how only 0.1% of the students surveyed had studied a book by a woman of colour, underscoring the intersectional implications of institutional racism, where the interrelated nature of race, class and gender creates cumulative discrimination. It is interesting to see that the official Curriculum and Assessment Review panel set up by the UK government in 2024 has expressed similar sentiments in its interim report (Department for Education 2025), noting that many people do not feel reflected in the curriculum they learn, and therefore, more efforts must be made to make the curriculum representative.

In announcing the review, Professor Becky Francis (the review body chair) outlined the newly elected Labour government's aims for a 'broader curriculum so that children and young people do not miss out on subjects such as music, art, sport and drama' and one that 'reflects the issues and diversities of our society' (Department for Education 2024, pp. 1–2). This highlights a need to diversify the educational experience – from the voices which dominate the classroom to the subjects being studied. However, whilst this is a welcome shift in tone from the new government, it sidesteps the more complex ways in which colonial legacies are embedded within education. This chapter offers a way to actualise Labour's intention by creating an innovative and inclusive curriculum that extends beyond merely diversifying content, such as the range of authors studied in English. Its relevance, however, extends around the globe, as teachers internationally are working to make their curricula representative and address colonial histories in their own contexts. In this chapter, I call for *decolonisation*, not simply diversification. My belief is that decolonial teaching is not only a way to deconstruct the legacies of our past but also to respond in the present to the changing direction of education and thus provide a more enriching learning experience for future students.

I will begin by examining the narrowness of the current Literature curriculum in England[2] and expand this to look more widely at coloniality in education. Whilst diversifying reading lists is a step forward, this response alone is not decolonisation, and so defining the concept is crucial. By laying out the theoretical basis, I intend to facilitate deeper understanding of how drama-in-English can contribute to a wider push for inclusion. Finally, I will offer examples of ways in which drama can be employed, demonstrating what this practice has to offer. Whilst Francis calls for Drama to be prioritised as a subject (Department for Education 2024, p. 1), these examples focus on drama as a pedagogical strategy,[3] as exemplified by Bryer, Pitfield and Coles' (2024) definition of drama-in-English, a form of integrated practice that is grounded in creativity and criticality. This chapter champions the use of drama-in-English to challenge the multifaceted ways in which coloniality remains embedded within the education system. In this sense, drama-in-English becomes not only a method we can use to engage students but also a significant embodiment of decolonial practice in the English classroom.

The current curriculum for English in England

Elliott et al.'s survey (2021, p. 30) reveals that '82% of youth survey respondents did not recall ever studying a text by a Black, Asian or minority ethnic author'. This evidences what Sinclair (2018, p. 189) calls the 'colonisation problem', where the curriculum is 'deeply rooted in white supremacy'. According to Iffath (2020, p. 370), 'the National Curriculum is perpetuating a narrative that is reminiscent of the colonial era whereby other cultures are forcibly excluded from what it means to be English and construed as indisputably inferior'. By muting voices of colour, educators risk suggesting that only the white voice deserves to be heard.

Such realities were amplified in England by Michael Gove, Secretary of State for Education (2010–2014), whose significant curriculum changes included a renewed emphasis on canonical literature and reading and writing (rather than spoken) English. Crucially, he emphasised literature written by British authors, removing popular American classics such as Lee's (1960) *To Kill a Mockingbird* and Steinbeck's (2001) *Of Mice and Men*, first published in 1937, from the curriculum, novels often used in secondary schools to teach racial literacy. Whilst it is important to note that the teaching of these novels is becoming increasingly controversial in both the UK and in some US states (for instance, because of the inclusion of overtly racist language and/or attitudes; cf. Flood 2020), these texts were removed in this instance to heighten a perceived sense of *'Britishness'*. It is a decision that feels reminiscent of the cultural imperialism evident in colonial times, where cultural artefacts such as works of literature were used to bolster the hierarchical position of European nations. Moreover, by teaching a curriculum entrenched in the voices of white males, curriculum-makers restrict what it means to be a British writer and thus challenge the multicultural identity of Britain. If the GCSE syllabus aims to provide students with the 'chance to develop culturally and acquire knowledge of the best that has been thought and written' (Department for Education 2013, p. 3), what are we telling our students if this excludes anyone from the Global Majority?

A plea for change

The international revival of the Black Lives Matter movement as a reaction to the murder of George Floyd[4] in the USA prompted greater critical introspection around race in schools. Strengthened by other political movements such as 'Rhodes Must Fall',[5] educational institutions globally began to consider the physical decolonisation of public spaces and how coloniality was entrenched in the institution itself – for instance, in staffing, pupil outcomes and the curriculum. In sum, as the world stood still at the height of the Covid-19 pandemic, voices of activism were mobilised. On a personal note, during this time, my doctoral thesis (concerned with decolonisation in the secondary English classroom) was born.

Underneath these movements lies an effort to challenge the presumed universality of the white experience, with commentators such as Eddo-Lodge (2017) not only highlighting how positive images of whiteness permeate society but also critiquing the ways in which colour-blindness is often offered as a sympathetic response to racism. Whilst colour-blindness encourages us to dismiss differences, true equity urges people to face them head-on and use affirmative action to create social justice. These movements have also galvanised a plea for anti-racism (cf. Kendi 2023), where people take an active stand against racism. In response, many English teachers in England have sought to diversify their reading lists and challenge the narrowness offered by Gove's National Curriculum by augmenting their Key Stage 3 syllabus (for learners aged 11–14 years) with novels by Black British writers or poems from other countries. Efforts to diversify are also evident in the International Baccalaureate (an examination syllabus studied widely outside of England), which promotes diversity in the curriculum for English by including literature from different times and places, and texts in translation. The growth of this programme may reflect a global emphasis on inclusion.

Beyond diversification

Whilst such changes indicate an 'appetite for change', Elliott et al. (2021, p. 35) believe diversification demands further work. For instance, they criticise efforts as being tokenistic, where authors of colour are only included in the form of short texts or during Black History Month, with the result that white voices still dominate curriculum time (p. 35). Landman (2015) exposes tensions around diversification in his criticism of Lee's (1960) *To Kill a Mockingbird*, reminding readers that whilst this novel is often used to discuss race in the classroom, it is a story told by white characters, by a white author, perpetuating a white focus. A further criticism could be the novel's use of the White Saviour Trope, where Black characters are depicted as 'passive spectators to their own oppression' (Jay 2015, p. 497), and thus, diversification demands further criticality.

Whilst literature's history as a tool for both cultural imperialism and cultural hegemony must be addressed, decolonisation also means addressing our pedagogy. Swapping in an author of colour will not necessarily result in decolonial practice, since the question remains: what will teachers do with it? In accordance with Sutherland (2023, p. 2), a central difference arises between inclusion, 'which seeks to extend *existing* teaching structures, syllabi, and delivery models to all students', and decolonising, 'a root and branch review of the foundations of academic knowledge, institutional classroom practices, learning materials, assessment aims and academic mindsets'.

In a recent report, the National Education Union (2024, p. 3)[6] states that:

> decolonising education means building a school system that supports all students, staff, and teachers…examining the limitations and biases of the current curriculum; the omissions in initial teacher education and training; and examining the political and societal legacies of colonialism and how they have influenced education policies.

This positions equity of opportunities and outcomes as part of challenging colonialism's legacy; it also reveals the complex ways in which colonialism impacts education, whilst showcasing how this work demands a whole-school approach. In recognising this, the NEU's (2024) definition highlights how decolonisation stretches beyond just one facet of education and is difficult to conceptualise. Moreover, whilst the NEU's definition arises out of their broader anti-racism framework, my argument is that teachers also need to understand manifestations of coloniality *as distinct from* other forms of racism, at the same time recognising how colonial ideas are facilitated by racist ideologies. In this chapter I invite English teachers to broaden their understanding of decolonisation and look to drama-in-English as a central resource in changing the wider, symbolic (and not just literal, textual) narrative.

Defining 'decolonisation'

To define decolonisation, we must first understand colonialism's legacy in education. Not surprisingly, my doctoral research indicated that most of the ten

English teachers I worked with in the Greater London area mentioned diversification when trying to articulate what decolonisation means to them. Alongside teacher interviews, I created professional development sessions aimed at furthering the group's understanding of decolonial education through creating lesson activities that could embody the principles of decolonisation but be used immediately. This was motivated by my intention to create practical solutions whilst also fostering decolonial research (cf. Smith 2012). Finally, this approach also enabled me to navigate my positionality as a white, middle-class woman from the UK who comes with experiences that are not shared by the students, teachers, and authors of colour I am discussing. In 2023, I first trialled my method and resources with trainee teachers at King's College London to test their appropriacy before sharing them with my core participant group of more experienced teachers in 2024. It is worth explaining these sessions in some detail as examples of approaches I have been developing.

Elliott et al. (2021, p. 43) identify teacher confidence and subject knowledge as barriers to curriculum change – a phenomenon also reflected in my own research. My professional development session began with participants considering where coloniality might emerge in the classroom, seeing this as an essential first step in understanding decolonisation as a response. Although initially invited to offer their opinion anonymously via an online forum, only 15 out of 28 trainees made a response. This is suggestive of a potential insecurity, where some lacked the confidence and knowledge to answer the question. Those who did respond echoed the group of more experienced teachers in citing a lack of diversity in the curriculum. The experienced teachers did, however, demonstrate more nuance. For instance, they mentioned the ways in which stories about Black characters, if used in isolation, can reiterate monolithic narratives (for example, the presentation of Black people as victims) and propagate stereotypes.

In talking with trainees as well as experienced teachers, a central lacuna was revealed in how we discuss decolonial education. Whilst the conversations were increasingly complex, we were still just talking about the books that largely constitute traditional literature curricula. It is only through a more nuanced understanding of the ways in which coloniality is embedded within the school system that possibilities for decolonisation will develop.

Coloniality in the classroom

Figure 3.1 demonstrates what the legacy of colonialism might look like in classrooms today. It is reflective of Maldonado-Torres' (2007, p. 243) concept of coloniality, which he defines as 'the long-standing patterns of power that emerged as a result of colonialism' and live on after independence. To avoid confusion, I will continue to use the better-known term 'decolonisation' in this chapter. However, according to Maldonado-Torres' logic, we are striving for *decoloniality*: we are disentangling education from the vestiges of colonialism

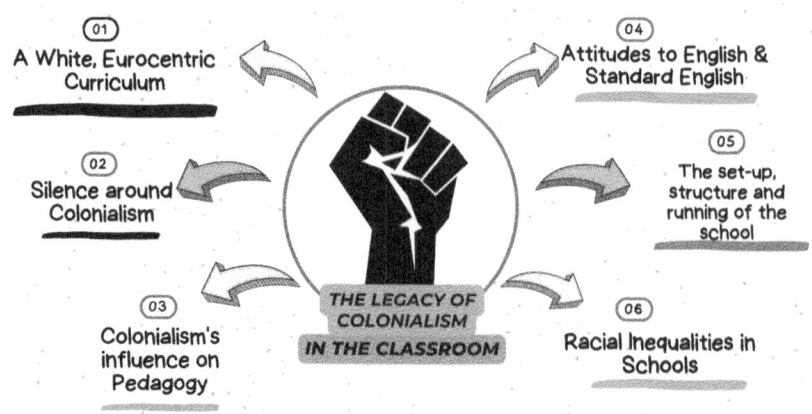

Figure 3.1 Author's mind map illustrating the different aspects of coloniality in education.

that permeate the classroom. Coloniality, for instance, can be felt in attitudes towards language. Hart and Risley's (1995) landmark US study claimed that working-class children suffer a 30-million-word deficit by the time they are four, a phenomenon often used to justify language intervention programmes. Identifying deficit attitudes to the speech of non-white speakers, raciolinguistics reveals the ways in which language and race are co-constructed to position racialised populations as inferior, with Flores (2021, p. 113) connecting language attitudes to a 'broader colonial history that [has] sorted populations into those deemed fully human (white) and those deemed not fully human (racialised)'. Relating this to UK schools, Cushing (2022, 2023a) investigates linguistic racism and attitudes towards Black working-class students, arguing that language policies highlighting the linguistic deficit of marginalised groups ultimately function to help children assimilate to white, middle-class behaviours. Identifying policies such as English Mastery[7] as being rooted in anti-Blackness, colonialism and white supremacy, Cushing (2023a) once again shows how racism and colonialism are distinct but intrinsically connected and how colonialism remains an influence in UK schools today. Furthermore, Cushing (2023b) also criticises the increasingly popular emphasis on a 'knowledge-rich' curriculum, asserting that this is a 'colonial, missionary and conservative narrative' (p. 1), grounded in the belief that students possess linguistic and knowledge gaps that only Western-centric curricula and linguistic intervention can fulfil, a narrative he describes as neocolonial.

Of further interest is Cushing's (2021) work on the policing of bodies in conjunction with the policing of language, where the control of students' movement (sit up straight, nod your head, walk on the left) creates an authoritarian environment. Additionally, he observes how even teachers' speech is controlled as they recite texts on PowerPoints or behaviour scripts. Thus, classrooms replicate not only colonialism's racialised hierarchy but also the sense of compliance that was evident in colonial times, denying space within which criticality and creativity might be cultivated. In the context of these observations, it is interesting to consider drama-based pedagogies, where students are invited to explore the possibilities of movement, to take control of their body for effect and to improvise. How can they do this if their voice and body are under surveillance?

Another consideration is the tendency to romanticise colonialism where it is mentioned in educational resources. Izzidien (2018, n.p.) observes how 'British textbooks still whitewash the British Empire' or direct the gaze to the violence of others. Alternatively, colonialism might be dissolved 'like a bitter pill into the much more palatable tonic of the nation's role in the story of abolition' (Manjapra 2018, n.p.), reiterating Goodfellow's (2019, n.p.) contention that 'amnesia and nostalgia sit side-by-side' in the teaching of colonialism. Said (1993, p. 63) asserts that colonialism exists as a 'codified, if only marginally visible, presence in fiction', with this invisibility creating a fictional narrative of Britain's past. He cites *Mansfield Park*, where 'colonial possessions help directly establish a social order' without explicitly being mentioned, and Rochester's West Indian wife in *Jane Eyre*, who is confined to the attic as a 'threatening presence' (1993, p. 62), demonstrating the ways in which colonies are depicted more vaguely as exotic realms and lands of opportunities, if mentioned at all, rather than sites of violence.

Recognising coloniality in education poses a thought-provoking response to the Sewell Report (Commission on Race & Ethnic Disparities, 2021), which was commissioned by the then Conservative UK Government with the aim of promoting a positive view of Britain's imperial legacy (arguably, instigated as a reaction to the BLM revival). The report's existence shows an effort to romanticise colonial history. As educators, how can we think about not just changing the literal narrative we teach but changing the historical narrative, or narrative emboldened by school policies and classroom decisions? In demonstrating how colonialism lives on in institutional racism within schools, Figure 3.1 challenges the report's assertion that racism is simply anecdotal.

Challenging epistemological hierarchies

Epistemology (the study of knowledge) is a further way in which coloniality manifests itself. Specifically, epistemological hierarchies exist that privilege knowledge from the Global North and instead present the Global South as the consumer, rather than the creator, of knowledge. Knowledge from some countries is seen as more valuable than others, which results in the presentation of the Global North as the epicentre of knowledge, helping others to progress.

Epistemological hierarchies are evident in the forms of knowledge that school systems prioritise. In many Western jurisdictions, lessons may privilege the written word in favour of knowledge formats more popular in the Global South – such as oral storytelling, drama, or art. In UK schools, this hierarchy is further entrenched in the approach to assessment, often focusing on academic essays dictated by exams that privilege written explanation. Here in England, the government's Curriculum and Assessment Review interim report (Department for Education, 2025) echoes similar sentiments, highlighting how non-exam-based assessment has been removed from many subjects and how diversifying assessment might ensure more skills are assessed and more students can excel.

For Mignolo (2009), this hierarchy is a by-product of colonialism, with colonial superpowers dictating who is knowledgeable and what counts as knowledge. Similarly, Smith (2012, p. 25) positions epistemological hierarchies as the consequence of racist, colonial ideas whilst simultaneously functioning to sustain them: 'one of the supposed characteristics of primitive peoples was that we could not use our minds or intellects...By lacking such virtues, we disqualify ourselves, not just from civilization but from humanity itself'. She suggests that, viewing knowledge through a Eurocentric lens, our classrooms contribute to the dehumanisation of marginalised groups. This is significant: educators cannot always change the curriculum to make it more inclusive, but we can use our pedagogy to make pupils feel a sense of belonging and a confidence in the knowledge that they demonstrate.

This discussion also encourages us to look critically at assessment, an enquiry which stretches beyond a consideration of the type of task being set to the freedom we give students in completing it. Hutchings (2015, pp. 4–5) suggests schools are being reduced to exam factories, where accountability pressures result in a drive for consistency of practice and 'shallow learning for the test', which Gillborn (2005, p. 494) explains is a result of the drive to raise standards and track progress through 'crude quantitative data'. There is a tendency that exam-orientated educational regimes, such as in England, give rise to a culture of rote-learning and memorising models at the expense of genuine comprehension (Department for Education 2025). Again, this suggests that criticality and students' own voices are being lost. For English teachers, decolonising our methods of assessment thus demands looking at how we encourage creative expression and independent thinking, both of which can be fostered successfully through an embedded drama-based approach. Ultimately, whilst diversifying the test materials is to be celebrated, we must also change our attitude to the test itself at both a governmental and classroom level.

Drama-in-English: a decolonial method

Figure 3.2 offers a way to conceptualise decolonising the classroom, reminding teachers to consider not just their curriculum but also their pedagogy.

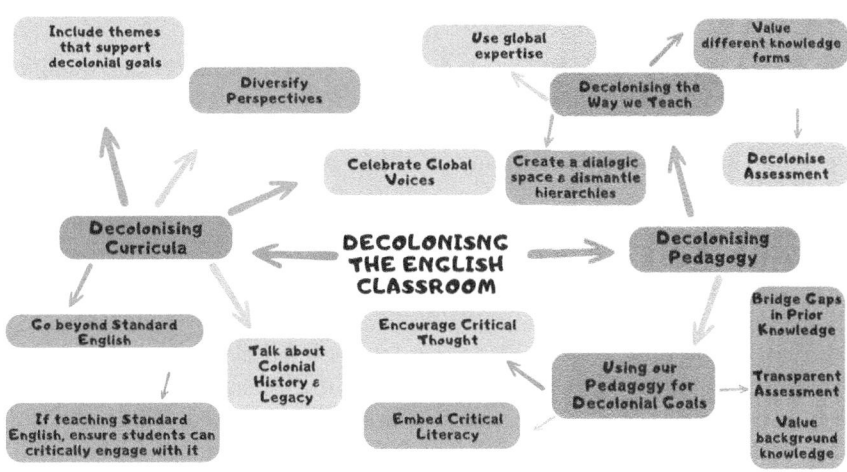

Figure 3.2 Author's mind map depicting different decolonial strategies.

As indicated by Figure 3.2, drama pedagogy offers a way in which knowledge can be diversified – and co-constructed – in English. Storytelling and oral traditions sit at the heart of drama, forms of knowledge that are often sidelined by the Global North. Drama-inflected pedagogy, therefore, offers a strategy by which Eurocentrism might be challenged. Moving forward, my aim in this chapter is to demonstrate ways in which drama-in-English can be used as a decolonial method, beginning with its ability to challenge epistemological hierarchies. The examples given below also show how drama-in-English has the capacity to challenge the silencing of colonialism and the creation of an authoritarian, censored classroom.

Crucially, drama-in-English gives learners back their voice, something essential for students to 'realise their potential, feel belonging and discover their identity' (Oracy Education Commission 2024, p. 7) and thus connects to the emancipatory goals of decolonial teaching. Moreover, dialogic pedagogy (for instance, exploratory talk and in-role work) fosters students' cognitive skills and deepens understanding, which consequently improves progress (Oracy Education Commission 2024; Education Endowment Foundation 2017). Framed in this way, drama-in-English can be used to narrow attainment gaps, essential when challenging institutional racism in schools: the Runnymede Trust (2021, n.p) for instance, highlights that learners from particular heritages (including mixed white/Black African, white other, Pakistani, Black other, mixed white/Black Caribbean, Black Caribbean, Irish traveller and Gypsy/Roma) all demonstrate lower achievement in comparison to their white peers in English secondary schools. In this context, I aim to illustrate decolonisation in action, not just in principle.

Example 1: the Victorian gentleman

My professional development workshops with both the trainees and qualified teachers were split into three sections: coloniality in education; an exploration of decolonial methods; and a planning workshop. Within the second section, the group imagined they were in my GCSE English class studying Stevenson's (1886) *Strange Case of Dr Jekyll and Mr Hyde*, imagining that they, like my students, were being introduced to the text for the first time. Starting off, I asked the group to walk around the space in the manner suggested by different tropes – from the damsel in distress to the archetypal hero figure. Quickly, the teachers jumped into action and transformed into various characters, all with noticeable similarity based on these well-established stereotypes. I then asked the group to walk in a way that suggests a British Gentleman. Immediately, they responded with chests out, noses to the sky, wearing pretend hats and with canes in hands...suddenly, the archetypal British Gentleman was before me.

Using collaborative discussion, the group were encouraged to reflect on the similarities between their walks, gestures, and expressions, eliciting the conclusion that despite not being a literary trope as such, the British Gentleman was a familiar concept. I prompted them to reflect on where these assumptions came from, using this to transition into teacher-directed instruction on etiquette rules and the unattainable image of perfection that was demanded in Victorian England. Then, I explained the colonial legacy of the British Gentleman: the construction of this gentleman was part of colonial rhetoric, and the facade of British gentility was essential to *legitimise* the subjugation of colonised peoples. As part of this, I included a brief history of European colonialism in Africa, using maps to demonstrate the wide expansion. I also included an African proverb ('Until the lion learns how to write, every story will glorify the hunter'), which we discussed as a group to further consider what this might reveal about literature or wider societal narratives about colonialism.

To further these ideas, I introduced the group to two poems: Kipling's (1899) 'The White Man's Burden' and Katwiwa's (2018) spoken word poem 'The Gospel of Colonisation'. These poems facilitated a discussion on the moral or religious justifications of colonialism, where the teachers worked in groups to consider how the concept of the British Gentleman further perpetuates these ideas. In doing so, the implications of their earlier role-plays were amplified as they connected their seemingly innocent enactment with colonial violence.

Constrained by time and the need to model activities for the teachers in an accelerated fashion, leaving time to unpick the rationale, it is important to recognise that with my own Year 10 students many of these discussions would have been more expansive. For instance, I might have asked students to mind-map together their prior knowledge of colonialism. A number of decolonial strategies were woven throughout the professional development workshops with the intention of showcasing a range of different dialogic methods, such as silent debates and body-line discussions. To expand the drama-based element of future workshops, I might include a still-images activity focused on contrasting lines from the two poems to help participants grapple with the different perspectives offered by the poets.

Finally, I moved on to an introduction of setting, using the earlier drama activity as a stimulus for an exploration of *Jekyll and Hyde*. Looking at descriptions of Dr Jekyll's house, we noticed the juxtaposition between the respectable front and the ominous back. Stevenson uses oppositions, with Victorian streets having moments of beauty and wealth, which are quickly followed by darkness. In pairs, the teachers considered how this could be interpreted through a colonial lens. Colonialism, for instance, had a sinister reality that was often masked by romanticised narratives. Finally, we touched on Stevenson's use of fog. Whilst many teachers may discuss the fog as a symbol for human nature (it's all a facade), I asked the group to consider how this could be interpreted from a post-colonial perspective: the rhetoric, like the fog, distorts our vision and prevents us from seeing colonial atrocities.

Drama-in-English, when used in this lesson, had not only opened up a space within which to talk about colonialism, but had also been crucial in demonstrating how colonial ideas had been propagated to such an extent that we could enact them almost identically at a moment's notice. The initial drama-based activity enables access to content that students may find challenging, for example, talking about historical issues and critical lenses. By its very nature, decolonial education values students' background knowledge and is connected to the students' world. In starting with their bodies, movement and assumptions, this enabled my workshop participants to personally connect with the curriculum in an inclusive way (Bryer, Pitfield & Coles 2024, p. 137). Moreover, in bringing together drama, written poetry, spoken word poetry, African proverbs and maps, this lesson was grounded in epistemological diversity and global expertise. Finally, it foregrounded discussion and criticality. Participants responded to prompts and moved between the text and the wider world. In this way, the activities cultivated critical literacy whilst also shifting the classroom into a collaborative space. Consequently, it inverted the typical lecturer-student dynamic and emphasised how all involved were active participants collaborating in the construction of their learning.

Example 2: play circles

The second example of decolonial practice I want to share is a 'play circles' unit I taught whilst working at an international school in Shanghai, which followed an American curriculum. I was teaching a non-exam class of 17-year-olds.

The summer term ended with a Lit Circles unit, where students were organised into simulated book clubs with the intention of encouraging independent reading. Modifying this, I created a unit focused on drama texts, where groups selected one play from a list that included Soyinka's (1962) *The Lion and the Jewel* and Garcia Lorca's (1936) *The House of Bernarda Alba*. Within each play circle (or group) there were various responsibilities which rotated: moderator; quotation expert; connector and context researcher. Students would spend one lesson taking parts and reading a particular section out loud and then completing a worksheet that supported their area of focus. The next lesson would be a Socratic Seminar, which amplified the talk-rich intention of the scheme.

Platforming decolonial learning, this unit was grounded in choice and independence – from students choosing the play they wanted to read, to the role they wished to take on, to the direction of their group's discussion. Returning to Cushing's (2021) critique of students speaking and moving almost robotically, this unit instead reimagined classroom hierarchies. To ensure students did not feel overwhelmed by increased autonomy, I created a list of plays from which students would select their choice and consciously curated this in a way that furthered the scheme's emancipatory intentions. When devising this list, I carefully considered plays that were from different parts of the world and could be used to prompt discussions around equity and social justice. In doing so, the unit was designed to be decolonial in its challenge to curriculum Eurocentrism and opened conversations that supported the liberatory goals of decolonial teaching.

Finally, the unit encouraged students to continually relate the play to real-world issues, supporting students' critical literacy. Inspired by bell hooks (1994), Dovey (cited in SOAS 2018, p. 18) comments, 'teaching has to be seen not only as an intellectual activity, but also as a form of activism and healing', and thus, my students were not just learning about different plays but also the world around them. An example of this was given in one student's response to *The House of Bernarda Alba* when Bernarda admonishes a young girl for speaking out in front of her elder, and my student drew a comparison to her own Korean culture. In this instance, a dramatic reading of the play was not simply the end product but was part of the meaning-making process (Bryer et al. 2024, p. 6), and thus, 'reading through drama' (Pitfield 2020) helped the student grasp the characters and relationships. Significantly, her personal connection was paramount, demonstrating critical reflection on the world around her. Such reflexivity is essential in society's quest for social justice, whilst also challenging the prescriptivism evident in colonial times.

Key to the design of this unit was my consideration of how drama could move towards a decolonising of assessment. Students were assessed on their holistic contributions to Socratic Seminars. A clear rubric ensured students were aware of what successful participation looked like (for example, asking thoughtful questions) and increased transparency. This embodies the idea that decolonisation is not only supporting all students to academically flourish but also privileging different forms of knowledge. Epistemological diversity was augmented through a weekly interactive notebook, where students had the choice to demonstrate their knowledge in any way they wished, which might include writing poems or creating set designs. My assessment model was grounded in giving students more autonomy over the learning whilst also emboldening students to express their own perspectives and creativity, something that stands in contrast to academic essays, constrained by prescriptivism (for instance, sentence starters and scaffolds).

Finally, I designed an end-of-unit assessment where groups performed two versions of a small scene in their play, using their performance skills (body language, tone of voice) and dramatic conventions (props, costume) to create different adaptations. Students were to select the extract as a group and work together to plan two versions, something heavily supported by prior units that had involved film comparisons. As a result of the pandemic, online learning disrupted this assessment, and it was eventually adapted into students recording two online performances of a monologue they wrote in response to their chosen play. As an example, one student played Walter from *A Raisin in the Sun* (Hansberry 1959) and used his tone of voice and levels to present the character as more dejected in version 1 and enraged in version 2, contrasting readings supported by physical movement and even a change of his bedroom lighting. Opportunities for enactment had clearly aided this student in portraying the character's complexity and, therefore, deepened his understanding.

In creating this assessment, I focused on students demonstrating not only their grasp of characterisation but also the impact of directorial decisions. Moreover, in making these interpretive changes, students were developing their command of English and understanding how it could be experimented with. Finally, retellings such as these effectively challenge 'single stories' (Adichie 2009), which are central in the replication of racist stereotypes. In asking students to create multiple versions, this point is accentuated. Looking forward, this would be a great opportunity to further discuss representation and stereotyping in cultural artefacts and the impact of complicating the narrative.

To assess students, I created a rubric with categories focusing on interpretation rather than on performance. This was written in the first person to promote self-assessment and provide transparent success criteria. To facilitate my summative assessment, each performance ended with students explaining the rationale behind their decisions. Through this Q&A, I was able to elicit how performance activities had supported students to make meanings and read through drama, as Pitfield (2020) puts it, encouraging students to think critically as they speculated how the scene could be imagined in different ways.

Conclusion

My aim in sharing these examples is to inspire fellow educators to realise that decolonising our pedagogy can happen even within the parameters of what we are mandated to teach – a much less daunting prospect. Furthermore, I have suggested that epistemological diversity can serve to foster creative *and* critical thinking. Whilst there is undoubtedly a time and place for exams and formal essays, these activities were essential in developing a comprehensive and nuanced grasp of the texts being studied. In summary, whilst these activities did not overtly 'teach to the test', they would help students succeed in conventionally academic ways. Moreover, they provided other ways of understanding students' knowledge and thus, remind us that drama-in-English and storytelling represent other ways in which we can demonstrate what we understand. And, surely, isn't *that* the whole point of assessment?

Significantly, I have showcased how aspects of drama-in-English offer English teachers a strategy that we can utilise to set up deep conversations, teach the tough histories, and shake up our preconceived ideas of what knowledge and knowledge-generating settings must look like. In this sense, we are innovative not only in the lessons we make but also in our approach to decolonisation, seeing it as more than updating book lists and instead a multifaceted task that is only just getting started.

Notes

1 A research project supported by Penguin Books and the Runnymede Trust to increase school students' access to more texts by writers of colour.
2 In the UK education policy decisions have been devolved by the Westminster government to its constituent nations: England, Northern Ireland, Scotland and Wales.
3 To clarify this distinction and to follow Bryer, Pitfield and Coles (2024), I will use 'Drama' to refer to the stand-alone subject, and 'drama' for its use as a pedagogical method.
4 George Floyd was an African American man who was murdered by a white police officer in Minneapolis, Minnesota, when he was arrested for using a counterfeit bank note.
5 This movement was initially inspired in 2015 by efforts to remove statues of Cecil Rhodes (founder of the British South Africa Company) in Cape Town but went on to galvanise the 'fallism' movement (cf. Frank & Mirjana Ristic 2020) and ignite wider exposure of institutional racism within universities (cf. Chaudhauri 2016).
6 The National Education Union (NEU) is the largest teachers' union in England and Wales.
7 English Mastery is a two-year intervention programme that aims to support students' literacy development at Key Stage 3. The programme was developed by the Ark multi-academy trust and prioritises literary heritage, explicit grammar and vocabulary instruction, and reading for pleasure.

References

Adichie, C. N. (2009). *The Danger of a Single Story*, TED Talk. Retrieved from www.ted.com/talks/chimamanda_ngozi_adichie_the_danger_of_a_single_story

Bryer, T., Pitfield, M., & Coles, J. (2024). *Drama at the Heart of English: Transforming Practice in the Secondary Classroom*. London: Routledge.

Chaudhauri, A. (2016). The real meaning of Rhodes Must Fall. *The Guardian*, 16 March. Retrieved from https://www.theguardian.com/uk-news/2016/mar/16/the-real-meaning-of-rhodes-must-fall

Commission on Race and Ethnic Disparities. (2021). *Commission on Race and Ethnic Disparities: The Report*. Retrieved from https://assets.publishing.service.gov.uk/media/6062ddb1d3bf7f5ce1060aa4/20210331_-_CRED_Report_-_FINAL_-_Web_Accessible.pdf

Cushing, I. (2021). Language, discipline and 'teaching like a champion'. *British Educational Research Journal*, 47(1), 23–41.

Cushing, I. (2022). Word rich or word poor? Deficit discourses, raciolinguistic ideologies and the resurgence of the 'word gap' in England's education policy. *Critical Inquiry in Language Studies*, 20, 305–331. https://doi.org/10.1080/15427587.2022.2102014

Cushing, I. (2023a). Challenging anti-Black linguistic racism in schools amidst the 'what works' agenda. *Race Ethnicity and Education*, 26(3), 257–276. https://doi.org/10.1080/13613324.2023.2170435

Cushing, I. (2023b). The knowledge-rich project, coloniality, and the preservation of whiteness in schools: A raciolinguistic perspective. *Educational Linguistics*, 2(1), 51–71. https://doi.org/10.1515/eduling-2022-0018

Department for Education (2013). *English Literature GCSE subject Content and Assessment Objectives*. Retrieved from https://assets.publishing.service.gov.uk/media/5a7ca069e5274a29d8363d20/GCSE_English_literature.pdf

Department for Education (2024). *Curriculum and Assessment Review: Review Aims, Terms of Reference and Working Principles*. Retrieved from https://assets.publishing.service.gov.uk/media/6699698f49b9c0597fdb0010/Curriculum_and_assessment_review_-_aims_terms_of_reference_and_working_principles.pdf

Department for Education. (2025). *Curriculum and Assessment Review: Interim Report*. Retrieved from https://assets.publishing.service.gov.uk/media/67e6b43596745eff958ca022/Curriculum_and_Assessment_Review_interim_report.pdf

Eddo-Lodge, R. (2017). *Why I'm No Longer Talking to White People about Race*. London: Bloomsbury.

Education Endowment Foundation (2017). *Dialogic Teaching: Evaluation Report and Executive Summary*. Retrieved from: https://d2tic4wvo1iusb.cloudfront.net/production/documents/projects/Dialogic_Teaching_Evaluation_Report.pdf?v=1727719710

Elliott, V., Nelson-Addy, L., Chantiluke, R., & Courtney, M. (2021). *Lit in Colour. Diversity in Literature in English Schools*. Retrieved from https://litincolour.penguin.co.uk/assets/Lit-in-Colour-research-report.pdf

Flood, A. (2020). American classics among most 'challenged' books of the decade in US. *The Guardian*, 28 September. Retrieved from https://www.theguardian.com/books/2020/sep/28/classics-books-most-often-challenged-and-banned-in-us-banned-books-week-to-kill-a-mockingbird

Flores, N. (2021). Raciolinguistic genealogy as method in the sociology of language. *International Journal of the Sociology of Language*, issues 267–268, 111–115. https://doi.org/10.1515/ijsl-2020-0102

Frank, S., & Ristic, M. (2020). Urban fallism: Monuments, iconoclasm and activism. *City*, 24(3–4), 552–564. https://doi.org/10.1080/13604813.2020.1784578

Garcia Lorca, F. (1936). *The House of Bernarda Alba*. London: Faber and Faber.

Gillborn, D. (2005). Education policy as an act of white supremacy: Whiteness, critical race theory and education form. *Journal of Education Policy*, 20(4), 485–505.

Goodfellow, M. (2019). Put our colonial history on the curriculum – then we'll understand who we really are. *The Guardian*, 5 December. Retrieved from https://www.theguardian.com/commentisfree/2019/dec/05/britain-colonial-history-curriculum-racism-migration

Hansberry, L. (1959). *A Raisin in the Sun*. New York: Vintage Books.

Hart, B. and Risley, T.R. (1995). *Meaningful Differences in the Everyday Experience of Young American Children*. Maryland, MD: Brooks Publishing.

hooks, b. (1994). *Teaching to Transgress: Education as the Practice of Freedom*. New York: Routledge.

Hutchings, M. (2015). *Exam Factories? The Impact of Accountability Measures on Children and Young People.* London: National Union of Teachers.

Iffath, H. (2020). Miss, what's colonialism: Confronting the English literacy heritage in the classroom. *Changing English,* 27(4), 369–392.

Izzidien, R. (2018). It is time to teach colonial history in British schools. *Aljazeera,* 30 August. Retrieved from https://www.aljazeera.com/opinions/2018/8/30/it-is-time-to-teach-colonial-history-in-british-schools

Jay, G. (2015). Queer children and representative men: Harper Lee, racial liberalism and the dilemma of 'To Kill a Mockingbird'. *American Literary History,* 27(3), 487–522.

Katwiwa, M. F. (2018). *The Gospel of Colonisation.* A Poetry Slam Inc Event. Retrieved from https://www.bing.com/videos/riverview/relatedvideo?q=katwiwa+the+gospel+of+colonisation+2018+pdf+download

Kendi, I. X. (2023). *How to be an Antiracist.* London: Vintage.

Kipling, R. (1899). The White Man's Burden. *McClure's Magazine,* 4 February. Retrieved from https://shec.ashp.cuny.edu/items/show/769

Landman, T. (2015). Is To Kill a Mockingbird a racist book? *The Guardian,* 20 October. Retrieved from https://www.theguardian.com/childrens-books-site/2015/oct/20/is-to-kill-a-mockingbird-a-racist-book-tanya-landman

Lee, H. (1960). *To Kill a Mockingbird.* Philadelphia: Lippincott.

Maldonado-Torres, N. (2007). On the coloniality of being: Contributions to the development of a concept. *Cultural Studies,* 21(2–3), 240–270.

Manjapra, K. (2018). *When will Britain Face Up to its Crimes against Humanity?* 29 March. Retrieved from https://www.theguardian.com/news/2018/mar/29/slavery-abolition-compensation-when-will-britain-face-up-to-its-crimes-against-humanity

Mignolo, W. D. (2009). Epistemic disobedience, independent thought and decolonial freedom. *Culture & Society,* 26(8), 159–181.

NEU (2024). *Framework for Developing an Anti-Racist Approach.* Retrieved from: https://neu.org.uk/sites/default/files/2024-09/NEU2532%20Anti-racist%20framework%202024%20WEB.pdf

Oracy Education Commission (2024). *We Need to Talk: The Report of the Commission on the Future of Oracy Education in England.* Retrieved from https://oracyeducationcommission.co.uk/wp-content/uploads/2024/10/Future-of-Oracy-v23-web-13.pdf

Pitfield, M. (2020). *Reading through Drama: The Contribution that Drama makes to Teaching and Learning in English (PhD),* University of Nottingham.

Runnymede Trust (2021). *Statement Regarding the Report from the Commission on Race and Ethnic Disparities.* Retrieved from https://www.runnymedetrust.org/news/statement-regarding-the-cred-report-2021

Said, E. (1993). *Culture and Imperialism.* New York: Vintage Books.

Sinclair, M. N. (2018). Decolonizing ELA. *The English Journal,* 107(6), 89–94.

Smith, L. T. (2012). *Decolonizing Methodologies: Research and Indigenous Peoples* (2nd ed.). London: Zed Books.

SOAS (2018). *Decolonising SOAS Learning and Teaching Toolkit for Programme and Module Convenors.* Retrieved from https://blogs.soas.ac.uk/decolonisingsoas/files/2018/10/Decolonising-SOAS-Learning-and-Teaching-Toolkit-AB.pdf

Soyinka, W. (1962). *The Lion and the Jewel.* London: Oxford University Press.

Steinbeck, J. (2001). *Of Mice and Men.* London: Penguin Books.

Stevenson, R. L. (1886). *Strange Case of Dr Jekyll and Mr Hyde.* London: Longmans, Green.

Sutherland, C. (2023). What's in a word? Modelling British history for a 'multi-racial' society. *Race, Ethnicity & Education,* 27(1), 1–19.

Chapter 4

Shakespeare on Zoom!

Erin Woodford

Introduction

Are drama-based approaches possible when students can't move freely, can't speak with ease, and can't physically interact or collaborate in groups? This was the question that faced my colleagues and me when the Covid-19 pandemic transformed our lively, energetic classrooms into atomised online learning and socially distanced in-person lessons. Drama-based pedagogy and 'active' approaches have long been integral to our teaching of Language Arts in my Singaporean secondary school. Pre-Covid, our classrooms were social and collaborative learning spaces, where students frequently worked in groups for activities such as discussions, role-plays, or debates. However, when the pandemic brought drastic changes and restrictions to our classrooms, it seemed more practical to replace these creative activities in favour of teacher talk and individual worksheets. Yet as our students grew more passive and disinterested, we realised that bringing back a sense of playfulness and collaboration in our lessons was even more important amidst these dispiriting constraints. Our answer to the question was to adapt 'active' approaches for the online space – and in doing so, we discovered a freedom that was no longer available to us in the physical classroom. In this chapter, I explore how my colleagues and I experimented with drama-based pedagogy online in teaching *The Merchant of Venice*, guided by the central principles of active Shakespeare and our own strongly held ethos of the classroom as a social and dialogic space, and our surprising discovery of how the online space offered unique opportunities for imaginative, learner-centred engagement with Shakespeare's work.

Active Shakespeare and our Language Arts department

My 14-year-old Language Arts students typically began their school year with a groan: 'Do we *have* to study Shakespeare this year?' *The Merchant of Venice* was a fixture on our Secondary 2 (Year 9) Language Arts curriculum, and it was generally greeted with trepidation and complaints of 'we can't understand this ancient English' and 'we are going to fail'. Their resistance was so great that we took to opening the unit with an activity called 'Shakesfears' so that we could address students' concerns. The 'fears' they shared all revolved around the same themes: it's boring, we don't understand it, we won't score well in exams. *The Merchant of Venice* not only felt culturally and linguistically distant to my multi-ethnic Singaporean students, it also seemed intimidating and impenetrable – a text that had to be correctly deciphered in order to achieve academic success. In response to this, my colleagues and I found that using 'active' and drama-rich strategies in the classroom was a powerful way of shifting students' perceptions of Shakespeare.

'Active Shakespeare' is a pedagogical approach to Shakespeare's plays that involves drama-based and other creative engagement. While it has a long history, perhaps its most well-known proponent is Rex Gibson (1998), who defines active Shakespeare as a form of imaginative engagement involving 'expressive, creative and physical activities' (1998, p. xii). While the idea of approaching a play through performance-based activities is perhaps not unintuitive, Gibson also extends his definition of 'active' pedagogies beyond acting and performance, broadening it to include any activities that engage the imagination, such as drawing, designing and creative writing. In their analysis of active Shakespeare pedagogies, Coles and Pitfield (2022) point to the pivotal influence of Gibson's work on similar, drama-based pedagogical approaches, including the Globe Theatre's 'creative Shakespeare' and the Royal Shakespeare Company's 'rehearsal-room' methods. In discussing the Globe education team's own rehearsal-room strategies, Fiona Banks (2014) acknowledges their roots in Gibson's work, particularly when she states that all the activities in her book 'draw on, and value, imaginative engagement and response' (Banks 2014, p. 5). My colleagues and I took inspiration from these definitions of 'active' approaches when designing our Shakespeare unit and adapted a number of our activities from those suggested by both Gibson and Banks.

Underscoring Gibson's approach are a set of clear principles. Two spoke most strongly to colleagues in my department: first, his exhortation to 'treat Shakespeare as a script' (1998, p. 7) as opposed to a text that is simply meant to be passively read. Gibson argues that the word 'script' suggests a sense of 'provisionality and incompleteness' (p. 8) that opens the door for students to engage with it imaginatively, rather than to mine the text for correct answers. The second principle that resonated strongly with us was Gibson's assertion that active Shakespeare is learner-centred and its aim is to create the social conditions for students to co-create their interpretation of the play together. Banks (2014, p. 8) echoes a similar learner-centric ethos in her assertion that 'creative Shakespeare' activities aim 'to put [students] in a position where they begin to experience a play from the inside as a creative interpreter – a player in all senses of the word – rather than to stare at it from without'.

The concept of co-creating meaning was particularly compelling for us. Singaporean classrooms are multi-ethnic, multicultural and multi-lingual – traits that are sometimes seen as stumbling blocks in the students' attempts to understand Shakespeare's plays by positioning learners on the 'outside'. Gibson's (1998, p. 9) assertion that students' 'rich variety of culture is a resource that Shakespeare lessons can celebrate and employ, rather than dismiss' was a powerful reminder to us to leverage our students' multicultural backgrounds as a strength. The activities that we created, therefore, often encouraged students to adapt the culture and language of the play to contexts that were more familiar to them – in doing so, learners not only became empowered interpreters of the play, they were also able to resonate much more deeply with its themes and nuances.

The principles and pedagogies of active Shakespeare aligned very naturally with our Language Arts department's focus on dialogic teaching and our view of the classroom as a collaborative and social learning space. We integrated drama-based and 'active' approaches routinely in our approach to all our Language Arts texts, not just Shakespeare; examples of such activities included choral speaking, role-play, debates, podcasts, writing-in-role, and artwork. In a signal of the importance we placed on creative and collaborative work, we also designed alternative assessments around these activities. We viewed this as a complement to traditional 'pen-and-paper' forms of assessment; while these were still an important part of our curriculum, alternative assessment allowed us a different means of assessing students' language and interpretive skills in an authentic setting. We also found that 'active' approaches gave students a strong sense of agency and ownership over their learning, which was central to developing their confidence as writers, speakers, and interpreters of texts. Above all, we found that our students responded naturally and eagerly to the invitation to 'play' with texts and language that was inherent in 'active' approaches – this greatly nurtured their interest in, and enjoyment of, Language Arts.

Our semester-long unit on *The Merchant of Venice* was structured around drama-based activities, leading towards a dramatisation of the play at the end of the unit – a clear highlight of the students' year. Each class was assigned an act of the play, which they then adapted and staged in a performance that was enthusiastically attended by their schoolmates, teachers and parents. The nature and focus of the dramatisation underwent several changes over the years. Initially, we focused on the adaptation aspect and encouraged students to set their assigned act in a different context that would appropriately highlight the key themes of the play. Our students were excited to modify the play to contexts that were relevant to them. These included: local settings, for instance, a Singaporean coffee shop; more 'modern' time frames, such as twentieth-century Italy (complete with the mafia); or different cultural contexts, for example, Ancient Egypt or China. We did not limit our students' options; rather, we encouraged them to make critical and intentional decisions by asking them to justify how their choices highlighted a particular theme or aspect of the play. More recently, we encouraged students to stage their act to foreground a particular view of a key character, for example, portraying Shylock as a sympathetic victim or Portia as the manipulative villain. Staging the play also offered a variety of activities that allowed each student the opportunity to choose their preferred way to engage with the play – from adapting the script to designing costumes, sets, posters or programmes, to acting. This echoed Gibson's definition of active Shakespeare as a variety of creative activities that offered imaginative engagement with the play.

Although the dramatisation was the culmination of the semester, it was not the only way in which we integrated the active Shakespeare pedagogy into our curriculum. We carefully designed and included accessible drama-based activities throughout our lessons, for example, writing-in-role activities to explore characterisation and drama activities like tableaux and role-play. Coles and Pitfield (2022, p. 16) term this approach 'process drama interventions', which they define as being 'characterised by the teacher's careful structuring of dramatic sequences, built across a number of lessons, utilising opportunities for participatory engagement, improvisation and interpretative approaches'. The concept of process drama is anchored in the work of Dorothy Heathcote, a key figure in educational drama. She argues that it allows students to draw collectively on their past experiences and their imaginations and encourages discovery and problem-solving (Johnson & O'Neill 1984). To further deepen students' critical appreciation of the performative elements of the play, we also showed them video clips from different film and theatre adaptations of *The Merchant of Venice*, encouraging them to compare and discuss various performative techniques and their effects. Significantly, we did not want students to only work towards a single showcase performance of *The Merchant of Venice* – rather, we wanted to embed drama-based approaches as a consistent feature of how they approached the play throughout the unit in order to firmly position our students as co-constructors of meaning in their engagement with Shakespeare's work.

Disruption and constraints

In 2020, the Covid-19 pandemic brought massive, unforeseen disruption to our lives and the regularity of our normal school routine. Singaporean schools closed for almost two months, and subsequently, students returned to in-person lessons on a staggered schedule, which alternated weekly between in-person lessons and home-based learning, with online lessons conducted via Zoom. This safety measure, intended to break any potential cycle of Covid-19 transmission, resulted in the somewhat disorienting experience of seeing students in person one week and on computer screens the next and affected the way we planned our lessons and activities. When students attended in-person lessons, the physical environment of the classroom was dramatically different. Strict social distancing measures were implemented to ensure everyone's safety. Students sat in single file, socially distanced with 1-metre gaps, and were discouraged from unnecessary movement. Teachers were similarly discouraged from moving freely around the classroom; instead, we remained at the front of the classroom. Students were not allowed to gather in groups. Furthermore, mask-wearing was compulsory at all times, which made students reluctant to speak up as they struggled to articulate themselves through their face coverings. These measures were necessary to ensure everyone's physical health and well-being, but they changed our lively, social classrooms immeasurably. As teachers, we were equally unsettled by these restrictive and unusual circumstances, and grappled with how to adjust our teaching accordingly – especially in terms of how to translate our usual classroom practice to online teaching. Increasingly, we relied on worksheets and teacher talk as the most practical and efficient way to teach. But our students, who keenly felt the strangeness and sense of confinement of these new arrangements, became increasingly passive and disinterested in response.

The onset of the pandemic and the sudden shifts in our school environment coincided with the start of our unit on *The Merchant of Venice*. My colleagues and I were surprised when our students eagerly asked us how we would continue with our plans for the dramatisation – it seemed obvious to us that this was a non-starter in the circumstances. At this point, we were mostly meeting online, and when we were in person, students could hardly get out of their seats; a large gathering in the school auditorium was certainly out of the question. When we explained this to our students, they were dismayed. They had heard about the dramatisations from their seniors and were eagerly anticipating it as a highlight of their Secondary 2 year. Meanwhile in the staffroom, we discussed with concern the students' growing lethargy and passivity, their frustration at their confined circumstances, and their lack of engagement with the desk-bound, individual work that had come to dominate their lessons.

Our concerns as teachers were certainly not unique – indeed, the Covid-19 pandemic had forced abrupt and unnatural changes to classrooms around the world. However, post-pandemic reflections from teachers have shown that innovative pedagogy can also arise from a situation of great constraint. For example, Gannon et al. (2021, p. 40) describe how a particular 'pandemic pedagogy' emerged amongst Australian teachers, characterised by 'collaboration, flexibility, personal reflection and professional collegiality'. Furthermore, they suggest that this emergent pedagogy 'advocated for a reimagining and transformation of teaching in order to value student voice and build confidence, independence, deep learning and understanding'. My colleagues and I had a similar experience as we grappled with how to engage our students in this new, socially-distanced reality. It was clear that we could not continue with our *The Merchant of Venice* dramatisations in their usual form, but we also knew we had to find some way to bring back the social, engaging and creative lessons which the students enjoyed and were looking forward to. As teachers, we approached this with an attitude reminiscent of Gannon et al.'s (2021) 'pandemic pedagogy', in that we worked collaboratively and with a spirit of experimentation as we reimagined what teaching and learning could look like in our new classrooms. Above all, we remained firm in our conviction that our classrooms – online or offline – would continue to be a learner-centred, social and dialogic space.

Active Shakespeare goes online

Ultimately, the answer lay in the flexibility of active Shakespeare as a pedagogy. Gibson, Banks and other proponents of this pedagogy emphasised that its ethos was imaginative, creative engagement; Gibson, in particular, was clear that this included non-drama-based activities such as drawing and writing. Guided by this ethos, we asked ourselves: how can our students engage imaginatively with Shakespeare online? This question inspired us to explore the possibilities offered by the online space, rather than just focusing on what we had 'lost' when we moved away from tried and tested classroom-based drama activities.

I describe our experience of taking our dramatisations of *The Merchant of Venice* online in the following section. However, taking a process drama approach, we did not focus solely on the dramatisation. Rather, we adapted several drama-based activities for our online classrooms. One which we called 'Soundtrack This Scene' turned out to be particularly impactful: I gave students short video clips of several key scenes from the Globe's 2015 production of *The Merchant of Venice* and asked them to overlay a song that would form an appropriate soundtrack to the action. This was a particularly effective lesson after we read Act 3.2, where Portia uses a song to slyly guide Bassanio to the right choice of casket. We discussed how music played an important part in the scene – besides conveying Portia's secret message, it also reflected key themes of love and desire and created an atmosphere that was playful and entertaining but also suspenseful. Students then applied what they had learnt to creating a soundtrack for their chosen key scene. They uploaded their soundtracked videoclips to a Padlet wall, accompanied by a short post which explained why this song formed an effective soundtrack to the scene. Their classmates then viewed the video clips and posts in a virtual Gallery Walk, followed by a discussion in a Zoom lesson.

Students' soundtrack choices proved to be immensely entertaining and surprisingly apt. Their song choices ranged from current pop hits from singers like Ed Sheeran and Taylor Swift to the latest K-pop stars. My students' song choices mirrored not just the themes but also the tempo and mood of the scene. Some students even used the songs to provide incisive commentary about the characters, for example, Kiara,[1] who chose Smash Mouth's hit song 'All Stars' as the soundtrack for the scene where Bassanio chooses the correct casket. In her explanation, she highlighted the song lyric 'all that glitters is gold, only shooting stars break the mould', cleverly pointing out that it ironically echoes the scene's famous line, 'all that glitters is not gold'. She further commented:

The mood after he selects the correct casket is a happy one and people are seen to be celebrating. I believe this is a suitable song as its fast tempo emphasizes the joyful mood in the scene. The lyrics also reflect Bassanio's personality as he can be very rash sometimes (lavishly spending money even when he should not).

Kiara's choice of song was not only witty, it also indicated that she was developing an insightful appreciation of the mood and pace of the scene. The activity not only displayed her perceptive understanding of the play, it allowed her to co-create its meaning with others in discussion: in adding this pop song, she provided wry commentary on Bassanio's character, as well as giving the scene a new level of playfulness and trendy relevance.

Another student, Imran, made a similarly thoughtful choice when he selected the theme tune from the film 'Schindler's List' as the soundtrack to Shylock's famous 'Hath not a Jew eyes' speech in Act 3.1. He described the use of music with great precision:

The theme would be played during the more sorrowful parts of the speech, specifically until 'and if you wrong us, do we not revenge.' The violin piece was made for a movie about a German protecting Jews during world war two, therefore dropping deeper meaning to the scene for the audience [who are familiar with the movie] ... the sorrowful trembling of the violin is in conjunction with each burst in which Shylock pleads for equality. After stopping at 1:10 of the video, the music will resume at 1:46. My intention is to help the audience sympathise with Shylock when he pleads for common humanity or when he is notified of his losses, but let the audience feel the full fury of his voice when he talks about revenge. This emphasises the theme of the speech, which is not solely about revenge but also about the sorrow Shylock feels when he loses his daughter and money, the inequality he has been struggling with, his ideals and shame.

I was surprised by the level of intentionality Imran showed in using music to bring out the emotional and thematic nuances of the speech. The act of using digital technology to overlay the soundtrack onto the scene seemed to have the effect of making him more keenly attentive to the text of the play – he not only 'matched' the music to specific lines, he also identified timestamps of the video which, to him, illustrated the exact moment Shylock's emotions shifted.

This activity showed me that there were unexpected benefits to using technology, beyond simply making the activities fun and engaging for students. In her discussion of digital and online activities, Emma Whipday (2023) argues that they can offer gains which are specific to this mode, in particular, 'opportunities for creativity, collaboration, peer-to-peer learning, and social engagement that equal or exceed those of in-person teaching […] and can, perhaps surprisingly, enable modes of close reading that are particularly alert to the embodied potential of performance texts' (p. 59). This was particularly relevant to my own experience of seeing my students' creativity flourish, perhaps in part because it was facilitated by digital devices that they were so familiar with. In fact, they ignored my painstaking instructions on how to overlay the soundtrack on the videoclip, telling me, 'oh there's an app for that' and deftly speeding ahead with the task! I also found that, as Whipday suggested, my students paid much closer attention to both the text of the play and its performative potential. In a typical lesson, I often had to prompt students to consider textual evidence in greater detail ('which line shows you this?'), but in this activity, I found my students, like Imran and Kiara, instinctively referring to lines from the play, even though I had not explicitly instructed them to do so. They also showed a sensitive awareness of the play as a performance. This was evident in their analysis of how the soundtracks would affect the audience, as well as their appreciation of the mood, pace and tempo of the performance. Later in the term, when students worked on their dramatised readings of *The Merchant of Venice*, they used this technique of including suitable music to complement the scene.

This activity also showed us the many other benefits that the online space offered our students. Brindley et al. (2021, p. 73) discuss how 'teaching English via a digital device may present opportunities for enhanced learning experiences as they are more intimate than a physical classroom'. They cite the wider variety of ways students can engage with content online, including direct messaging, online polls, and the ability to do online research. Myfanwy Edwards (2021, p. 19) sounds a similarly optimistic attitude about moving in-class activities online, noting 'there are not only ways to replicate this in an online classroom, but there are aspects that work more effectively'. In Edwards' experience of teaching *Hamlet* online to Year 7 students in the UK, she describes how the use of Google Classroom allowed her students to articulate their views in ways they perhaps might not have done in the classroom – for example, the chat function which allowed students to seamlessly comment on an ongoing lesson in ways they might not have done in person, for fear of interrupting the class. As a teacher, she also found the chat function useful, as it allowed her to 'deal with each idea and interpretation in turn, something I could not do in a classroom' (p. 19). These examples of classroom practice illustrate what my colleagues and I found as we transitioned from in-person lessons to online activities – that online technology presented many unexpected benefits to learning, in a way that was different from what our physical classrooms offered us.

To Zoom or not to Zoom: *The Merchant of Venice* dramatic reading project

While our students greatly enjoyed activities like 'Soundtrack this Scene', they were anxious to know what would happen with their much-anticipated dramatisations. Some elements of the dramatisation would remain the same as before the pandemic: for example, students were still able to work on the posters and programmes that would accompany their dramatisations. The real conundrum was what to do with our on-stage performance, which could no longer be done under the new social distancing guidelines. The solution that my colleagues and I eventually came up with was to adapt the performance to what we called dramatised readings, which would be video-recorded.

We were inspired by an online 'Reader's Theatre'-style performance of *Hamlet* by middle school teachers from America, which took the form of a Zoom call between the characters (see Hamlet For Kids, 2020). The format of a video-recorded Zoom call was both novel and, given the current circumstances, timely and relevant. Most importantly, it was practical for our students to execute. Furthermore, the concept of Reader's Theatre was helpful in clarifying for us how we could adapt 'active' approaches for an online context. Beverly Busching (1981, p. 331) defines Readers' Theatre as a 'formalized dramatic presentation of a script by a group of readers', with characterisation and emotion being primarily conveyed through the reader's voice as opposed to the usual performative conventions of action, costume, staging and props. While we eventually incorporated the use of costumes and a few other dramatic elements, the concept of Readers' Theatre gave us a meaningful way to translate our dramatisation to an online platform, where students would not be able to rely heavily on stagecraft and physical movement. Beyond these practical affordances, the ethos of Reader's Theatre struck a chord for us, in particular, the way it not only encourages students to strongly empathise with the characters that they role-play, it also allows for a 're-creation' of the literary text, where 'children search for personal meaning in the characters and situation and build their own individual interpretations' (Busching 1981, p. 331). This echoes Gibson's principle of learner-centredness in active Shakespeare, where 'every student seeks to create his or her own meaning, rather than passively soak up information' (1998, p. 9). Therefore, in both its form and principles, Reader's Theatre seemed, to us, an appropriate way to transition our 'active' approaches to an online space.

These dramatised readings offered another powerful example of how the online space enabled students to both circumvent physical restrictions and engage imaginatively with Shakespeare's work. To complement the Reader's Theatre format, my students used the choral reading skills that they had learnt in a previous Language Arts unit, such as collective voice, echoing, and antiphonal reading. This also encouraged students to be more playful and creative in their interpretation of the play. For example, one group of students found the technique of collective voice to be particularly impactful in representing the shifting power dynamics between Portia and Shylock in the trial scene. When students felt that Portia was more empowered, they represented this by having two or three students speak her lines in unison: a chorus of Portias, instead of a single student playing the character. However, when her power decreased, so did the number of Portias. In justifying her group's choice, one student wrote:

> As Portia becomes more and more vindictive and ruthless with Shylock's sentence, I imagine more Portias slowly descending on the scene. With each new (line of) dialogue, a new Portia will appear. At the final line, "Down, therefore, and beg mercy of the duke" they all will say the line together. This line feels important to me and is sort of underrated in my opinion, as Portia kept asking Shylock to have mercy on Antonio. Now, she denies him of any mercy and he has to physically beg for it. It feels particularly powerful and vindictive.

The use of collective voice was vivid, but what made it especially powerful was how my students complemented it by manipulating the layout of the Zoom screen, conveying a metaphorical level of interpretation. As the number of students playing Shylock decreased, each 'Shylock's' square box on the Zoom screen dramatically faded to black, signifying his absence – while several 'Portias', each in their own square box, dominated the screen. This had great visual impact in illustrating the shifting power relations between the two characters at pivotal moments in the scene. While this could perhaps also have been achieved physically on stage, it might have felt more clunky or forced; here, the black Zoom boxes signifying the character's diminishing status were integral to the dramatic effect of the scene.

In fact, working in an online mode appeared to encourage my students to think more playfully and metaphorically, creating more room for a learner-centred interpretation of the play. To illustrate the settings of their scenes, students used Zoom background images, such as a grand staircase to represent Portia's Belmont house or a courtroom for the famous trial scene. These were the obvious choices, but there were also others which were less literal, though no less highly evocative. For example, one group incorporated a meme as a backdrop to Shylock's 'Hath not a Jew' speech. The meme displayed a room on fire while a cartoon dog ironically declares 'this is fine', which to them reflected Shylock's suppressed rage at living in a society which treated him with such contempt. The use of a meme, much more natural in an online context than it would be in person, gave students yet another way to express their interpretation of Shylock's experience. They also seemed to enjoy trying to convey a sense of performance despite the restricted, static format of the Zoom screen. They dressed in simple but symbolic costumes – a student who played Portia in the trial scene expressed what she saw as the character's sinister intentions through a forbidding black cape. They also used simple props, occasionally 'passing' the props from one Zoom window to another – in one dramatised reading, Bassanio gave up his wedding ring to Portia by 'dropping' it between their Zoom windows into her impatient, outstretched hand.

My students seemed to experience what Whipday (2023, p. 72) describes, somewhat paradoxically, as 'embodiment in a disembodied way'. She acknowledges that the online space is essentially a disembodied one, as students are not in the same physical location and are simply represented by images of their faces – or, possibly, not represented at all. In these circumstances, the online classroom itself requires students to make 'imaginative leaps' that are similar to how they need to imagine a written text being performed. Whipday explains,

> When I ask students to read aloud a stage direction and to imagine it in performance, the task is not so very far removed from the work they are already doing in imagining the series of boxes on their Zoom screen as a learning community.
>
> (p. 73)

This resonated with what I saw in my students' dramatised readings. Despite the disembodied space, their approach to the play was still an embodied one – particularly in their use of voices, as well as their use of gestures, costumes and props. It also broadened their concept of performance beyond simply 'acting out' the play. Unlike previous years, where students put most of their energy into acting and 'accurately' representing the script, the students who worked online were more imaginative, playful and non-literal in how they introduced performative elements into their work – for example, through disappearing Zoom boxes, witty soundtracks, memes, and symbolic props. While our classroom circumstances may have been restrictive, working online seemed to liberate students in other, unexpected ways. In addition to Whipday's suggestion that online learning engages students' imaginations, I think my students were empowered by working in a medium in which they felt completely comfortable. In a digital realm, they were able to confidently draw on their knowledge to access a play that they otherwise perceived as 'ancient' and remote from them. This lent a freshness and relevance to their interpretations of Shakespeare.

Conclusion

The project culminated in widely-anticipated screenings of the dramatised readings, which we held online as well as in small, in-person class groups. At the end of the screenings, we grandly held our own version of the Oscars, called the LALA Awards (named after our subject, Language Arts, often referred to by the acronym 'L.A.'). Students and teachers cast their votes for a range of awards which acknowledged every category: in addition to the awards for acting, we also had Best Sound and Technical Effects, Best Poster, and Best Script. The winners were presented with shiny trophies and, of course, bragging rights, which they gleefully claimed. We did not assess the dramatised readings as it was the first time we were experimenting with this project, but we wanted to give students an opportunity to showcase their work in front of an audience – even if, in this case, the audience was a virtual or socially distanced one. Banks (2014, p. 170) observes that

> performing for an audience gives them status. They have the authority. They are the interpreters of the play and have shaped their version of the story to share with the audience. Nobody knows this version of the play as well as they do.

She further explains that an audience shifts students' relationship with the text from understanding it to becoming co-creators of meaning. Ensuring that our students had an audience not only created an atmosphere of excitement and enthusiasm, it also ascribed them the 'status' that Banks describes – positioning them 'within' the play and showing that their interpretation has credibility and impact.

Taking active Shakespeare online was a response to unusual circumstances that changed our classrooms in ways that we could not have foreseen. In a true case of necessity driving invention, we found ways to adapt our in-class drama-based pedagogy to the online mode – and in the process, discovered surprising benefits to the online space that we had not encountered in our face-to-face lessons. In reflecting on this experience, what stands out is the resilience and flexibility of drama as a pedagogy. While it required us to reimagine our classrooms – from a physical space full of free movement and group work to an online space – we discovered that the principles of active Shakespeare, particularly in terms of its imaginative, learner-centric engagement with the text, continued to be enduring regardless of the mode of enactment. Not being confined by our physical environment, in fact, freed us up in some ways to explore even more imaginative, more compelling engagement with the play. As teachers, we already knew how transformative the active Shakespeare approach was in developing critical, engaged readers, but amidst hugely restrictive circumstances, we were able to find freedom in how we encouraged our students to engage with the play online. This had additional resonance with the constraining backdrop of Covid-19. In a time of passivity, fear and isolation, it offered us what we were sorely missing: imaginative engagement, collaboration and co-creation.

Note
1 Students' names have been anonymised.

References
Banks, F. (2014). *Creative Shakespeare: The Globe Education Guide to Practical Shakespeare*. London: Bloomsbury.
Brindley S., Alexander, P., Amis, D., Lownds, S., Shaw, C., & White, S.S. (2021). Teaching and learning in UK English classrooms: Tales from the Pandemic. *English in Australia*, 56(2).

Busching, B. (1981). Readers Theatre: An education for language and life. *Language Arts*, 58(3), 330–338. https://www.jstor.org/stable/41961305

Coles, J., & Pitfield, M. (2022). *Reading Shakespeare Through Drama*. Cambridge: Cambridge University Press.

Edwards, M. (2021). The Tempest explored online by year 7. *Teaching Shakespeare*, 21, 19–20.

Gannon, S., Jacobs, R., D'warte, J., & Naidoo, L. (2021). 'But w'rry not we shall banquet again someday': Creativity and socially distanced English. *English in Australia*, 56(2), 38–48.

Gibson, R. (1998). *Teaching Shakespeare*. Cambridge: Cambridge University Press.

Hamlet for Kids – Readers Theatre – The Teacher Edition. (2020) Retrieved from: https://www.youtube.com/watch?app=desktop&v=hDlB6mZ0KE0&amp%3Bfeature=youtu.be

Johnson, L., & O'Neill, C. (eds.) (1984). *Dorothy Heathcote: Collected Writings on Education and Drama*. London: Hutchinson.

Whipday, E. (2023). *Teaching Shakespeare and his Sisters: An Embodied Approach*. Cambridge: Cambridge University Press.

Chapter 5

Writing-in-Role
The Significance of Visualising Fictional Worlds Through Drama

Theo Bryer

Writing-in-role as a pedagogic strategy has a distinctive history in English classrooms. This chapter draws on data from two research projects (2015, 2021) conducted with student-teachers on a Post Graduate Certificate of Education course[1] to develop an understanding of aspects of the relationship between writing-in-role and active drama. The student-teachers' writing-in-role which emerged from these projects is indicative of their heightened awareness of the visual dimensions of the drama they engaged in, and hence of features of the literary texts that inspired both the drama and their writing. The emphasis in this chapter is on the effects of watching as well as making and performing, and listening as well as speaking.

Drama-in-English (Bryer, Pitfield and Coles 2024) offers opportunities for students to engage with texts in creative ways by bringing characters, incidents, atmosphere and metaphor into a physical and visual dimension. According to O'Neill and Rogers (1994, p. 51), the process creates 'a bridge between the abstraction of the written word and the students' understandings'. I refer to the acts of remaking a text in the form of drama, digital media or creative writing as 'transmedia approaches' (Bryer 2020; Coles and Bryer 2018), drawing on Louise Rosenblatt's (1978) 'transactional' reader response theory to explain how this process supports students' reading, their critical awareness and insights. This chapter is about what constitutes such a bridge to meaning-making, or how seeing can become make-believing, as evidenced in students' writing-in-role.

For many people, reading and making meaning from literary texts encompasses some form of visualisation of the locations, environments, characters and incidents that inform narratives. Creative writing may involve communicating similarly vivid visual details to dwell in a moment or to develop a story. One of my recent English with Drama PGCE student-teachers explained to me what it was like to have aphantasia, meaning that she did not create involuntary mental images when reading. She reported how adapting a text in dramatic form and watching others do the same made her engagement with texts more immersive, enjoyable, and meaningful and supported her creative writing. Although only a small percentage of students might have aphantasia, not everyone is readily able to make sense of the texts that they encounter in English lessons.

Moving from reading a text to enacting it involves a neglected aspect of dramatic interaction: watching, as well as making and performing, and listening, as well as speaking. Of course, in classrooms populated with desks and chairs rather than stage scenery, students have to work as hard to derive meaning from the dialogue and movement that emerge from their peers' dramatic interactions as they do when grappling with the words on the page. Assuming a role facilitates this process, involving a more nuanced awareness of the signs made by bodies, props, movement, use of space and the ways that these are framed in classroom contexts (Bryer 2020; Bryer and Coles 2022; Coles and Bryer 2018). I have identified evidence of particular attention to the visual dimensions of narratives in the two research projects (2015, 2021) I draw on here. I will focus particularly on what the literacy specialist Myra Barrs (1987, p. 9) refers to as 'drama on paper' to explain these insights.

Writing-in-role: a historical perspective

Writing from the perspective of a fictional character emerged out of a tradition of progressive English teaching and creative writing, sometimes allied with active drama. The English teacher Marjorie Hourd (1949) followed Harriet Finlay-Johnson's (1911) and Henry Caldwell Cook's (1917, p. 188) habits of 'dramatizing nearly everything' that their English classes read, through forms of acting 'extempore' rather than spending too long discussing or envisaging a final performance. Creative writing was integral to this process, and Hourd was one of the first English teachers to recognise the power of writing-in-role specifically, as recorded in an article about the power of dramatisation inspired by the study of literary texts. Hourd (1940, p. 152) notes how the 11-year-old Margaret succeeds in capturing the 'essence and spirit' of de Cervantes' *Don Quixote* and Bunyan's *The Pilgrim's Progress* and 'unconsciously borrowed in style from both books' in her imagined conversation between Don Quixote and Christian, the protagonist of *The Pilgrim's Progress*.

Observing and visualising

An interest in the significance of close attention to visual signs emerges from research into drama's role in English teaching undertaken by the internationally renowned drama practitioner Dorothy Heathcote, working with Barrs (Heathcote 1980). Characteristic of Heathcote's practice was to draw attention to the semiotics of the image created with the resources of bodies, economically selected props or symbolic pieces of costume. In Heathcote and Barrs' project, Shelley's 'Ozymandias' provided a stimulus for drama, talk and writing with primary children. The children created depictions or still images representing waxworks in a museum to show important moments in the gradual decline of the dynasty of Ozymandias (Heathcote 1980). The children also assumed roles as expert archaeologists and museum guides, explaining the significance of the visual details in the 'exhibits' created by their peers. Heathcote invokes Britton's (1970) spectator role, implying observation and reflection on experience, in order to understand the children's considered spoken and written responses, identifying the conscious examination of the implications of the action that they engaged in through the process. She recognises the meaningful way that the drama prompted the children to call 'upon language *to serve their needs*; using language to help make sense of the situation' (Heathcote 1980, p. 22, her italics). In this account, making meaning from visual prompts was obviously central to the experience, informing the dramatic action and the ways that the children were able to adopt particular registers in their talk and writing.

Since Betty Jane Wagner (1976, pp. 193–196) documented the many examples of what she called Heathcote's 'press for language', including prompts to writing-in-role as in the 'Ozymandias' project, there have been a number of case studies undertaken to establish the ways that role-play can provide a stimulus or model or frame for writing. These involve heightening awareness of purposes and audiences, particularly in primary schooling (e.g., Booth and Neelands 1998; Dunn, Harden and Marino 2013). As part of Andy Kempe's (2001) drama and literacy research project with 10- and 11-year-olds, he asked the children what mental pictures certain words induced and noted the ways that words spoken in a dramatic context were ascribed meaning by those listening 'not only through their sound and semantic meaning, but through the visual resonances they evoke' (p. 4). Kempe is also attentive to the way that the 'rhythms and patterns' of his assumption of the role of Prospero, including wielding a staff in significant ways, informed the pupils' writing. In other classroom-based research, Cathy Burnett (2015, p. 203) is alert to the way that a boy assuming the role of a zombie 'seemed to generate (or affirm) a shared frame of reference', serving to inform the mystery stories his peers in the primary classroom went on to write.

In an important year-long research project in primary schools, Cremin et al. (2006, p. 279) found that writing informed by drama was characterised by 'powerful language choices and the inclusion of details'. A sense of the significance of the journey from visualising to dramatic activity and writing emerges from their conclusion (Cremin et al. 2006, p. 289):

> While improvising in drama, children are involved in thinking, feeling, visualising and creating multiple possibilities; in their related writing, they are often able to make this thinking visible as they shape their understanding further.

Widening perspectives: a critical dimension

In *Drama at the Heart of English* (Bryer et al. 2024), my co-authors and I strongly made the case for creative and critical responses realised through writing inspired by drama. Designed to meet conventional curricular demands, such as reflection, evaluation and writing-in-role, our examples of practice include journalistic, letter and diary writing. We drew on evidence from a lesson sequence based on Swindell's *Stone Cold* about homelessness and another with A-Level[2] students (aged 16–18 years old) that involved imagining what Goneril from *King Lear* might say were she present at the mock trial in which she is represented by 'a joint stool' (Act 3 Scene 6 of the 1608 quarto). Both of these examples prompted students' critical insights about the positioning of relatively voiceless or vulnerable characters. In Pitfield (2020, p. 221) research, she quotes from a student, Zemar, who explains that drama-inspired activities, including writing, have helped him 'get attitudes to the text'. There are links here with Saunders' (2022) insights about the ways that drama was 'applied to explore the gaps, silences and critical moments' within texts, including Marsden and Ottley's *Home and Away*, with a class of primary pupils in Sydney. This has been characterised as 'perspectival learning', offering the potential to open up 'new ways of looking at the world which reflect the complexity of living and that ensures alternative positions and different views are examined' (Grainger, Goouch and Lambirth 2005, p. 109). Through their research into processes of creative writing in primary schools, Grainger and her colleagues (2005) clearly recognise a connection between ways of looking and different perspectives or views. They identify that the 'ambiguity and tension' (p. 116) implied in dramatic action provides a significant stimulus to writing that is enriched by the assumption of the stances, registers and words of the characters drawn from literary texts, such as Sachar's *Holes* and Kurtz's *Almaz and the Lion*. The authors also identify the ways that the language of the text is echoed in the writing that the pupils do if the text is revisited or consciously integrated into the drama.

In two articles that focus on drama with secondary-age school students, O'Neill and Rogers (1994) write about a drama-based sequence focusing on Williams' *A Streetcar Named Desire* and Lee's *To Kill a Mockingbird* (O'Neill, Rogers and Jasinski 2006). The authors see the potential in the creation of fictional worlds and 'possibilities of meaning not only through word but also through gesture, visualisation, and movement' (2006, p. 93). In this case, a recognition of the metaphorical implications of the ways that their peers use their bodies to make meaning clearly enhances the students' reading of the text.

The importance of writing-in-role for A-level students is explored by Kate Bomford (2022). She recognises the significant relationship between criticality and creativity. She draws on evidence of two students' 'interpretative insights' (p. 427) into the way Frankenstein's creature is positioned in the novel to argue that writing-in-role, 'although ostensibly a "creative" activity, involves hard intellectual work' (p. 433). The creature's paradoxical feelings about his creator and his surprising eloquence are captured in the students' assured writing-in-role. For those less conversant with the characters and situations of a text than Bomford's A-level students, seeing others embodying a role can provide a visual prompt to focused in-role writing.

Drama on paper

Barrs (1987) was inspired by watching Heathcote's work to develop an account of the reading process closely connected to forms of enactment. Central to Barr's argument is her claim that role-play paves the way for writing and that the passage between the two media is facilitated by students remaining in-role as they shift from speaking, moving and watching each other to writing. Key to the process is a clear sense of the reader or audience, meaning that if their roles are established, children can effectively sustain them on paper. She explains that she began to recognise the potential of drama on paper through the ways that the children involved in Heathcote's 'Ozymandias' drama 'were able to access linguistic registers that they might not normally be expected to be able to use' (1987, p. 9), taking on the voice of an appropriate genre. In research that Barrs conducted with Valerie Cork (2001, p. 209) in primary classrooms, they demonstrated that drama and associated writing-in-role 'can provide a strikingly immediate route into a fictional situation'. With an emphasis on the way that 'readers are led to create or reenact the text or to picture the text as they read' (p. 36), Barrs and Cork identify explicit links between visualisation, reading, writing and drama. The possibilities brought into play in the shift from embodied enactment to writing are something that I aim to draw out further.

The drama practitioner and editor of Heathcote's (2015a, 2015b) writings, Cecily O'Neill, explains how Heathcote's work in-role gave students the 'permission to stare', a challenge 'to make sense of what they see, to become aware of their own responses, and to use these responses as an impetus to action' (O'Neill 2006, p. 109). O'Neill's interpretation of the call to action initiated by a teacher assuming a role provides a particularly apt description for the drama that I analyse later, involving students writing in-role as witnesses to a significant event.

Teacher-in-role as a prompt for writing

I am particularly interested in what is visualised or imagined, as well as what is seen. My focus here is on the visual impact of the work that is created, acting as a prompt to the imagination, and on the ways that students work to translate their insights into writing, making artistic and aesthetic choices through the process. With this in mind, I interrogate the ways that a communal classroom-based activity focused on the Old English text *Beowulf* provided a platform for a writing activity with specific outcomes. In this case, a brief but charged multimodal intervention involving a teacher-in-role was key to the visual detail and play of ideas that emerged in the resulting writing-in-role. I supplement these insights with an example of writing-in-role derived from a similarly intense dramatic interaction based on Shelley's *Frankenstein*.

I have previously referenced this account of a teacherly interaction in-role because it offers such a significant yet economical conduit to writing-in-role (Coles and Bryer 2018; Bryer et al. 2024). Here, I present a more detailed analysis of the effects of an English teacher drawing on the resources of her voice and body in significant ways; this was particularly notable because of the visual dimension of the writing that it gave rise to. The evidence that I refer to emerged from a two-day workshop conducted with student-teachers. This research is related to my doctoral work exploring the affordances of role (Bryer 2020), although my case study formed part of a larger research project about transmedia adaptations of a canonical text, the Old English poem *Beowulf*.[3]

Although much of my argument rests on the power of a moment of teacher-in-role, I aim to highlight how accessible this kind of interaction is for an English teacher. This form of teacher-in-role might be described as narration through the lens of a particular character. Our aim in working with *Beowulf* was to open up different narrative perspectives, including those that might be meaningful for our largely female cohort of student-teachers. Our colleague Morlette Lindsay had assumed a storytelling or narrator role in introducing the group to *Beowulf*. Her subsequent subtle shift from narrator to the character of the female monster, Grendel's Mother, as she set up a writing-in-role task, prompted vivid responses. Taking account of the combination of Morlette's precise choice of words and syntax helps to explain some of the power of her artistic intervention in-role. More telling than this is the way that she used her body and gaze to activate students' imaginations so that they appeared to have found space to dwell in the moment or to immerse themselves in the story in a visceral and visual way. This was a momentary intervention that could happen in any classroom space.

Initially, Morlette pulled a cloak-like piece of fabric around her shoulders and addressed the students as if they were in role as one of Beowulf's followers ('ceorla') waiting for the hero to return from his encounter with Grendel's Mother at the bottom of the mere or lake. She used a heightened tone and gestured with her hands in a way that seemed reminiscent of mediaeval depictions of religious figures, turning her palms towards the listeners as she spoke:

> You watch the water. You keep watch loyally because you want to see Beowulf come back to rise victorious out of the water. And you think, what has this hero meant to you? Why are you loyal to this hero?
> [Her hands flat, palms open, gesturing to them]

The lilting tone that she adopted signalled that she was now in role as the storyteller, her language carefully chosen to echo that of Heaney's (2000) version of the *Beowulf* text with which the student-teachers were familiar. In addressing the watchers as *you*, rather than *we*, she retained some distance. But her emphasis on loyalty to the hero was suggestive of what is sometimes known as a twilight or 'shadowy role'. This liminal, facilitating role is close to that of a narrator or storyteller but with a stake in the dramatic action; a vested interest, attitude or opinion that the teacher communicates clearly (Wagner 1976). Thus, through this act of identification, Morlette emphasised that the warrior community's overwhelming concern was with their leader and his fate and that what they must do is 'watch' and 'watch loyally'. From their physical responses, it seemed as if the student-teachers were indeed in-role, watching, as if waiting for Beowulf's return. From their writing, it is clear that several were open to this suggestion and that they recognised what this implied about their attitudes of devotion and concern, referring to the warrior as 'our hero' and 'our brave leader', for example.

Morlette's next move sent a frisson around the circle of student-teachers. Having reminded the group what might lie in store for their hero Beowulf, she dropped the piece of cloth that she had draped over her shoulders and walked slowly and deliberately to the centre of the circle, summoning up a vision of the mere, or deep lake, that everyone was supposedly seated around, as she did so. She crouched down in what appeared to be a defenceless position, without the protective covering of the cloak. Through this subtle yet powerful transition, she embodied the role of the monster, Grendel's Mother, offering through her posture, positioning and expression a suggestion of the monster's perspective, awaiting an attack by the man who had fatally wounded her son by tearing his arm off with his bare hands (Heaney 2000, lines 815–820). This move to a physical assumption of the role was made particularly poignant by the way she swivelled around quite awkwardly, on the spot, reinforcing the sense of the character's entrapment. She spoke in a low tone as she deliberately looked several of the students in the eye:

> But deep in the waters is Grendel's Mother. She has lost her son, he is mutilated - here she is in the cold, cold water... she has been banished here with the monsters in the deep, dark and cold and all she wanted to do was avenge her son. That's why she attacked, that's why she left the fens and the moors and the water and now she's here, under the water, cradling the arm of her son. She knows that someone is come, someone is coming to revenge, she is waiting in the water, with the arm of her son.

As before, Morlette did not speak in the first person, but this time her words and actions were clearly associated with the role that she embodied. When standing on the edge of the circle, her words had embraced the group of warriors with reference to their communal concerns and values, implying a shared identity with those sitting around it. Now, in an instant, she had begun to speak from the perspective of an isolated individual. Speaking in the third person made it clear that this performance of the text was not a moment of realist acting but a reading or interpretation, albeit from the character's perspective. This is an instance of teacher-in-role work that involves directing students' attention to a significant aspect of the text and inviting a critical response.

Morlette's embodiment reminded us that the monster is female and that her body is subject to viewing in a different way from that of the male warrior. Yet despite the character's subjugation in this position, Morlette's words maintained a critical distance, an aspect of what might be interpreted as a Brechtian 'gestus' or form of symbolic action with socio-political implications. Morlette deliberately showed us the monster in her abject state with the intention of inviting comment while also eliciting some sympathy. In her bitter tone and words that were indicative of rejection, 'banished here', she spoke of the absences in the text in which Grendel's Mother is not even honoured with a name, as well as the circumstances of the imminent attack. A particularly noteworthy aspect of this improvised text was the way that Morlette described the monster's body in an imagined landscape. She emphasised that she is 'deep in the waters ... now she's here, under the water, cradling the arm of her son'. There was also a sense of depth called to mind by the way she crouched and then, fleetingly, appeared to look up.

Heathcote (2015a) underlines that the function of the teacher-in-role is to address and question the participants in the drama, to draw them into the action. This was a powerful moment of enactment because Morlette was clear about the provocation she was offering, but it was very brief and did not require that the students respond verbally or with their bodies, or that the space be transformed in order for them to imagine being in a particular time or place. Such immersion into fiction might happen in the classroom with students at desks and the teacher moving towards them or between them. On a school visit, I observed one of my student-teachers assuming the role of Pandora (the first woman, according to Greek mythology) as a stimulus for some writing-in-role about the character's dilemma. She moved closer to individual students to emphasise Pandora's desperation by scooting up the centre aisle of the classroom on a wheeled office chair. This intensity had the desired effect, and the pupils had so much to express about her situation in their writing-in-role that they were reluctant to stop when the bell rang at the end of the lesson.

The transition into writing-in-role

The student-teachers' ready engagement in this moment of the *Beowulf* project was familiar to me from the many occasions that I have set up writing as an extension to some drama activity. With an unusual shift of the lens onto the physical responses of the students, Barrs (1987, p. 10) points out that 'Some residual physical activity, in the form of minute bodily adjustments, seem likely to accompany any attempt to take on a role in writing, as in a way of getting physically in tune for the performance'. It was hard to discern whether the frantic way that Arthur[4] dropped his head and set to writing before Morlette had finished speaking denoted a kind of shift into seeing through the eyes of a character, somehow channelling what the character might be thinking.

I noticed Sumaya and Emma raising their heads, pausing and staring into the middle distance, possibly summoning up an imagined landscape. In Vygotsky's (2004, p. 68) formulation of the creative process, he analyses the way that as a child told a story, they drew on what they saw or had seen so that their 'imagination reproduced and combined external visual images, and made a new picture out of them'. Heathcote reflects on how she wanted a class of nine-year-olds in a historical drama about the surgeon Dr Joseph Lister and his pioneering antiseptic innovations to look '*with* Lister, not *at* Lister' (Heathcote 2015b, p. 90, her italics). This form of immersion or prompt to the imagination involved the children interpreting what they envisaged from a historical perspective.

Morlette's appeal to the spectators to watch and to respond clearly had an impact on the majority of the student-teachers whose writing starts with a visual description of the place that the monster inhabits. Thus, most of their accounts begin with scene-setting, as Morlette did, and then develop into the character's stream of consciousness. Sophie's writing starts with the 'Icy cavernous depths' that seem 'thick with fear' because of the violence that is about to ensue. Arthur writes about the darkness, contrasting it with the 'brightness' of the monster's fury. Similarly, Emma starts:

> On the floor of my home, is it water, is it blood, the blood of my own, my own son, I cannot tell. It is dark now, the light that once lit this cave extinguished, cradled in my arms, the only source of light left, dripping into the sea. And he is coming.

As in Arthur's writing, the darkness, light and blood that she envisages assume a metaphorical aspect as her writing develops. There is something elemental in both Emma and Arthur's writing that appears to emerge from their imagining of physical elements.

For those students who chose to write from the point of view of Beowulf's followers, visualising where they are and what they might be seeing from their particular vantage point is just as significant. Richard starts his graphic account with a mention of 'the craggily cliff-side' that marks the warriors' journey. Through Sumaya's account of the landscape in which the men are trapped, she captures a sense of collective fear, conveying the way that time passes painfully slowly for those who wait in this alien land:

> Oh, if only we'd never set foot on this doomed land with these roaming man-eating monsters and swamps that hold secrets of evil misfortunes. Every time the bubbles in the water increase, heavy sighs are heard among the men.

Reference to the specifics of the mere that they crouch around positions the warriors as they are in the printed text, in the thrall of the murky water.

Both Richard's and Sumaya's accounts situate their drama on paper within a recognisable heroic genre that includes those elements that they identify as significant to the telling of a powerful story, in which they have, in some sense, become the active protagonists. Heathcote's method of lending students agency when working in-role is signalled, as she puts it, by the teacher using 'delicate linguistics in vocal sign, plus the equally selective body and space sign' (Heathcote 2015a, p. 77). This 'act of conscious self-representation' invites action, provokes a response, or implies a sharing of responsibility and expertise with the participants (O'Neill 2006, p. 109). Selective signing means that a teacher-in-role can also offer a conduit to a specific genre or form of narrative that, in this case, provided a cultural frame of reference to inform the students' writing, their choice of words and associated register. What students see and how they see it are as significant in positioning them as what they hear.

Those students who chose to 'speak back' to the text, through their writing as Grendel's Mother, are clearly arrested by the way that Morlette shifts the narrative perspective from warrior to monster in her brief assumption of the latter role. Grendel's Mother's reactions are less clearly defined by the prescriptions of the text and by our cultural knowledge of what monsters that are also mothers do in such circumstances. Cremin et al. (2006, p. 279) note that powerful writing-in-role emerges when there is more tension in the drama that precedes it. The waiting warriors and the monster are poised in anticipation in this moment, making the way that Morlette moves Grendel's Mother to the centre of the dramatic action, both physically and metaphorically, all the more striking. Through her framing of the role and this moment in the narrative, Grendel's Mother is positioned as a significant antagonist, with a hint at the power she might exert in defence of her mutilated son.

Several of the students reflect on Beowulf's imminent arrival. Emma writes, 'And he is coming. I can sense his malevolent presence crawling closer to me. Beowulf'. Arthur also vividly expresses Grendel's Mother's point of view:

> I will not go meekly but with my final flicker of life I will burn bright with fury. One of us will be extinguished. I await him now in the darkness. I await.

He ends on a cliffhanger, a point of tension and a pause suggestive of a recognition of the way the *Beowulf* narrative is structured. In the Heaney text we shared with the students, Grendel's Mother 'sensed a human/observing her outlandish lair from above' (2000, lines 1499–1500). We know that the monster has a long time to await her fate, as it takes nearly a day for Beowulf to swim downwards to reach her. But the tension is not just about time – it also has to do with the perspective that the poet introduces, suggestive of Grendel's Mother's awareness of Beowulf's position above her.

Through this research, I have come to recognise how the kind of framing that Morlette brought into play helps students to develop their own point of view about the dramatic action and the characters involved. In a later reflection, one of the student-teachers, Alex, claimed that through the dramatic improvisations:

> From Beowulf seeing Grendel's Mother [*making a gesture of seeing, involving pulling pretend rays from his eyes.*] I could then put myself in, really in… in the weirdest way. I was in Beowulf, I was seeing her, then I was in her… every activity we've participated in, we've been reliving it.

This sense of seeing through another's eyes may not necessarily be as vivid for all the participants. But it is clear that the student-teachers' visualisation of the characters within a very specific setting had been framed by Morlette's economical narration and positioning. This served as a conduit to the characters' thoughts or ideas at the point at which the student-teachers articulated their insights expressed through the medium of writing-in-role. Although the student-teachers' writing is reflective, it is also dynamic and dramatic. This role-play on paper is critical and active. When the student-teachers gathered to read their work aloud, they were performing their characters' reactions with echoes of Morlette's powerful gestus, albeit articulated in words.

These findings informed another research project, which focused on my student-teachers' experiences of using drama-in-English in schools (2021) and involved further writing-in-role. As part of that project, I modelled some dramatic approaches based on Shelley's *Frankenstein* and reflected on the outcomes with my English with Drama PGCE group (see Bryer et al. 2024). The student-teachers had developed a scene involving the creature coming to life and then assumed the roles of accidental witnesses to the event, responding to what they saw. Exploring different perspectives of this iconic moment led to writing that involved the creature addressing his maker, Dr Frankenstein, about his memories of the traumatic circumstances of his birth. Having created and also been an audience to the drama of the creature's first moments and its horrific implications, many of those writers started with a vision of the world that first came to the creature. Hope, Rachel and Bethan's visceral descriptions echo some of the dramatic action that they had physicalised. Hope writes, 'What is happening? Who are you? What am I? A fuzzy image becomes clear – a being stands before me'. Rachel's sparse writing similarly captures the creature's confusion and despair as he opens his eyes for the first time: 'All I see is unknown. Nothing. Nothing. Nothing… Send me back to the darkness'. Bethan starts from the creature's first breath to his vision of a bleak future, 'I sucked life into my aching lungs and made my eyes wide, to see your world. I saw emptiness, and I saw the bile rise in your throat'. The Gothic tone emerges from the ways that the writers are able to locate the action in a particular moment, envisaging the world through the creature's eyes and then speculating about what the future holds for him. This involves generalising about the significance of where the character finds himself in pithy yet emotive terms.

Conclusion

Heathcote (2015a, p. 74) claims that 'Role helps them [the students] *do*, and the teacher helps them *see*' (her italics). In a final evaluation, one of the student-teachers involved in the *Beowulf* project reported how Morlette's visual stimulus in-role had provided her with inspiration to write. As Alex's insight, quoted above, suggests, it is the teacher and students assuming a role that can help students to really 'see'. It also foregrounds the visual, bringing it into play in subtle but pervasive ways that deserve greater acknowledgement. The interactions between seeing, observing and visualising, and between embodiment, enactment and writing, are multilayered. In the cases cited here, being able to watch a significant interpretation of the narrative in bodily form supported the development of the kinds of judgements and criticality that the student-teachers expressed in their writing. The variety in their responses is suggestive of the ways that the process enabled them to develop their own attitudes or opinions about the action that they viewed and that they were implicated in. The roles that they assumed on paper enabled them to widen their perspective (Heathcote 1984), so that they developed different interpretations, readings or views of the events that constitute the *Beowulf* and *Frankenstein* narratives. Introducing an explicitly visual and embodied dramatic interaction as a prompt to the imagination enables readers and writers to visualise fictional worlds in vivid ways so that 'the text lives outside of the original', as one student-teacher put it. Moments of drama also appear to open up more dynamic and meaningful written responses that are suggestive of the stake that students have in the narratives that they take ownership of through the act of writing-in-role.

Acknowledgements

I am very grateful to the student-teachers, now teachers, involved in the research projects referenced here.

Notes

1 The PGCE is a one-year post-graduate course leading to qualified teacher status in the UK.
2 Subjects at Advanced Level (A Level) are typically studied as part of a 2 year course. Success in A Level examinations represents the most common route to higher education for students in the UK.
3 This two-day Beowulf workshop was conducted with a group of PGCE English and English with Drama students in 2015. Our research was part of a Digital Transformations project funded by the Arts and Humanities Research Council

(AHRC) which involved university departments of English and of Education, the British Library and five London schools (for a further account of the research project see https://darecollaborative.net/?s=beowulf+gaming+the+library). Over the two days our student-teachers were positioned as school students might be, following which we reflected on the pedagogic processes involved.

4 The names I use here are culturally appropriate pseudonyms.

References

Barrs, M. (1987). Voice and role in reading and writing. *Language Arts*, 64(2), 8–11.

Barrs, M. and Cork, V. (2001). *The Reader in the Writer: The Links Between the Study of Literature and Writing Development at Key Stage 2*. London: Centre for Language in Primary Education.

Bomford, K. (2022). Critical or creative? The creature writes to Victor Frankenstein. *Changing English*, 29(4), 421–439.

Booth, D. and Neelands, J. eds. (1998). *Reading, Writing and Role-Playing across the Curriculum*. Ontario: Caliburn Enterprises.

Britton, J. (1970). *Language and Learning*. Harmondsworth: Penguin Books.

Bryer, T. (2020). *What Are the Affordances of Role in Learning through Transmedian Forms of Pedagogy?* (PhD), University College London.

Bryer, T. and Coles, J. (2022). Re-animation: Multimodal discourse around text. *Literacy*, 56(2), 150–159.

Bryer, T., Pitfield, M. and Coles, J. (2024). *Drama at the Heart of English: Transforming Practice in the Secondary Classroom*. London: Routledge.

Burnett, C. (2015). Investigating children's interactions around digital texts in classrooms: How are these framed and what counts? *Education 3–13: International Journal of Primary, Elementary and Early Years Education*, 43(2), 197–208.

Caldwell Cook, H. (1917). *The Play Way: An Essay in Educational Method*. London: William Heinemann.

Coles, J. and Bryer, T. (2018). Reading as enactment: Transforming Beowulf through drama, film and computer game. *English in Education*, 52(1), 54–66.

Cremin, T., Goouch, K., Blakemore, L., Goff, E. and Macdonald, R. (2006). Connecting drama and writing: seizing the moment to write. *Research in Drama Education: The Journal of Applied Theatre and Performance*, 11(3), 273–291.

Dunn, J., Harden A. and Marino, S. (2013). Drama and writing: Overcoming the hurdle of the blank page. In M. Anderson and J. Dunn, eds., *How Drama Activates Learning: Contemporary Research and Practice*. London: Bloomsbury Academic, pp. 245–259.

Finlay-Johnson, H. (1911). *The Dramatic Method of Teaching*. Boston, New York, Chicago and London: The Athenaeum Press/Ginn and Company.

Grainger, T. Goouch, K. and Lambirth, A. (2005). *Creativity and Writing: Developing Voice and Verve in the Classroom*. London: Routledge.

Heaney, S. (2000). *Beowulf: A New Translation*. London: Faber and Faber.

Heathcote, D. (1980). Drama as context for talking and writing: The Ozymandias saga at Broadwood Junior School. In M. Barrs, ed., *Drama as Context: NATE Papers in Education*. Aberdeen: NATE in association with Aberdeen University Press, pp. 4–24.

Heathcote, D. (1984). From the particular to the universal. In L. Johnson and C. O'Neill, eds., *Dorothy Heathcote: Collected Writings on Education and Drama*. London: Hutchinson, pp. 103–110.

Heathcote, D. (2015a). Signs and portents. In C. O'Neill, ed., *Dorothy Heathcote in Education and Drama: Essential Writings*. Abingdon: Routledge, pp. 70–78.

Heathcote, D. (2015b). Meeting Doctor Lister. In C. O'Neill, ed., *Dorothy Heathcote in Education and Drama: Essential Writings*. Abingdon: Routledge, pp. 88–93.

Hourd, M. (1940). Dramatization. *The New Era*, 21, 149–152.

Hourd, M. (1949). *The Education of the Poetic Spirit: A Study of Children's Expression in the English Lesson*. Melbourne, London and Toronto: Heinemann Educational Books.

Kempe, A. (2001). Drama as a framework for the development of literacy. *National Foundation for Educational Research (NFER)*, 25, 1–7.

O'Neill, C. (2006). Dialogue and drama. In P. Taylor and C. Warner, eds., *Structure and Spontaneity: The Process Drama of Cecily O'Neill*. Stoke-on-Trent: Trentham Books, pp. 101–112.

O'Neill C. and Rogers, T. (1994). Drama and literary response: prying open the text. *English in Australia*, 108, 47–51.

O'Neill, C., Rogers, T. and Jasinski, J. (2006). Transforming texts: Intelligences in action. In P. Taylor and C. Warner, eds., *Structure and Spontaneity: The Process Drama of Cecily O'Neill*. Stoke-on-Trent: Trentham Books, pp. 91–100.

Pitfield, M. (2020). *Reading Through Drama: The Contribution that Drama Makes to Teaching and Learning in English* (PhD), University of Nottingham.

Rosenblatt, L. (1978). *The Reader, the Text, the Poem: The Transactional Theory of the Literary Work*. Carbondale: Southern Illinois University Press.

Saunders, J. N. (2022). Using drama-rich pedagogies with the episodic pre-text model to improve literacy. *Teachers and Curriculum*, 22(2), 49–61

Vygotsky, L. (2004). Imagination and creativity in childhood. M. Sharpe (trans.) *Journal of Russian and East European Psychology*, 42(1), 7–97.

Wagner, B. J. (1976). *Dorothy Heathcote: Drama as a Learning Medium*. London: Hutchinson and Company.

Chapter 6

Drama-Rich Translanguaging for Multilingual Meaning-Making

Rafaela Cleeve Gerkens and Julie Choi

Introduction

Recent developments in translanguaging research emphasise the role of the arts in facilitating multimodal and multilingual expression (Bradley et al. 2018; Choi et al. 2023, 2024; Oniţă 2022). Drama is increasingly central in translanguaging pedagogies (Dutton and Rushton 2022; Galante 2022). Translanguaging's value for supporting multilingual learners is well understood (Aleksić and García 2022). However, enacting embodied and translanguaging pedagogies may present a challenge for teachers operating in writing-centric, English-medium countries (Tian and King 2023).

Our research collaboration explores the alignment of drama-rich pedagogy (Ewing 2019a) and translanguaging. We are teacher educators and researchers in Language and Literacy and Arts education. Raf's research interest in drama-rich pedagogy emerged from her work as a primary classroom teacher, using drama with her students, particularly to support their language and literacy learning. Julie's expertise in translanguaging stems from her own multilingual learning journey and autoethnography. Together, we investigate the potential of drama and translanguaging to activate deeper conceptual and linguistic understanding, supporting students' writing. Drama-rich pedagogy creates multimodal, aesthetic spaces for engaging with complex concepts and language (Cleeve Gerkens 2024; Ewing 2019a; Saunders 2019). Translanguaging theory recognises multilingual individuals' unified linguistic repertoires and the need for dedicated spaces to facilitate meaning-making (Li 2018). Both approaches aim to tap into students' full meaning-making repertoires.

In this chapter, we present a collaborative exploration of arts-rich translanguaging in primary literacy classrooms. Through our professional dialogue as specialists in drama pedagogy and translanguaging, we revisit a case study of a drama-rich experience (Cleeve Gerkens 2024), developing primary students' knowledge for writing an explanation text. We examine how embodied drama builds students' conceptual and linguistic knowledge for writing within a genre approach. Drawing on drama's emerging role in translanguaging pedagogy, we discuss how we could enhance this inclusive approach for multilingual learners.

DOI: 10.4324/9781003655664-6

Recent research has explored drama's role in establishing 'creative translanguaging spaces' (Dutton and Rushton 2022, p. 159) and affirming student identity. Building on this work, our dialogue analyses how key concepts of drama and translanguaging overlap to create deeper learning experiences engaging students' full cognitive and linguistic resources.

Through our collaborative analysis and dialogue, we contribute to conversations about creating intellectually rigorous, culturally responsive learning environments. We know that such environments require collaborative knowledge-building across disciplines. That is why we have worked together to develop approaches that leverage multilingual students' diverse meaning-making resources as assets in academic learning.

In the following section, we will introduce the theory underpinning drama-rich translanguaging through a collaborative dialogue designed to help us discover possible areas of theoretical synergy between the two areas of study.

Theoretical framework

i Embodied learning and linguistic fluidity

Julie: Raf, I've been reading your publication (Cleeve Gerkens 2024) on the potential of a drama approach in developing academic language for children and was thinking about the benefits for multilingual learners. Could you elaborate on how drama-rich pedagogy supports language development? I'm particularly interested in how it creates those embodied learning experiences you described.

Raf: Drama-rich pedagogy has many characteristics that support language and literacy learning. It uses multimodal, multisensory techniques to create embodied, aesthetic experiences where, as Dunn (2016) notes, 'cognition, imagination, memory and the body work in complex interrelation' (p. 129) to engage students (Dawson and Kiger Lee 2018) and support deep learning. These experiences can both support and challenge students in building new conceptual and linguistic understandings. Martello's (2002) work shows how embodiment fosters nuanced shared understandings through symbolic representation, and more recent studies by Branscombe (2019) and Paige et al. (2021) demonstrate that embodied drama experiences support discipline-specific knowledge development and student engagement. When we combine these experiences with reflective dialogue, they have been shown to enhance children's writing abilities. That reflective component is crucial. Reflection on the drama experience solidifies language learning and is essential for transformative learning. Carroll (1978), Freebody (2013), Heathcote and Bolton (1995) have all emphasized this in their work.

A skilfully planned drama experience can also support students' experience of 'metaxis' (Bolton 1984) or 'dual affect' (O'Toole and Dunn 2002), of being 'simultaneously' within and a contributor to the fictional world of the drama and a spectator of that world, monitoring and reflecting on the impact of their actions within the evolving drama. The drama world is the fictional world created by students and teachers through their participation in classroom drama. This world creates a safe space for experimentation where learners can try stepping into new roles, ideas and identities while also observing and analysing their experience as a spectator. This experience of metaxis further supports the deep processing of new language and concepts by combining the analytical thought of the spectator with the felt experience of the participant (Carroll 1980). In this space, students can monitor and evaluate their language choices within the drama experience, considering whether they support their intended meaning (Morgan and Saxton 1988). These considered language choices can then translate into students' writing.

Julie: That concept of metaxis fascinates me because I see strong connections to translanguaging theory. Both drama-rich pedagogy and translanguaging seem to share fundamental principles that could make them highly complementary approaches in creating transformative learning experiences. Both challenge traditional boundaries, between languages, and between reality and fiction, creating spaces where these boundaries become permeable. Unlike traditional views that compartmentalise languages as separate systems, translanguaging argues that multilingual individuals possess one integrated linguistic repertoire from which they strategically draw to make meaning. This perspective challenges the notion of multilinguals as 'two monolinguals in one person' (Grosjean 1989, p. 3), instead recognising that languages exist as a 'unitary [linguistic] repertoire' (Li and García 2022, p. 313) where individuals develop their own unique 'idiolect' (Li 2018, p. 18) of self-expression.

What strikes me when learning more about metaxis is that multilingual students already navigate between different languages, cultures, and identities daily. The idea of simultaneously inhabiting two worlds that underpins metaxis is very familiar to them. Yet despite their experience of 'in-between-ness' (Davis 2015, p. 68) of language, culture and identity, multilingual students usually don't encounter the zone for safe experimentation that you describe being created by the drama world in enacting their linguistic identities across different educational contexts.

Raf: That's an important insight I hadn't fully considered. What kinds of challenges do these students typically face?

ii Drama and translanguaging: empowering multilingual voices in safe creative spaces

Julie: In moving between languages, cultures and identities, they are often harshly judged and viewed through a deficit lens as language and literacy learners in English-medium instruction settings. Many multilingual students live with a constant fear of being perceived as intellectually inferior or as outsiders who don't belong simply because their English is still developing. This anxiety frequently silences them in classroom settings, where they avoid speaking rather than risk judgment from peers or teachers who might equate their emerging English proficiency with limited cognitive ability, as research by Motha (2014), Bell and Pomerantz (2014), and Conteh and Brock (2011) has shown.

I can see a lot of potential in bringing metaxis and translanguaging together. Creating a protected space for students to try out different aspects of their linguistic identities is vitally important. Drawing on the concept of metaxis could help us to do so within the safety of the fictional drama world. Dutton and Rushton (2022) demonstrated how drama and translanguaging can work in tandem to create a 'creative translanguaging space' (p. 159) that affirms student identities and draws on their multilingual resources. When deliberately combined, drama and translanguaging create powerful learning environments in which students can develop important school literacies while harnessing their funds of knowledge and identity from their out-of-school lives.

Raf: Yes, I think that aligns with what you and I have seen in our own research (Choi et al. 2023, 2024) on arts-rich pedagogy. We found that in allowing learners to draw on their full semiotic repertoires in playful and creative ways, we were able to see the emergence of their unique voices and identities as authors and meaning makers. In addition, learners were able to develop confidence in academic settings without fear of judgment based on their developing language proficiency.

iii Enriching a genre approach to writing through drama

Julie: There's another dimension of your work that I would like to know more about. In your case study, you explored how drama-rich pedagogy could enrich a genre-based approach to teaching writing. Could you explain a bit more about that connection? I'm wondering how these approaches might work together to support multilingual learners specifically, especially as the genre approach is widely used with English as an Additional Language learners.

Raf: As you know, the genre approach emphasises teaching purpose, structure, and language features of key school knowledge genres (Rose 2015). It stems from a functional approach viewing language as a resource for meaning-making in social contexts, drawing on Halliday and Matthiessen's (2014) work. The approach emerged from critiques of personal and process approaches that often disadvantaged students from diverse backgrounds, as Martin (1985) and Rose (2008) have argued. As you remarked, it remains widely used in Western English-dominant countries (Myhill 2011), especially for English language learners.

A key initial stage of the genre approach involves building students' knowledge of the field of study. Teachers aim to engage students with key language and concepts through multimodal experiences and oral language emphasis. Drama-rich pedagogy addresses these requirements and opens multimodal entry points to language and literacy for diverse learners, as Dutton and Rushton (2022) as well as Piazzoli (2018) have demonstrated in their research.

Julie: I'm excited by the possibilities of bringing drama and translanguaging together and how each area can enrich the other. By looking at the intersection of drama and translanguaging pedagogies, we can explore how literacy learning can be transformed by creating spaces where students' full linguistic and embodied meaning-making resources are not only recognised but strategically leveraged to deepen conceptual understanding and academic language development. This approach could address the emotional barriers many multilingual students face by creating safe spaces where their identities are affirmed, and their fears of speaking are acknowledged and mitigated.

Introduction to the case study

The case study that served as the catalyst for this collaborative analysis was undertaken as part of Raf's doctoral research (Cleeve Gerkens 2022). This study investigated how using drama-rich pedagogy could support development of students' academic language proficiency in the middle primary years (eight to ten years), a key competency, as students are required to interpret and create increasingly complex texts across the curriculum. Raf worked with three teachers in middle primary classrooms in three schools in Victoria, Australia, to develop a drama-rich literacy unit of work based on the identified learning goals of the teachers. The three-session, drama-rich portion of the unit formed part of a broader, term-long (ten-week) focus on chemical science and the writing of a scientific explanation text.

Methodology

A qualitative interventionist case study approach (Merriam 2009; Stevenson 2004) was employed in the original study (Cleeve Gerkens 2024) to examine how drama-rich pedagogy could support students' academic writing as part of a genre-based teaching approach. The case focused on a year 3/4 class (ages eight to ten) at a multilingual Catholic primary school in Melbourne, Australia.

i Case study: Brendan's year 3/4 class

The key participant was Brendan (all names of teachers and students are pseudonyms), a teacher in his fourth year of teaching, who viewed the study as valuable professional development. Brendan's class of 22 students participated in three 80-minute integrated science and literacy sessions over three weeks as part of the drama-rich intervention. These sessions incorporated drama conventions like improvisation and mime to build students' conceptual and linguistic understanding around chemical science topics in preparation for writing scientific explanation texts. Raf acted as both observer and co-teacher, planning and implementing the drama-based lessons with Brendan.

ii Data collection and analysis

Data collection methods to ensure a diversity of data sources (Mills 2003) included video recordings and transcripts of the drama-based lessons, researcher field notes from lesson observations, semi-structured interviews with the teacher before and after the intervention, focus group interviews with students after the intervention, student work samples and written reflections and teacher planning documents. Data analysis used deductive and inductive coding (Miles and Huberman 1994; Saldaña 2009) to identify moments of linguistic and conceptual engagement in drama experiences. Codes were grouped into themes related to building knowledge for writing.

In revisiting the case study, Raf and Julie employed collaborative analysis through a translanguaging lens. We identified drama experiences with the potential to integrate translanguaging and support multilingual learners. Key drama concepts from the original analysis were used to suggest ways of activating students' home languages. New connections between drama and translanguaging pedagogies emerged, drawing on second language acquisition theories.

Case study: drama-rich pedagogy builds conceptual and linguistic knowledge for writing

The drama-rich lessons, developed collaboratively by Raf and Brendan, aimed to build students' knowledge for writing a scientific explanation text. Our goal was to build students' understanding of water changing states and the language required to express these concepts. Using genre pedagogy, we planned to use drama in the 'building knowledge of the field' stage. We built students' knowledge through various activities, including videos, a Word Wall, handling physical objects, drama games, and improvised scenes. A warm-up game called 'Categories' was played at the beginning of each session, where students had to name and justify examples of solids, liquids, or gases.

In the second of three drama-rich sessions, we used mime to help students understand how water molecules react to energy or temperature changes.

82 Transforming English Through Drama

Figure 6.1 Illustration of students using their heads and fists to embody H2O. Credit: Hana Kinoshita Thomson.

The following vignette illustrates how this embodied drama experience created an inclusive, multimodal space that both supported and challenged students in developing conceptual and linguistic understandings for their writing.

i Vignette: embodied translanguaging in a scientific explanation

This session began with the class watching and discussing a short video about the changing states of matter that reinforced the key concepts and vocabulary they had been learning about the topic in the previous session. The students took notes as they watched and decided on vocabulary that should be added to the Word Wall. After creating a space for movement in the classroom, Brendan explained to the students that they were going to become water molecules. To embody the molecule, they used their two fists to represent the hydrogen atoms and their head to represent the single oxygen atom, embodying a concrete representation of the abstract concept of H2O (see Figure 6.1).

In this mime, we used light to represent energy being added or removed from the molecules. Brendan started the mime by lowering the blinds and turning off the lights in the classroom, representing very low energy being applied to the molecules, and asked the students to show how they, as water molecules, would be moving. The students began to vibrate in place. Throughout the mime, Brendan both narrated the students' movement, linking their embodiment with language, and invited them to describe what they were doing, supporting them to make these links themselves.

Brendan: Using your words, what were you acting out?
Student: Starting off freely and then slowly slowing down 'cause as the temperature's' cooling down 'cause the light and energy …'
Brendan: There's not much, is there? Would you be moving much?

Class: No
Brendan: Not really. What state of matter is it probably going to be?
Class: Solid.

Brendan raised the blinds, representing slightly more energy being applied to the molecules. The students began to move more quickly, sliding past each other in the space. Two students began to debate whether they had reached boiling point. Through dialogue guided by Brendan (see Cleeve Gerkens 2024), they concluded they were no longer solid but lacked the energy to become gas. This embodied experience facilitated higher-order thinking about the concept of 'boiling'. The mime provided a physical context for their arguments and seemed to support their understanding of the concept in an almost visceral way. Bringing the mime to an end, Brendan turned on the lights, representing more energy. Students moved rapidly, agreeing they had become gaseous (see Figure 6.2).

Figure 6.2 Students embodying water molecules in solid, liquid and gaseous states. Levels of classroom lighting are increased to represent energy being added to the molecules. Credit: Hana Kinoshita Thomson.

Collaborative analysis

i Building multimodal and multilingual knowledge for scientific writing

As we observe this rich drama-based literacy experience through a translanguaging lens, we see multiple dimensions where translanguaging approaches could enhance students' learning. While Raf and Brendan's activity successfully engaged students through multimodal expression, there remain untapped opportunities to activate students' full linguistic repertoires. Here, we examine specific elements of this drama experience where 'translanguaging spaces' naturally emerged and suggest additional strategies that could deepen multilingual students' meaning-making experiences.

From the beginning of the lesson sequence, we notice everyday learning resources that offered perfect entry points for translanguaging integration. The introductory video about changing states of matter, presented solely in English, could have been offered with multilingual subtitles or parallel language versions, including but not limited to Italian, Greek and Mandarin. When multilingual students can access content in both their home languages and school language simultaneously, they develop stronger conceptual frameworks and transfer this knowledge more effectively into academic tasks (Creese and Blackledge 2015; García and Kleyn 2016). Similarly, the Word Wall created in the classroom represents another missed opportunity for multilingual expansion. While multilingual labelling – where key terms appear in all languages represented in the classroom – would be valuable, an even more inclusive approach would be a truly multimodal Word Wall that incorporates visual symbols, tactile representations, gestural demonstrations (captured as photos), and sound recordings – making vocabulary accessible through multiple semiotic channels rather than privileging written language alone. These practical translanguaging strategies would set the foundation for deeper engagement with the embodied learning experience that followed.

The mime involved the core dramatic elements of 'transformation of space' and 'the symbolic use of space' (Bird et al. 2017, p. 110) through the manipulation of lighting levels within the classroom to represent changes in energy levels. The physical removal of light (representing energy) by closing blinds and turning off lights was coupled with Brendan's verbal narration and discussion with students, incorporating elaborated verb groups like 'starting off freely' to describe movement and subject-specific nouns such as 'heat' and 'energy' to discuss factors influencing changes in molecular structure. This dramatic transformation of classroom space perfectly mirrors what we conceptualise in translanguaging theory as transformative spaces where boundaries between languages and modes of expression become permeable. The mime activity exemplified this integration of multiple dimensions – physical movement, spatial positioning, visual stimuli through lighting changes, and verbal description – into a cohesive learning experience. For multilingual learners who might struggle to articulate molecular behaviour verbally, we would invite them to demonstrate understanding through their bodies or articulate their observations about molecular movement in their home languages alongside English, creating additional cognitive connections and deepening conceptual understanding. While teachers may not speak students' home languages, they can still validate and encourage this expression through peer collaboration, technology-assisted translation, visual documentation of understanding, and creating a classroom ethos where all languages are valued as thinking tools.

Brendan's narration of the mime allowed students to experience the embodied and abstract simultaneously by hearing academic language associated with changing state while embodying it, supporting an experience of 'metaxis' (Bolton 1984) or 'dual affect' (O'Toole and Dunn 2002), being both inside the drama and observing it simultaneously. This experience of metaxis further supports the deep processing of new language by combining the analytical thought of the spectator with the felt experience of the participant (Carroll 1980). In this space, students could monitor and evaluate their language choices within the drama experience, considering whether they support their intended meaning (Morgan and Saxton 1988).

We see metaxis as providing a particularly powerful connection point between drama pedagogy and translanguaging theory. As mentioned above, for multilingual learners who often hesitate to speak in class due to fear of judgement or ridicule, this liminal space becomes especially valuable. It allows them to experience and process new language while actively participating without being singled out for additional language support. The collective embodied experience provides a non-threatening context to encounter academic language, allowing students time to comprehend meaning and rehearse language mentally before producing it themselves. Unlike traditional classroom interactions that can provoke anxiety, this drama-based approach enables multilingual students to engage with complex concepts without the pressure of immediate verbal performance, addressing a fundamental barrier to their participation and learning.

The social context of the whole class mime meant that students' conceptual understanding could be supported by observing and moving alongside peers, developing shared understandings of the target language and concepts. It also provided context for the use of molecular language as students attempted to describe why they were moving in specific ways. As demonstrated in the quoted interactions above, Brendan invited the students to pause and distil their embodied experience into language out of frame, supporting them to take ownership of the abstract explanation of their embodied experience. This approach is particularly valuable for multilingual students, as not all students have knowledge of scientific concepts in their stronger languages either. Using embodied activities like mime engages all students through physical demonstration before verbal explanation. When teachers encourage reflection in whichever language(s) feel most natural – or through translanguaging practices that blend features from multiple named languages – students can demonstrate knowledge without being limited by their developing proficiency in the school language.

ii From embodiment to multimodal representation

The students' written reflections and diagrams recorded in a preliminary writing task immediately following the mime demonstrated a strong grasp of the subject matter, reflective of their embodied experience of the mime. For example, their diagrams of water molecules resembled their miming using their heads and fists, as can be seen in Antony's diagram (Figure 6.3) and Matteo's diagram (Figure 6.4), which also includes a visual depiction of the 'crystal lattice' made by the molecules in their solid state. Their descriptions of the movement of molecules reflected their movement in the mime. The language of movement, such as 'slowly move', 'gather together', and 'get faster', characterised most student reflections, including Felix's explanation (Figure 6.5).

Drawing labelled diagrams of the mime functioned to further bridge the gap between the contextualised, embodied experience of the drama and the decontextualised written account of the process of matter changing state. Ewing (2019b) identifies drawing as a step along the journey of 'playing with language orally, and subsequently through drawing and writing … to investigate how it works, explore how its rules operate and then how to break them' (p. 10). Following oral experimentation, drawing can precede or accompany writing in this process. In this episode, the students' diagrams, which formed part of their written reflections, provided a visual representation of their experience of

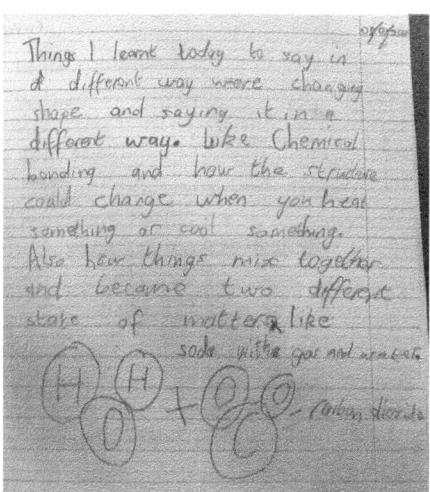

Figure 6.3 Antony's diagram of a water molecule.

Figure 6.4 Matteo's diagram of a water molecule and the 'crystal lattice'.

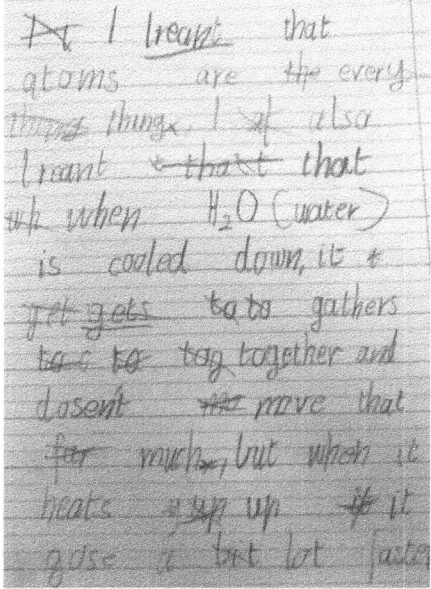

Figure 6.5 Felix's explanation of the movement of molecules.

metaxis: being within the mime as a molecule and observing it from the outside. The experience of metaxis is particularly marked in Sienna's diagram (Figure 6.6), which shows her and her classmates embodying the water molecules alongside a more abstract depiction of molecular structure.

From a translanguaging perspective, these diagrams represent perfect opportunities for multilingual meaning-making. For students with emerging literacy in English, combining visual representation with labels in their strongest language offers a powerful bridge to eventual academic expression in English. Additionally, diagrams leverage universal visual logic through spatial

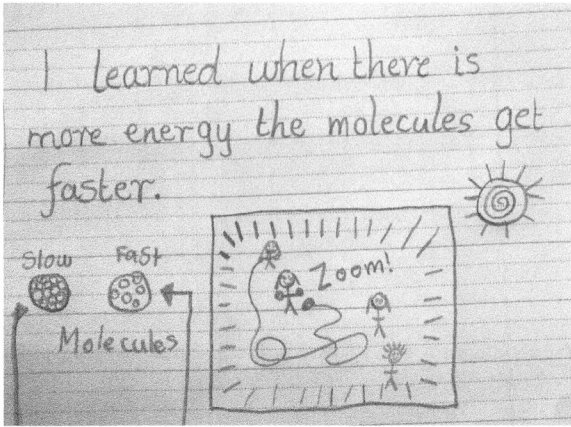

Figure 6.6 Sienna's diagram and explanation of molecule movement.

arrangements, arrows, and hierarchies that follow patterns recognisable across cultures and languages. This visual reasoning transcends linguistic boundaries, allowing multilingual learners to demonstrate conceptual understanding regardless of their English proficiency. Furthermore, diagrams significantly reduce language dependency by communicating relationships and processes with minimal text, making scientific concepts accessible even for students with limited vocabulary in the classroom language. Numerous studies support the efficacy of visual diagrams for second language learners (Cummins 2008; Mayer and Moreno 2003; Tang 1992, 1993). Tang's research with second language science learners demonstrates that visual representations significantly improve comprehension of scientific concepts, while Cummins' work highlights how visual supports bridge the gap between basic communicative skills and cognitive academic language proficiency. The visual nature of diagrams in combination with the visual element of embodiment essentially creates a scaffold that supports meaning-making while students continue developing their academic language skills.

Sienna's reflection also demonstrates her growing ability to explain the abstract concepts she embodied. This ability is evident in her use of a complex sentence with the subordinating conjunction 'when' to describe cause and effect and subject-specific nouns 'molecules' and 'energy', demonstrating scientific knowledge: 'when there is more energy the molecules get faster'. In these reflections, many students employed complex sentences using the subordinating conjunction of time, 'when'. It could be argued that the embodied experience of the mime, with its sequence of events as Brendan changed the 'energy' levels in the room, facilitated a natural use of this complex syntax by the students to explain how the experience had played out in real-time.

While this can be beneficial for all students, for multilingual learners, these keywords and grammatical structures need to be pointed out explicitly, as we cannot assume they have this specific language knowledge already. Teachers should prepare explicit explanations of scientific vocabulary and sentence patterns that they can review with the whole group, acknowledging that such explicit language instruction benefits first language speakers as well. The use of subject-specific language by students in their reflections on the mime also aligns with findings in studies by Dobson and Stephenson (2019), Ewing and Saunders (2016), O'Mara (2004), Rosler (2005) and Winston (2004). These studies showed that drama provides substantial experiences on which students can draw in their writing, fostering richer output, including more 'sophisticated' (Dobson and Stephenson 2019, p. 75) and 'heightened' language use (O'Mara 2004, p. 102).

This attention to language structure can be complemented by leveraging students' existing linguistic resources as they move between embodied understanding and written expression. For multilingual learners, this progression from embodied experience to written expression could be further enhanced through translanguaging writing strategies. When writing scientific explanations, encouraging students to draft or brainstorm in their home languages before crafting English versions supports deeper thinking. In our everyday work with multilingual graduate student teachers, we have found that strategic use of students' full linguistic repertoire prevents disengagement when facing challenging writing tasks. Lin's (2013) research provides excellent examples of how bilingual note-taking strategies in science classrooms enable learners to maintain the thread of meaning in their thinking and writing.

As Brendan reflected, students were 'getting it [concept and language knowledge] from all angles at once'. Brendan identified the effectiveness of the combination of embodiment and verbal reflection, commenting that by 'talking it through and acting that out from what I've seen … I absolutely have confidence that that's a way in which they can engage with that subject matter and have a better understanding'. Brendan reflected on the power of the embodied mime to 'pu[t] those [subject-specific] words in context'; students were able to encounter the language 'embedded in the context of experience' of becoming a molecule (Carroll 1980, p. 35). This supporting context enabled students to process the target language more deeply while building and demonstrating their knowledge of key concepts related to the changing states of matter. In line with the findings of Garret et al. (2018) using creative body-based learning in primary numeracy, in our context, students were able to initially build and demonstrate their knowledge and understanding using their bodies and through dialogue rather than writing. Through the shared embodied experience of the mime, they then developed deeper and more nuanced understandings of the target concepts and language that fed into their writing.

For multilingual learners, this process aligns with Swain's (2005) 'output hypothesis' (p. 471), which emphasises that producing language – not just receiving input – is crucial for language acquisition. Swain argues that 'languaging' (Swain and Watanabe 2019, p. 1), or using speech to mediate cognition, helps learners notice gaps in their knowledge, test hypotheses about language, and reflect on their understanding. However, in taking a bird's eye view of the multimodal aspects of this lesson sequence, from the initial video to the embodied mime and dialogue to the drawing of diagrams and writing, we see how 'languaging' in this process is more than just language but is about making meaning in embodied ways. By talking through their embodied experience of molecular movement, multilingual students engage in precisely this kind of productive 'languaging', simultaneously deepening their conceptual understanding through embodied experience and developing their academic language proficiency. Such spaces are not merely 'translanguaging spaces' but can be better understood as translanguaging aesthetic spaces. In these spaces, learners are encouraged to make meaning fluidly across languages, modes, and artistic expressions, fuelled by the engagement of their senses, imagination, and aspirations.

Recommendations for collaborations between teachers

Finding time to collaborate across disciplinary boundaries is becoming increasingly difficult in schools. However, in line with the aim of this volume to support a wide range of learners through the integration of drama and English, we offer suggestions for meaningful collaboration between teachers' different but potentially complementary areas of expertise. While the collaborative analysis presented in this chapter comes from our perspectives as researchers and teacher educators in drama and translanguaging, we know that teachers draw on deep expertise of what works for students in their contexts. Therefore, we present some ideas for how teachers might collaborate in a similar way to integrate drama and translanguaging practices. Based on our experience, we recommend the following principles:

- cross-disciplinary planning: where possible, pair language/English as an additional language specialists with generalist primary teachers and drama specialists to co-plan lessons that address curriculum objectives. In the Australian context, the presence of specialist EAL and drama teachers is variable across primary schools. Where such specialists are not employed within the school, professional learning opportunities with such specialists for teachers are vitally important. In the example provided in this chapter, the collaboration between Brendan and Raf was one example of a generalist primary teacher and an outside drama specialist collaborating to enrich learning
- lesson sequence selection: select a sequence of lessons that have the potential to integrate translanguaging

- lesson-by-lesson analysis: examine each lesson component to identify specific moments where multilingual practices could enhance learning (e.g., pre-teaching key concepts in home languages before embodied activities)
- gradual implementation: begin with small, manageable translanguaging elements before attempting full integration

While teacher agency is a powerful force for innovation in teaching practices, we understand the immense pressure teachers face and the systemic barriers that make the collaborations we suggest challenging. Therefore, as teacher educators and researchers, we need to advocate for structural changes that would create environments where translanguaging can thrive without placing additional burdens on already overworked teachers.

Conclusion

This chapter has explored the synergy between drama-rich pedagogy and translanguaging theory in supporting multilingual students' language and literacy development. Through analysis of a drama-based integrated science and writing lesson, we have demonstrated how embodied learning experiences create inclusive spaces activating students' full linguistic and semiotic repertoires. We argue that this drama-rich translanguaging approach can challenge the deficit lens often applied to multilingual learners in mainstream classrooms. However, this pedagogy is equally valuable for all learners and all subject areas. Drama conventions like mime serve as catalysts for conceptual and linguistic understanding, with metaxis aligning closely with translanguaging theory to create transformative learning spaces. By combining these approaches, educators can create intellectually rigorous, culturally responsive environments that recognise all students' diverse meaning-making resources as assets. We encourage collaborative planning between language specialists and drama teachers, gradually implementing translanguaging elements into drama-rich lessons, despite systemic challenges, for the benefit of multilingual learners in our increasingly diverse classrooms.

Acknowledgements

The authors wish to acknowledge Hana Kinoshita Thompson as the illustrator of Figures 6.1 and 6.2.

References

Aleksić, G., and García, O. (2022). Language beyond flags: Teachers misunderstanding of translanguaging in preschools. *International Journal of Bilingual Education and Bilingualism*, 25(10), 3835–3848. https://doi.org/10.1080/13670050.2022.2085029

Bell, N., and Pomerantz, A. (2014). Reconsidering language teaching through a focus on humor. *EuroAmerican Journal of Applied Linguistics and Languages*, 1(1), 31–47. https://doi.org/10.21283/2376905X.1.15

Bird, J., Donelan, K., and Sinclair, C. (2017). Drama: social dreaming in the 21st century. In C. Sinclair, N. Jeanneret, and J. O'Toole, eds., *Education in the Arts*. Victoria, Australia: Oxford University Press, pp. 107–127.

Bolton, G. (1984). *Drama as Education*. London: Longman.

Bradley, J., Moore, E., Simpson, J., and Atkinson, L. (2018). Translanguaging space and creative activity: Theorising arts-based learning. *Language and Intercultural Communication*, 18(1), 54–73. https://doi.org/10.1080/14708477.2017.1401120

Branscombe, M. (2019). *Teaching Through Embodied Learning: Dramatizing Key Concepts from Informational Texts*. London and New York: Routledge. https://doi.org/10.4324/9780429462986

Carroll, J. (1978). A language functions approach to learning areas in drama in education. *National Association for Drama in Education*, 3, 19–27.

Carroll, J. (1980). Language, the role of the teacher and drama in education. *English in Australia*, 53, 35–43.

Choi, J., Cleeve Gerkens, R., and Ohki, S. (2024). Multilingual authors 'standing taller' in arts-rich translanguaging spaces. *Language and Education*, 39(3), 586–613. https://doi.org/10.1080/09500782.2024.2348599

Choi, J., Cleeve Gerkens, R., and Tomsic, M. (2023). 'My book ideas were spinning in my head': Arts-rich bookmaking experiences to create and sustain multilingual children's meaning making flows and authorial voices. *TESOL Quarterly*, 58(4), 1372–1400. https://doi.org/10.1002/tesq.3279

Cleeve Gerkens, R. (2022). Drama as a Pedagogic Tool for Developing Academic Language Proficiency in the Middle Primary School. [Doctoral dissertation, University of Melbourne].

Cleeve Gerkens, R. (2024). Using drama to enrich a genre-based pedagogy for teaching academic writing across content areas. *Australian Journal of Language and Literacy*, 47, 427–449. https://doi.org/10.1007/s44020-024-00072-8

Conteh, J., and Brock, A. (2011). 'Safe spaces'? Sites of bilingualism for young learners in home, school and community. *International Journal of Bilingual Education and Bilingualism*, 14(3), 347–360.

Creese, A., and Blackledge, A. (2015). Translanguaging and identity in educational settings. *Annual Review of Applied Linguistics*, 35, 20–35. https://doi.org/10.1017/S0267190514000233

Cummins, J. (2008). BICS and CALP: Empirical and theoretical status of the distinction. In B. Street and N. H. Hornberger, eds., *Encyclopedia of Language and Education: Vol. 2. Literacy* (2nd ed.), New York: Springer, pp. 71–83.

Davis, S. (2015). Perezhivanie and the experience of drama, metaxis and meaning making. *NJ: Drama Australia Journal*, 39(1), 63–75. https://doi.org/10.1080/14452294.2015.1083138

Dawson, K., and Kiger Lee, B. K. (2018). *Drama-Based Pedagogy: Activating Learning Across the Curriculum*. Bristol: Intellect.

Dobson, T., and Stephenson, L. (2019). 'I think It fits in': Using process drama to promote agentic writing with primary school children. *Literacy*, 53(2), 69–76. https://doi.org/10.1111/lit.12145

Dunn, J. (2016). Demystifying process drama: exploring the why, what, and how. *NJ: Drama Australia Journal*, 40(2), 127–140. https://doi.org/10.1080/14452294.2016.1276738

Dutton, J., and Rushton, K. (2022). Drama pedagogy: Subverting and remaking learning in the thirdspace. *Australian Journal of Language and Literacy*, 45, 159–181. https://doi.org/10.1007/s44020-022-00010-6

Ewing, R. (2019a). *Drama-Rich Pedagogy and Becoming Deeply Literate*. Sydney, Australia: Drama Australia.

Ewing, R. (2019b). Embedding arts-rich English and literacy pedagogies in the classroom. *Literacy Learning: The Middle Years*, 27(1), 7–17. https://search.informit.org/doi/10.3316/aeipt.222610

Ewing, R., and Saunders, J. (2016). *The School Drama Book: Drama, Literature and Literacy in the Creative Classroom*. Sydney, Australia: Currency Press Pty Ltd.

Freebody, K. (2013). Discourse in drama: Talk, role, and learning in drama education. *NJ: Drama Australia Journal*, 37(1), 65–75. https://doi.org/10.1080/14452294.2013.11649564

Galante, A. (2022). Translanguaging drama: Embracing learners' *perezhivanie* for embodiment of the repertoire. *International Journal of Bilingual Education and Bilingualism*, 27(9), 1258–1270. https://doi.org/10.1080/13670050.2022.2069460

García, O., and Kleyn, T. (eds.) (2016). *Translanguaging with Multilingual Students: Learning from Classroom Moments*. London and New York: Routledge.

Garret, R., Dawson, K., Meinters, J., and Wrench, A. (2018). Creative body-based learning: Redesigning pedagogies in mathematics. *International Journal for Learning Through the Arts: A Research Journal on Arts Integration in Schools and Communities*, 14(1).https://escholarship.org/uc/item/5396b47c.

Grosjean, F. (1989). Neurolinguists, beware! The bilingual is not two monolinguals in one person. *Brain and Language*, 36(1), 3–15. https://doi.org/10.1016/0093-934X(89)90048-5

Halliday, M. A. K., and Matthiessen, C. M. I. M. (2014). *Halliday's Introduction to Functional Grammar* (4th ed.). London and New York: Routledge.

Heathcote, D., and Bolton, G. (1995). *Drama for Learning: Dorothy Heathcote's Mantle of the Expert Approach to Education*. Portsmouth, NH: Heinemann.

Li, W. (2018). Translanguaging as a practical theory of language. *Applied Linguistics*, 39(1), 9–30. https://doi.org/10.1093/applin/amx039

Li, W., and García, O. (2022). Not a first language but one repertoire: Translanguaging as a decolonizing project. *RELC Journal*, 53(2), 313–324. https://doi.org/10.1177/00336882221092841

Lin, A. M. Y. (2013). Toward paradigmatic change in TESOL methodologies: Building plurilingual pedagogies from the ground up. *TESOL Quarterly*, 47(3), 521–545. https://doi.org/10.1002/tesq.113

Martello, J. (2002). Four literacy practices *roled* into one: Drama and early childhood literacies. *Critical Studies in Education*, 43(2), 53–63. https://doi.org/10.1080/17508480209556402

Martin, J. (1985). *Factual Writing: Exploring and Challenging Social Reality*. Oxford: Oxford University Press.

Mayer, R. E., and Moreno, R. (2003). Nine ways to reduce cognitive load in multimedia learning. *Educational Psychologist*, 38(1), 43–52. https://doi.org/10.1207/S15326985EP3801_6

Merriam, S. (2009). *Qualitative Research: A Guide to Design and Implementation*. Hoboken, NJ: John Wiley and Sons.

Miles, M.B., and Huberman, A.M. (1994). *Qualitative Data Analysis: An Expanded Sourcebook*. Thousand Oaks, CA: SAGE.

Mills, G. (2003). *Action Research: A Guide for the Teacher Researcher* (2nd ed.) Upper Saddle River, NJ: Merrill Prentice Hall.

Morgan, N., and Saxton, J. (1988). Enriching language through drama. *Language Arts*, 65(1), 34–40.

Motha, S. (2014). *Race, Empire, and English Language Teaching: Creating Responsible and Ethical Anti-Racist Practice*. New York: Teachers College Press.

Myhill, D. (2011). Grammar for designers: How grammar supports the design of writing. In S. Ellis and E. McCartney, eds., *Applied Linguistics and Primary School*

Teaching. Cambridge: Cambridge University Press, pp. 81–92. https://doi.org/10.1017/CBO9780511921605

O'Mara, J. (2004). At Sunny Bay: Building students' repertoire of literacy practices through process drama. In A. Healy and E. Honan, eds., *Text Next: New Resources for Literacy Learning*. Sydney, Australia: Primary English Teaching Association Australia, pp. 119–136

O'Toole, J., and Dunn, J. (2002). *Pretending to Learn*. Sydney, Australia: Pearson Education Australia.

Oniță, A. (2022). Articulating an arts-based language pedagogy. In E. Lyle, ed., *Re/Humanizing Education*. Leiden: Brill, pp. 109–123

Paige, K., Brown, L., O'Keefe, L., and Garrett, R. (2021). Dramatising the S and M in STEM. In P. White, J. Raphael, and K. van Cuylenburg, eds., *Science and Drama: Contemporary and Creative Approaches to Teaching and Learning*. Cham, Switzerland: Springer, pp. 73–92. https://doi.org/10.1007/978-3-030-84401-1_5

Piazzoli, E. (2018). *Embodying Language in Action: The Artistry of Process Drama in Second Language Education*. London and New York: Palgrave Macmillan.

Rose, D. (2008). Writing as linguistic mastery: The development of genre-based literacy pedagogy. In R. Beard, D. Myhill, J. Riley and M. Nystrand, eds., *Handbook of Writing Development*. Thousand Oaks, CA: SAGE, pp. 151–166.

Rose, D. (2015). Genre, knowledge and pedagogy in the 'Sydney School'. In N. Artemeva and A. Freedman, eds., *Genre Studies Around the Globe: Beyond the Three Traditions*. Edmonton, AB: Inkwell, pp. 299–338.

Rosler, B. (2005). Improving content area writing through process drama. *Ohio Reading Teacher*, 37(1), 49–58.

Saldaña, J. (2009). *The Coding Manual for Qualitative Researchers*. Thousand Oaks, CA: SAGE.

Saunders, J. N. (2019). Dramatic Interventions: A Multi-Site Case Study Analysis of Student Outcomes in the School Drama Program. [Doctoral Dissertation, University of Sydney]. Retrieved February 24, 2024, from https://hdl.handle.net/2123/21249

Stevenson, R. (2004). Constructing knowledge of educational practices from case studies. *Environmental Education Research*, 10(1), 39–51. https://doi.org/10.1080/1350462032000173698

Swain, M. (2005). The output hypothesis: Theory and research. In E. Hinkel, ed., *Handbook of Research in Second Language Teaching and Learning*. Mahwah, NJ: Lawrence Erlbaum Associates, pp. 471–483.

Swain, M. & Watanabe, Y. (2019). Languaging: Collaborative dialogue as a source of second language learning. In C. A. Chapelle, ed., *The Encyclopedia of Applied Linguistics*. Wliey Online Library. https://doi.org/10.1002/9781405198431.wbeal0664.pub2

Tang, G. (1992). The effect of graphic representation of knowledge structures on ESL reading comprehension. *Studies in Second Language Acquisition*, 14(2), 177–195. https://doi.org/10.1017/S0272263100010810

Tang, G. (1993). Teaching content knowledge and ESL in multicultural classrooms. *TESOL Journal*, 2(2), 8–12.

Tian, Z., and King, N. (eds.) (2023). *Developing Translanguaging Repertoires in Critical Teacher Education*. Berlin, Germany: De Gruyter. https://doi.org/10.1515/9783110735604

Winston, J. (2004). *Drama and English at the Heart of the Curriculum: Primary and Middle Years*. London: David Fulton Publishers.

Chapter 7

Embodied Approaches to English 'Exam Prep' in an Attainment-Driven Climate

'Coming in through the pleasurable route'

Camilla Stanger

Introduction: 'Coming in through the pleasurable route'

In the latter part of 2020, the UK's National Literacy Trust collaborated with author Jude Yawson to host 'Game Changers', a series of discussions with public figures around the impact of reading and writing on their lives. Author Derek Owusu and lyricist MC Angel spoke powerfully on this matter, with anecdotes of literary encounters that had, significantly, taken place outside of school:

> I was just wandering on the wind, not in school. And [my mentor] was like, Shana, write a poem about it girl. […] I'm a big advocate for writing with your own voice, your own experiences – tapping into the power that's already within your own life.
>
> MC Angel, October 2020

> I didn't like school – I felt stupid. I just wasn't feeling it […] everything changed after I read that first short story [from a book found in a local library] – I was just like whoa, this is what it's like to read – it was just so immersive – I'm having fun doing this - it was important I came in through the pleasurable route.
>
> Derek Owusu, October 2020

In this chapter, I discuss the importance of coming in 'through the pleasurable route' and 'tapping into the power that's already within' when it comes to learning (and teaching) English – especially for young people who may be marginalised from and within a particular schooling context.

In terms of what may produce experiences of disengagement and disenfranchisement when it comes to reading and writing, researchers have argued that the current UK English curriculum is centred around a canonical understanding of what counts as worthy literature (Elliott et al. 2021; Nelson-Addy 2020), with a view of young people's own writing that favours functional and technical skill in Standard English over free and authentic expression (Barrs 2019;

DOI: 10.4324/9781003655664-7

Cushing 2021). A third theme within the research is how these features of the English curriculum take particularly rigid shape through an educational climate that prioritises measurable outcomes and thus invites an acute focus on preparing students for performance in examinations (Gibbons 2019; Nevin 2020). The research cited above suggests that such a curriculum- and assessment-driven format invites teaching approaches and learning experiences that can disenfranchise many students from their pleasure and power as readers and writers – something to which the 'Game Changers' interviews attest. However, the interviews also locate spaces for hope. Owusu and MC Angel speak respectively to experiences of reading that are 'immersive' and 'fun', and approaches to writing creatively that 'tap into the power' of young people's 'own voice [and] experiences'. I take this forward to discuss an 'embodied' approach – one that mobilises feeling and lived experience (hooks 1994) and draws on drama-inflected approaches (Barrs 1987; Bryer et al. 2024) to unleash authentic expression in writing analytically about literature, and creatively through narrative.

The examples I explore in this chapter are drawn from three extracurricular English projects I co-designed to support Year 11 students (aged 15–16) towards success in their imminent GCSE[1] English Language exams. The students who accessed these projects attended different state schools in an economically underserved and culturally and linguistically diverse area of inner London. I interviewed eight students for this chapter, and their words play a key role in guiding its arguments alongside my own reflections as a teacher-researcher. The teaching approaches detailed here were developed in collaboration with two brilliant colleagues, Monika and Josie, both of whom taught English at the participating schools, and whose perspectives also inform the arguments of this chapter. A key perspective we all shared is an understanding of the above work as a social-justice-informed approach to 'doing English', especially within an exam-orientated education system shaped by a limiting cultural hegemony. So, before further exploration of the embodied approaches we developed, it is important to consider the particular constraints presented by GCSE English requirements at the time of writing and the common forms of classroom practice they invite.

The GCSE English exam: formula v. freedom

The discussions of this chapter are rooted in the experiences of teaching and learning in England post-2014 reforms to the secondary[2] curriculum and assessment. These reforms have drawn much criticism, particularly from English teachers (Pitfield et al. 2021; Palmer 2014), regarding a 'knowledge rich curriculum' that prioritises canonical knowledge and requires didactic teaching methods to cover the sheer amount of content, coupled with a heavy load of examinations that invites 'teaching to the test' (Gibson 2024). I suggest that teaching and learning under this particular system is revealing of how examining English in any context – especially where there is a narrow curriculum – can flatten it as a subject, or worse still, render it inaccessible.

Two key features of the English Language exam – analysis of an 'unseen' literary extract and a creative writing task, both set under tightly timed conditions – are ones that no doubt many English teachers will recognise. As part of GCSE preparation, it is common for analytical writing frames to be explicitly taught and used, with the goal of facilitating thinking and writing within the limited time given. While research suggests students may find such scaffolds helpful, it is also clear that writing frames can feel prescriptive and that overreliance on them can limit thinking and expression, ultimately lowering students' confidence to articulate their ideas (Gibbons 2019; McKnight 2020). It is interesting then that the bright and outspoken young women I was helping prepare for this exam would often resort to 'feature spotting' (simply identifying literary devices) as a way in to their pre-structured essays, with one student admitting to feeling 'blank', even with this approach in her toolkit. Veitch (2022, p. 133) indeed acknowledges that 'technique-spotting' mirrors the way we expect students to answer exam questions but that it also 'objectifies reading by divorcing form from content', thus emptying texts, and readers, of their power.

The rather dry creative writing task is assessed largely in relation to technical skill and accuracy.[3] This also invites particular forms of 'exam prep', especially as the reorienting of the writing assessment around the demonstration of technical skill can transform creative writing into, at best, an artificial tick-box exercise (Smith 2023). For example, some students and schools with whom I have worked focus on practising technical approaches, such as how to craft *in-media-res* openings and how to blend long and short sentences. Others develop a strategic approach of preparing a whole story in advance – one that can be partially memorised and then adapted to fit that year's writing prompt. One student I interviewed even shared that 'we never really did any creative writing in lessons – we just did analysis, and yeah, I kind of forgot about it'. As for students forgetting about their voice as free and creative writers, there is another matter at play here: that of a limiting cultural hegemony.

The excellent *Lit in Colour*[4] report (Elliott et al. 2021) offers an unsparing critique of how Anglocentric and middle-class cultural norms govern the current UK English curriculum, despite the diversity of the UK and its imperial 'past'. In regard to the literature element of the GCSE exam, the authors argue this disadvantages some students through requiring an unspoken familiarity with the dominant cultural norms that inform setting, character, storyline and of course language – while also centring experiences to which many students would be less likely to relate and therefore potentially less confidently analyse (see also the work of Nelson-Addy 2020). As Joy Mbake puts it, 'many of our students have been gazing at the curriculum from the outside […] we have subtly communicated with them that their lives, their language and their stories do not matter' (cited in Elliott et al. 2021, p. 7). The creative writing element of the exam can be critiqued through a similar lens: not only is Standard English the one dialect deemed acceptable (see Cushing 2021), but the examination writing prompts can at times be anything but culturally neutral (for example, past exam papers have asked candidates to write a description of a fishing village or an extremely grand-looking library). While discussions of this kind are complex and are certainly not intended to denote or limit what types of text, experience and writing young people can engage with, it is telling to hear Josie's interpretation of what was taking place in her inner London classrooms:

> These are the texts you must experience. This is the way that you must write. […] it teaches there's only one way and you can see students who can articulate themselves very well, with a lot of confidence verbally, when it comes to trying to express themselves in writing, it's like they're afraid to even get started.

It therefore seems vital to try something different in the classroom. Namely, approaches that might help students experience this kind of exam-driven curriculum from the *inside*, without fear, and with the kind of fluency, flow and joy that writers and readers can experience outside of exam conditions. We turned to an embodied pedagogical approach: one that encourages students to trust what they know, how they feel and who they are in responding to unseen prose and writing creatively.

An embodied approach: engaged pedagogy and drama-in-English

The work of bell hooks (1994) is helpful in defining an embodied approach for an exam-driven and canon-dominated English classroom. As a literature teacher herself, hooks advocates for what she calls an 'engaged pedagogy' (p. 13). Crucially, hooks' engaged pedagogy foregrounds and never loses sight of 'wholeness' (p. 6), namely the idea that students and teachers are never less than full human beings in the classroom, with lived experiences and feelings brought to bear on their learning. An 'engaged' classroom would be founded through building a learning community where each member can bring their own narratives of lived experience as valid and valued criteria for meaning-making. Following this, hooks also advocates for recognising 'the notion of pleasure in the classroom' and its liberatory but also purposeful effects in 'stimulating serious intellectual…engagement' (p. 7), referring to the sensual, physical and emotional energy that can charge a learning process and 'excite the critical imagination' (p. 195). It is no surprise that educators have continued to draw on the work of bell hooks to serve as a tonic within, or even an antidote to, the mechanistic character of teaching and learning within an attainment-driven and unequal education system. As Sosa-Provencio et al. (2020, p. 345) put it, 'education as freedom repairs the disconnectedness and invisibility minoritized students often experience within Eurocentric, socially reproductive, market-driven schooling'.

To further imagine the embodied pedagogy of hooks within the secondary English classroom, I turn to the relationship between English and Drama. Bryer et al. (2024) suggest there is nothing less than a 'natural affinity between drama and English', in that both subjects 'promote affective and intellectual understanding of ourselves as individuals and social beings' (p. 3). The authors articulate an approach stretching beyond 'traditional' and 'atomised' (p. 5) drama methodologies, proposing an embedded form of drama-in-English. Such an approach would allow students to experience and create texts in ways that exploit the 'creativity and criticality', the 'everydayness' and the 'enjoyment' (p. 5) of dramatic play. This would be through approaching reading as an immersive experience in which 'textual investigation happens from the inside out' (p. 6), and a 'creatively expansive' (p. 5) approach to writing that incorporates improvisation and writing-in-role. The work of Myra Barrs is foundational here. Barrs (1987) also sees the absolute connectedness of drama, reading, and writing, referring to reading as 'drama in the head' (p. 9) and writing as 'drama on paper' (p. 9), informed by theories of how children acquire language, learn to read, and make meaning through embodied play and enactment in role. Barrs therefore suggests that 'intelligent use of drama in education can tap into precisely the same capacity', describing this process as nothing less than 'empowering' (p. 11). It is with these ideas of engaging and empowering students within an exam-driven system that I now explore three embodied approaches to English exam preparation.

Empowered English: an *'in-her-shoes'* approach to teaching unseen prose

The first of the three examples of this chapter is taken from a project called 'Empowered English', a weekly after-school lesson focused on the Reading section of the GCSE exam. It was attended by ten young women (aged 15–16), all friends from the same school, and during the sessions, we experimented with what we named an *'in-her-shoes'* approach: imagination- and empathy-driven and subtly dramatised ways of reading and writing analytically about prose.

i The unseen prose extracts: 'A bit of spice'

The first step in developing an embodied and empowering approach was in the selection of extracts. I wanted the students to engage with challenging literature that required them to transport themselves to other worlds, while also featuring characters and relationships that were relatable. Through emotionally engaging material, I hoped we could 'excite the critical imagination' (hooks 1994, p. 195) first off, but then apply it back onto the page of the exam paper. This hooksian approach was further inspired by a previous collaboration with a colleague whose praxis is illuminating regarding teaching

English to racially marginalised young women in the UK (see Stanger and Ali 2025). So, I ultimately chose complex extracts that might still speak to the students' experiences as young women and as friends. We experimented with the following:

1   *The Haunting of Hill House*, by Shirley Jackson (2009): the moment Eleanor and Theodora are harassed by a ghostly presence outside their bedroom door, leaning on the wit and care within their friendship dynamic in this moment of threat
2   *The Handmaid's Tale*, by Margaret Atwood (1996): the opening of The Ceremony (a ritual rape in service of repopulating the dystopian North American setting of the novel), following the protagonist Offred's viscerally uncomfortable experience as she enters the grand living room of the house where the formalities begin.

Asked about our lessons together a few months on, all the girls vividly remembered these texts, with one student exclaiming, 'ah, we loved those extracts!' And as another put it, 'those extracts brought a bit of spice, Miss'. This was the starting point for inviting convincing and critical exam responses, and developing skill and mastery in doing so.

ii   Preparing to read: stepping into her shoes

As Donna Boam suggests, 'there is a strong moral imperative in English to explore empathy – it is the only [core GCSE] subject where students are asked to step into someone else's shoes' (cited in Elliott et al. 2021, p. 55). Drawing on the power of this in establishing a hooksian 'engaged' approach, each lesson started with a series of 'juicy debate questions' (as one student put it), pertaining to the extracts and essay questions they would soon be working with. For example, 'what would you do if you were in a haunted house with your best friend?' and 'would you rather have a relationship that gives you a comfortable and luxurious life, or one that allows personal freedom?' Students discussed these in pairs before being invited into a whole-class sharing and discussion of the issue. Each debate finished with a not-at-all subtle segue into the extracts: 'well, let's now see how the characters deal with these issues shall we… will you see yourself and your views reflected, or not?'

It was clear how engaged students were in these debates, within which they referenced their own lived experiences and expressed ideas that already captured the nuance of Jackson's and Atwood's writing. The emotional and critical engagement ignited by the debates immediately translated into the gusto with which they then attacked the extract, with the students often eagerly starting to read as soon as I handed extracts to them, rather than waiting for the 'exam activity' to formally begin. This evokes Owusu's (2020) reference to 'coming in through the pleasurable route' and the importance of being 'immersed' in a text, which was facilitated here by engaging the young women's sense of self and lived experiences. Indeed, there seemed to be power in allowing students to start 'in their feelings' and with a sense of (potential) connection to the character, rather than getting too 'in their heads' with the feature spotting and the formula of essay writing in mind. As one of the young women in these sessions put it, 'it was good that we started with those discussions as then I was already bringing ideas – I usually start English [essays] blank, but not now'.

iii A reading methodology: the head and the heart

In discussing the title for their book *Drama at the Heart of English*, Coles and Pitfield (2024) assert that 'heart is as much of a key word as drama' (p. 33), rooted in a belief that English should be 'reclaimed' as a 'humane' subject, with 'enjoyment and playfulness' at its own heart (p. 35). I thus describe the approach we took to reading the extracts as one that alternated between 'the head' and 'the heart' in efforts to create an immersive reading experience that activated the students' capacity to enter the text, to stand alongside the character, and to even see and feel themselves inside the narrative.

First, I asked students to devise a colour-coding system based on the essay question, embedding room for different interpretations. The next step was modelled by me reading the extract aloud to the class, or more so, performing it for them. This was something of a cross between teacher as (dramatic) narrator and 'teacher-in-role' (Bryer et al. 2024), in that my reading of the text was one that aimed to bring all characters, feelings and actions to life and immerse students in the world of the extract. Barrs (1987, p. 8) suggests, very simply, that 'Whether we read aloud or silently, in some way we enact, or perform, the text', drawing on Dorothy Heathcote's (1980) metaphor of becoming 'lost' in a text as a reading audience. The examination experience and forms of teaching discussed earlier in the chapter may well serve to flatten or block students from this otherwise natural process, and so I sought to reintroduce (or permit) this experience for students by asking them to imagine that, rather than a 'reader', they were an audience watching a film or a play in their mind's eye. To assist and ease them into this process, I would mobilise my voice (tone, volume and pace) and body (moving around the classroom to depict certain actions) to bring the narrative and characters to life. As we journeyed through the extract in this way, I asked students to use their colour-coding system to note evidence for the essay question, encouraging them again to be led by the heart rather than the head. The final step, once the reading had finished, was to identify material for analysis of authorial style and methods within their highlighted evidence, annotating if they had time.

This three-step methodology, moving between 'head' and 'heart', proved a quick and snappy, easily replicable yet powerful bit of 'exam prep'. Regarding the inclusion of the middle 'heart'-based method, especially within such tight exam-time constraints, Bryer et al. (2024, p. 13) suggest that such approaches have the power to 'prise open texts'. This certainly appeared to be true for my students, who throughout the dramatised readings demonstrated clear emotional responses (widening eyes, smiles), alongside confident highlighting, and an immediate desire to discuss character and theme before going back in to annotate for techniques. I explained to the students this is something they would then do for themselves 'in the exam', reading with as much drama as they could muster via their *own* internal reading voice, bringing the action and characters to life for an imagined audience – as a way to 'put you in the story' (Bryer et al. 2024, p. 3) and bring the evidence for the essay to life and therefore to light. The clarity this process gave to the students' understanding and analysis of the extract was clear in their resulting evidence selection and annotations, and Josie noticed something similar when she observed sessions with her own students:

> Initially there was little technique-spotting, but it was about emotionally engaging with the text. How would the character feel? Do you agree? What was really interesting was how enthusiastic they were and [their] confidence to share their ideas, how excited they got. It just gave them that sense of, oh I can read a text and understand it and see what the writer's doing and make actually quite deep level interpretations and only then move into analysis.

These embodied approaches indeed helped transform stale and formulaic writing (the kind that writing frames can produce) into more authentic analytical discussions that felt fresh, conveyed in the students' own voices, and grounded in their own experiences. For example, one young woman wrote with fluency about how bodily descriptions of self-protection depicted in *The Haunting of Hill House* (arms wrapped around oneself) created imagery of a fiercely loving, motherly protection, supporting her thesis that Eleanor overcomes her own fear to protect her friend. Interestingly, this student had spoken in a passionate way in our opening debate around how she too would hide her fear in order 'to look out for' her own best friend. Another student's noting of parallels between the experiences of Atwood's 'handmaids' and those of enslaved African American women led to a sophisticated discussion of narrative voice, in which she argued Offred engages in a process of emotional detachment from her luxurious surroundings as a form of survival. These approaches, therefore, allowed these young women to read 'heritage texts through the prism of diverse histories' as opposed to an 'assumed deficit' (Shah 2013, cited in Elliott et al. 2021, p. 18), another marker of an empowering pedagogy. This was an important opportunity for these students to experience their capacities outside deficit narratives – a similar opportunity also presented itself in the creative writing approaches we trialled.

Internalising the drama: embodied approaches to creative writing

Both creative writing sessions took place in extracurricular contexts: a girls-only revision and well-being day and a revision residential, taking place in a beautiful woodland location. In a hooksian sense, these settings acknowledged the 'wholeness' (hooks 1994, p. 6) of each young person: their feelings, bodies and friendships. The value of this in supporting students to 'tap into the power of their own voices' (MC Angel 2020) should not be overlooked. Indeed, Christine Nevin (2020) argues, in relation to teaching English in an exam-driven system, that young people's experiences outside of the classroom should be 'respected' as a valid starting point for writing. Nevin draws on a Vygotskian (1931) understanding of the teenage imagination as operating through a visceral sense of self in the world, thus being a powerful fuel for creativity. Again, the role of drama-in-English becomes clear: as Pitfield (2016) puts it, prompted by the work of Franks (1997), 'drama in schools, by legitimising adolescent play, [can] externalise inner desires which are dynamic, socially orientated and responsive to context' (2016, p. 110). Following this, the sessions discussed here encouraged students to externalise internal experiences when preparing for their creative writing exam.

i Free writing through fantasy and feeling: YA fiction on the girls' well-being day

I had started my own planning for this day with close reference to the assessment criteria – a common approach with the exam date looming. My colleague Monika, however, with whom I was co-leading the day, confessed she found this uninspiring as a starting point and wanted to try something different, namely using 'the books and media these girls are into - things like *Twilight*, *The Hunger Games*' as an inspiration. As Fenn (2023) explores, teenage girls are not often given the opportunity to see themselves reflected in the literature they study in school. Researchers such as Moss (1989) and Bode (2010) take this further to suggest that the texts (literary and media) often enjoyed by teenage girls are openly derided and undervalued, with echoes of the early positioning of 18th-century female novelists' work as trivial, sentimental stories for an equally trivial, sentimental (female) audience (Spender 1986; Kennedy 2019). Monika's session arguably served as an important antidote to the marginalising of girls' perspectives, investments and voices from the English curriculum and assessment.

Monika began by showing the students an iconic scene from the film adaptation of *Twilight* (2008): the moment the protagonist Bella sees her love interest Edward, 'the new boy in school', in the canteen for the first time. As Monika puts it:

> I loved how [Bella] almost didn't have anything to say - she was more observing. I thought it would be interesting to ask the girls to write from her perspective, because it's also contextualizing for them. They've all been in a canteen, all seen someone that they fancy or hadn't seen before and then have all these thoughts and feelings flooding their mind. So, I played them the video [and then] okay, why don't we write from Bella's perspective? You don't need to rewrite the exact scene - you are a better source - what would be going on in your mind?

In terms of how Monika helped her students access themselves as source material via the prism of Bella (or vice versa), we can again turn to the pedagogy of Barrs (1987, p. 11), who suggests writing-in-role makes use of 'powers that they [learners] naturally possess'. This sits neatly alongside Nevin's (2020) positing of the adolescent imagination as its own powerful source for creativity. Indeed, this blending of writing-in-role and writing-as-self led to a writing experience only too rare in the GCSE English classroom:

> As soon as I said 'write' there wasn't like a, 'oh, I don't know how to start'. The room was silent, the heads were down and no one hesitated at all. When I said all right stop writing you can see they were yearning to write more.

It was not just the confidence that was remarkable here – with none of the 'fear' Josie detected in her students – but also how the students seamlessly embedded their own lives, perspectives and languages into their imaginative retelling of this scene. As Monika explains:

> I then asked them to write from Edward's perspective and it was so interesting as some wrote from the perspective of a like '[name of local town] boy', and the slang, the colloquialism they were bringing in, the way that they were describing Bella through his eyes - it said a lot about the environment they had grown up in and things they had experienced. It was amazing.

What the students did here, transforming an existing story from 'the inside', demonstrates a real flair for conveying narrative perspective and character and considerable skill in weaving together different linguistic registers. Increased confidence and skill in manipulating language is something Barrs (1987) also noticed in her explorations of young people writing-in-role, and indeed, we would hope to see it rewarded by an examiner.

It seems that allowing these young women to write immersed in a relevant fantasy world merged with their own lives, and thus engage in the internalised kind of enactment, unleashed a fluency, precision and power in their writing. However, this session also did something beyond renewed confidence and flair in a style of 'exam writing'. It also showed respect for and offered a tool for navigating their lives beyond the exam:

> A lot of them were like thank you for allowing us the space to just write [...] it was almost like journaling - perhaps a form of writing that isn't deemed 'serious' but it's like – they're teenage girls. And their writing was beautiful.

This is reminiscent of the work of Sosa-Provencio et al. (2020), who advocate for a 'body-soul rooted pedagogy', nothing less than a 'salve' to 'remedy the wounds' inflicted 'by dominant schooling upon the academic, emotional well-being of marginalised communities' (p. 345). This work was developed specifically in relation to the experiences of Chicana youth studying in US high schools, but it does not feel unwarranted to apply the same thinking to the experience of working-class teenage girls studying in a UK school system that undervalues and even erases their textual and emotional lives and interests. Something similar was *also* true, however, for a group of young men who attended the revision residential.

ii Framing your feelings: embodied writing in the woodland revision residential

This session was developed with my colleague Josie and delivered to a group of Year 11s from four different schools. I interviewed three of these students, friends from different schools. All three young men had complicated relationships with creative writing:

Student (1): I really loved doing English [in primary school] because I could write about what I'm imagining and my own world. But then when I came secondary, after I just didn't like it because I didn't have that space or freedom.

Student (2): I feel like there was like a systematic like way of doing it, like only one way. You were given the techniques to do it because obviously you need to use them to get marks. But they don't promote, like, expressing, your own way of writing

Student (3): We went detail about how to analyse texts, break apart them, the tools. But what about your imagination, what you want to be able to see?

However, when asked to describe their experiences during the revision residential, they had the following to say:

Student (1): Yeah after I did that the first sentence, I just felt that, I'm ready - everything I was feeling, it just somehow went all through my mind. So it was like the inspiration was there and then it just kind of flowed after that.

Student (3): I was not even expecting to be able to compose a story that good. I actually feel like it was, in essence, one of the best-creative writing sessions I've had - I don't think I've ever had a lesson like that.

The session the students were referring to started with me sharing a specific yet loose writing structure with the group: Drop (your reader into the scene); Zoom (in or out to explore particular details); Flash (back, forward, or somehow out of the current moment); Return (to the opening to create a conclusion of some kind). To prevent this frame from feeling prescriptive and stale (Gibbons 2019), I modelled, with the help of a student volunteer, how this structure could be viewed as taking your reader on a journey. We physically journeyed around the classroom with me as 'writer' and the student as 'reader', experimenting with vantage points in both space and time. I hoped this would help students understand the writer's 'sense of the reader' as having something in common with a dramatist's sense of an actor' (Barrs 1987, p. 9) – both producing material for others to bring to life, whether on stage or in the mind's eye. Meanwhile, the rest of the class used the given structure to help us co-create and indeed dramatise an interesting and stylised tale about a school lesson, zooming in on two students having a whispered conversation, revealing, with the use of flashbacks, a dramatic (and perhaps not entirely fictional!) love triangle that subtly dominated the classroom dynamics. Pitfield (2016, p. 100) refers to 'fold[ing] the experience gained from the embodied composition into written composition', and the embodied composition experimented with here certainly seemed to prepare students for their writing. As one student put it, 'the type of explanation you did, like going through the structure like that, helped us to know our ideas but it also gave us a freedom' and as Josie noticed, 'the stories they all wrote – they were all well-crafted but very distinct, and you couldn't then really see the frame in it'. This underlines the importance of sharing frames with students, but doing so in ways that bring them to life – so they become malleable structures to be filled with the living, breathing ideas and voices of young people.

Next, we invited the students to plan out their own story – but this time, one inspired by their stay in the residential. There were two further criteria: use something real as inspiration, even if it then becomes fictional; select a genre through which to shape the tone and events. The genres suggested were dystopia, horror, gritty realism and... romance. And it was interesting, if not entirely unsurprising, that many students selected romance, including the young men interviewed for this chapter. This again speaks to Nevin's (2020) discussion of how the teenage imagination, replete with fantasy and self-discovery, can form powerful material for sophisticated creative writing. The final step before writing, however, was to offer support with the 'techniques' referred to by the students earlier – the ones that 'get you marks' – but again, in ways that lifted the 'tools' off the page and brought them to life within the context of the students' imagined worlds. Students were therefore given a list of sensory adjectives and told to spend at least 10 minutes outside in nature to finish planning their story. They were encouraged to interact physically with and take photographs of their environment to help choose their sensory language but also to help them imagine or 'stage the scenes' they would go on to write. This responds to Barr's avocation that 'the old adage that child's play is imagination in action must be reversed: we can say that imagination in adolescents is play without action' (1987, p. 10) – except in this instance, the action was reintroduced, to powerful effect. For example, one student told me with shy excitement as she re-entered the room, 'Miss, I have an idea', subsequently going on to write a vivid scene of eyes meeting over a crackling campfire, one that again would not be out of place in a compelling YA novel. This again underlines the importance of the material chosen by the teacher for stimulating the students' drama in the head, supported in this case by dramatic embodiment of the writing frame and being asked to imagine scenes while physically 'in situ'.

In a similar way to Monika's creative writing session, Josie noticed the following:

> There was just a complete shift in confidence – so many students had said 'I can't write a story', but when they came back into the room they just sat down and wrote and it felt very free flowing, it didn't feel forced or constrained by anything. I certainly didn't see any mnemonics [to remind students to use particular techniques] being written on bits of paper - it just felt free.

So, just as with the girls' well-being day, this creative writing session used lived experiences relevant to young people's lives as source material, and just as with the first session, this one also drew on visceral and drama-inflected methodologies for unleashing authentic writing. However, instead of inviting students to re-imagine a relevant YA text through the prism of their own lives, students were invited to re-imagine their own lives through the prism of a particular literary genre and embodied narrative structure. And instead of drawing on internalised dramatic techniques – such as creating an inner monologue to further explore a film scene – students were invited to engage imaginatively, viscerally and playfully with the physical environment around them, including co-creating a story in dramatised form before writing their own. It is therefore interesting to note that a few of the students elected to read their stories for the group afterwards. As Josie put it, 'the sense of pride that it fostered, that they wanted to read them out – perform them almost – it was quite dramatic and then how appreciative they were of each other's writing - that's not [something] you'd usually experience in a classroom'.

Conclusion

An embodied approach to teaching English in an exam-driven climate would mean helping students develop their confidence as readers and writers through mobilising their feelings, lived experiences, imaginations and ingrained capacity for role-taking when dealing with unseen prose and the blank page of a creative writing exam. A key UK exam board's *own* advice is not far from all this in highlighting the importance of 'thinking before writing' (AQA 2018, p. 8). I am suggesting here, however, that *feeling* and *imagining* before writing also have a place. The power of this for young people is clear, with the students I interviewed repeatedly using the following words to describe how they felt during and as a result of the approaches we tried: 'free', 'energised', 'confident', 'like I can be myself'.

An obvious limitation, or challenge, within the approaches detailed here is how they are worlds apart from the examination format itself. Indeed, in the exam hall students won't have space to debate 'juicy' issues with friends before writing about an extract that speaks to their lived experiences. They won't be able to disappear into nature with their friends to stage scenes before starting their individual crafting of a story. However, the purpose of these sessions was to support students in experiencing literature beyond flattened text for formulaic analysis and in experiencing creative writing as a space for actual creativity rather than a mere demonstration of skill. The approaches articulated here, therefore, can be viewed as a step towards exam confidence and a way to unlock a deeper and more authentic (rather than performative) set of skills for the exam.

Finally, while what prompted these experimentations was coping with the current curriculum and examination format in England, I suggest that the approaches discussed can apply more widely, wherever 'exam prep' is part of an English teacher's job. Not least because there is another equally important outcome to this pedagogy: to honour and unleash young people's pleasure and power as readers and writers outside of and perhaps in spite of 'the exam'. For example, the students I taught for Empowered English asked to borrow copies of *The Handmaid's Tale* and *The Haunting of Hill House* to read in their own time, while some students on the residential proudly submitted their work for publication in their school magazine. Indeed, it seemed these sessions achieved 'moments of spark' (Nevin 2020, p. 210) in apparent opposition to 'didactic' and 'exam-rehearsal'-based approaches that can leave students and teachers alike feeling 'jaded' (p. 212). So, to return to the words of MC Angel and Owusu, perhaps English teachers should continue to explore ways to 'come in through the pleasurable route' – not only to circumnavigate barriers to exam success, but to help students (re)discover themselves as readers and writers, all the while affirming 'the power that already exists in their own lives' within a school system that arguably does not.

Notes

1 General Certificate of Secondary Education: national school-leaver exams in the UK, usually taken by 16 year olds in a range of subjects.
2 Five years of education from 11 to 16 years old, concluding in national school leaver examinations.
3 See AQA 2021, for exam specification and details. AQA is one of the most popular examination boards for GCSE English.
4 A campaign launched by Penguin Books UK in 2020, in partnership with The Runnymede Trust, a race equality think tank, aiming to make the teaching and learning of English literature more inclusive.

References

Angel, M. C. (2020). 'Game Changers' interview with Jude Yawson. *National Literacy Trust*. Retrieved from https://www.youtube.com/watch?v=TNtZ4bTi1bI
AQA (June, 2018). *Report on the Examination – GCSE English Language Paper 1, 8700/1*. Retrieved from https://www.cienotes.com/wp-content/uploads/2020/02/AQA-87001-WRE-JUN18.pdf
AQA (14th October 2021). GCSE English language specification: For Teaching from 2015 Onwards. Retrieved from https://cdn.sanity.io/files/p28bar15/green/dbb5a2227be7d057a13894c32aded01133433e8c.pdf
Atwood, M. (1996). *The Handmaid's Tale*, London: Vintage.
Barrs, M. (1987). Voice and role in reading and writing. *Language Arts*, 64(2), 8–11.
Barrs, M. (2019). Teaching bad writing. *English in Education*, 53(1), 18–31. https://doi.org/10.1080/04250494.2018.1557858
Bode, L. (2010). Transitional tastes: Teen girls and genre in the critical reception of *Twilight*. *Continuum*, 24(5), 707–719. https://doi.org/10.1080/10304312.2010.505327
Bryer, T., Pitfield, M. and Coles, J. (2024). *Drama at the Heart of English: Transforming Practice in the Secondary Classroom*, London: Routledge.
Coles, J. and Pitfield, M. (2024). Revitalising English through drama. In J. Coles and M. Pitfield (eds.), *Teaching English* (Special Issue: Drama-in-English) NATE, 35, 33–36.
Cushing, I. (2021). Policy mechanisms of the standard language ideology in England's education system. *Journal of Language, Identity & Education*, 22(3), 279–293. https://doi.org/10.1080/15348458.2021.1877542
Elliott, V., Nelson-Addy, L., Chantiluke, R. and Courtney, M. (June, 2021). *Lit in Colour: Diversity in Literature in English Schools*. Runnymede Trust. Retrieved from https://litincolour.penguin.co.uk/assets/Lit-in-Colour-research-report.pdf
Fenn, R. (2023) Pride and Who? Jane Where? The missing women in GCSE English literature. *End Sexism in Schools*. Retrieved from https://endsexisminschools.org.uk/wp-content/uploads/KS4-Gender-Representation-in-the-English-Curriculum.pdf
Franks, A. (1997). Drama, desire and schooling. Drives to learning in creative and expressive school subjects. *Changing English: Studies in Culture and Education*, 4(1), 131–147.
Gibbons, S. (2019). 'Death by PEEL?' The teaching of writing in the secondary English classroom in England. *English in Education*, 53(1), 36–45. https://doi.org/10.1080/04250494.2019.1568832

Gibson, J. (May 2024). Testing patience: Reducing the burden of the English school curriculum. *Social Market Foundation*. Retrieved from https://www.smf.co.uk/wp-content/uploads/2024/04/Testing-patience-May-2024.pdf

Heathcote, D. (1980). Drama as context for talking and writing. In M. Barrs (ed.), *Drama as Context: NATE Papers in Education*, Aberdeen: NATE in association with Aberdeen University Press, pp. 4–24.

hooks, b. (1994). *Teaching to Transgress*, London: Routledge.

Jackson, S. (2009). *The Haunting of Hill House*, London: Penguin Classics.

Kennedy, V. (2019). Haunted by the Lady Novelist: Metafictional anxieties about women's writing from Northanger Abbey to The Carrie Diaries. *Women: A Cultural Review* 30(2), 186–205. https://doi.org/10.1080/09574042.2019.1600308

McKnight, L. (2020). Since feeling is first: The art of teaching to write paragraphs. *English in Education*, 55(1), 37–52. https://doi.org/10.1080/04250494.2020.1768069

Moss, G. (1989). *Un/Popular Fictions*. London: Virago.

Nelson-Addy, L. (2020). A journey of discovery: Breaking away from the single story. *Teaching English: NATE*, 23, 35–36.

Nevin, C. (2020). Paying Attention: The respectful work of teachers to enable remarkable achievements by adolescents. *Changing English*, 28(2), 208–222. https://doi.org/10.1080/1358684X.2020.1756742

Owusu, D. (2020) 'Game Changers' interview with Jude Yawson. *National Literacy Trust*. Retrieved from https://www.youtube.com/watch?v=_R5KsvY4wCM

Palmer, L. (2014). How Michael Gove's reforms drove me out of teaching. *The Guardian*, 5 August. Retrieved from https://www.theguardian.com/education/2014/aug/05/how-gove-reforms-drove-me-out-teaching

Pitfield, M. (2016). A pedagogy of possibilities: Drama as reading practice. In A. Hickey-Moody and T. Page (eds.), *Arts, Pedagogy and Cultural Resistance*, London: Rowman and Littlefield, pp. 95–111.

Pitfield, M., Gilbert, F., Asamoah Boateng, C. and Stanger, C. (2021). Selective amnesia and the political act of remembering English teaching. *Pedagogy, Culture and Society*. https://doi.org.libproxy.ucl.ac.uk/10.1080/14681366.2021.1990988

Shah, M. (2013). Reading canonical texts in multicultural classrooms. *Changing English*, 20 (2), 194–204.

Smith, L. (2023). Responding to a cry in the wilderness: Teachers' perceptions of teaching the Apprentice of Fine Arts in Creative Writing and its impact on the signature pedagogies of English. *Cambridge Journal of Education*, 53(6), 743–759. https://doi.org/10.1080/0305764X.2023.2237955

Sosa-Provencio, M. A., Sheahan, A., Desai, S. and Secatero, S. (2020). Tenets of body-soul rooted pedagogy: Teaching for critical consciousness, nourished resistance, and healing. *Critical Studies in Education*, 61(3), 345–362. https://doi.org/10.1080/17508487.2018.1445653

Spender, D. (1986). *Mothers of the Novel: 100 Good Women Writers Before Jane Austen*, London: Pandora.

Stanger, C. and Ali, A. (2025). The power of extracurricular pedagogies with young Black women in 21st century British schools. In J. A. Bustillos (ed.), *Questioning Gender Politics: Contextualising Educational Disparities in Uncertain Times*, Oxon and New York: Routledge, pp. 43–58.

Twilight (2008). [Film]. Directed by C. Hardwicke, USA: Maverick Films.

Veitch, R. (2022). Reading the Word Instead of the World: GCSE English Re-sits and the Divorce of Literacies from Their Lifeworld Use. *Changing English*, 29(2), 124–140. https://doi.org/10.1080/1358684X.2021.2024427

Vygotskian, L. [1931] 2004. Imagination and creativity in childhood. *Journal of Russian and East European Psychology*, 42(1), 7–97. https://doi.org/10.1080/10610405.2004.11059210

Chapter 8

Multilingual Digital Storytelling
Enhancing the Learning of English Through Drama

Vicky Macleroy

Introduction

The research I present here looks at how the learning of English and other languages can be enhanced through drama and the process of multilingual digital storytelling. I examine how and why drama has become a key feature of learning languages in a global literacy project. Critical Connections (2012–ongoing) was launched to reconnect young people with language learning and involves learning English and other languages through the process of digital storytelling. Originally working with teenagers, the project expanded its reach across all school stages (3–18 years old) in over one hundred pre-school, primary, secondary, and community-based complementary schools in 17 countries (Algeria, Australia, Brazil, Cyprus, Egypt, Germany, Iceland, India, Italy, Luxembourg, Malaysia, Palestine, Taiwan, Turkey, the UK, the USA, and Zimbabwe).

In this chapter, I examine how drama played an integral part in the emergence of digital storytelling and look at the ways in which combining drama and storytelling with digital technology transforms how young people explore texts, ideas, and narrative. This builds on research findings and work from the Critical Connections (CC) Project that clearly demonstrate how 'drama can be used in the pre-production, production, and post-production stages of digital storytelling to open up possibilities for creative and imaginative uses of language' (Macleroy 2024, p. 74). I investigate how drama enables young people to move from talk about texts to performance and filmmaking.

Drama is explored and conceptualised here as transformative pedagogy in practice, with learner agency, identity, and voice seen as key to young people creating stories that matter to them. I look at how young people use drama to portray difficult truths and how the art of collaborative filmmaking can allow students the 'space and time to make their own metaphors, and decide exactly what kind of truth they want to tell' (Bramley & Rowsell 2024, p. 1022). Young digital storytellers in the CC project learn English and other languages through 'experimenting, improvising, problem-solving and working things out through repetition, resilience, and imagination' (Macleroy 2024, p. 74). Rehearsal, performance and reflection become part of this digital storytelling process, and young people improve their dramatic, linguistic and technological skills. The CC pedagogical approach is underpinned by Project-Based Language Learning (PBLL) and recognises the benefits and challenges of this type of more sustained and in-depth learning. PBLL emphasises the importance of understanding both process and product through analysing how the digital stories are crafted, and the digital stories themselves are analysed as artefacts or 'embodied objects' (Alexandra 2017, p. 168).

In the CC project, young filmmakers seek out new ways of telling their stories and use these digital storytelling spaces to connect with multiple others, play with a plurality of personae, and 'experiment with being multiple selves' (Craft 2011, p. 43). Lambert (2018), founder of the digital storytelling movement, centres story and argues for the key role of digital storytelling in making sense of experience in an age of 'infoglut' when the memory bank is overloaded. Lambert views a digital story as a place of calm and hopefulness, describing story work as 'the quiet place around which the storm blows' (Lambert 2018, p. 3). In our digital storytelling work, we look at how children and young people create stories of hope and resilience (Macleroy & Chung 2023) and open up spaces for activist citizenship.

This chapter focuses on the ways drama has been utilised in our multilingual digital storytelling project in the learning of English and other languages across four countries (India, Italy, Taiwan, and the UK). The schools in these countries were part of a funded research project, 'Re-imagining Adolescent Wellbeing (RAW): A Young Adult Digital Storytelling Study' (2023–2024) within the wider Critical Connections project, contributing to the Care, Community and Hope Festival 2025. In the following sections, I look at the connections between drama and multilingual digital storytelling, drama as transformative pedagogy in practice, and enhancing the learning of English and all languages. I then turn to analysing the digital storytelling process and four digital stories to demonstrate these ideas in practice.

Multilingual digital storytelling and drama

Digital storytelling comes from a background of experimental theatre, folk culture, and cultural activism. It is rooted in ideas of social justice and democratised culture, seeking ways to tell stories that capture a 'sense of the extraordinary in the ordinary comings and goings of life' (Lambert 2018, p. 26). This type of storytelling, with its rootedness in community, has the 'potential to illuminate the lifeways and lifeworlds of those telling the stories' (Willox et al. 2012). Digital storytelling recognises the power of shared stories and how a story that is crafted, performed, and shared using digital technology can have 'totemic power for the storyteller' (Lambert 2018, p. 11). Lambert convincingly argues that a healthy community is grounded in plurality, understanding, and belonging: 'Being the author of your own life, of the way you move through the world, is a fundamental idea in democracy' (Lambert 2013, p. 2).

The story circle is at the heart of the digital storytelling process and involves young people sharing oral stories in the circle under a common theme and developing deep listening skills. In the CC project, we took digital storytelling into schools and classrooms, and students worked collaboratively to create their stories. We discovered opportunities to bring drama, poetry, artwork and props into the story circle. Role play, developing characters' backstories, and experimenting with how the story is told are crucial stages in the digital storytelling process. Connecting these dramatic processes with digital storytelling supports young people in facing difficult truths and complex, contradictory realities. Lambert argues that what works in digital storytelling is truth and that 'each word and each apparent digression is critical to the final resolution of the character's action' (Lambert 2018, p. 101). Young people need spaces to discuss stories and lived experiences that resonate deeply with them and consider the power of stories to bring about change. Bertolt Brecht (1935), renowned playwright, grappled with the difficulties of writing the truth and argued for courage, keenness, skill, judgement and cunning.

In the CC project, we brought in new ways to work with story, character, and cameras during the filmmaking process. Drama researcher and practitioner Chryso Charalambous expanded the story circle with cultural artefacts, personal objects, and props and enabled participants to experiment with characters, play with presenting and framing objects, build tension, and shift emotions. Film educator Jo van de Meer devised film workshops for the Critical Connections project that extended these drama and storytelling practices into filmmaking. Participants played with objects and with creating characters, experimented with camera angles and shots, tried out different sound effects, and improvised short scenarios. Young filmmakers were given the courage to try things out, make mistakes, and find imaginative and creative solutions to telling their stories. In digital storytelling work, participants are asked to 'tell something about the stuff in your life and what it reveals about you' (Lambert 2018, p. 96). Research in digital storytelling as a pedagogy continues to expand and has moved (within education) from technology training to a focus on understanding 'story-based pedagogy as a tool for transformative learning' (Lambert 2018, p. 117).

Drama as transformative pedagogy in practice

In conceptualising a framework for learning languages within a model of transformative pedagogy, Cummins (2000) identified three core elements for transformative orientation: 'critical literacy, critical language awareness and acting on social realities' (p. 280). Transformative pedagogy (creative, critical, and performative) is one of the key design principles in the CC project with multilingual digital storytelling at the centre (Macleroy et al. 2023). In our research into transformative pedagogy, we look critically and carefully at whether drama and digital storytelling can transform language pedagogy in some of the following ways:

> Shift ownership of learning to the students; engage students in grappling with multiple viewpoints; break down barriers of language and culture; change the way students perceive others; research and problem solve; value student-generated creative-critical-performative success criteria; promote multilingual literacy and multilingual activism.
>
> (Macleroy 2025, p. 135)

This process of constant experimentation, revision and reflection is viewed 'as the essence of successful Digital Storytelling' (Lambert 2017, p. 26). Teachers must rethink their role in classrooms and ensure young people are provided with scaffolded support and have agency to devise, direct, perform, and edit their digital stories. A lead educator in Taiwan combines students' learning of English with citizenship and digital storytelling. He commented on the profound and long-lasting influence of the CC project and how this pedagogical approach continues to have an impact on teachers and students (Chung & Macleroy 2022, p. 266):

> I suddenly realised that this was something I had to learn. I always gave feedback and expected them to accept my comments. I should have respected their ownership of their story and raised questions when I had doubts. I should have allowed them time and space to review their story and consider whether any improvements were needed; just as I expected they would do with their classmates. I had forgotten I should have done the same.
>
> (EFL Teacher, Fengshan Senior High School, Taiwan)

In viewing drama as transformative pedagogy in practice, I recognise the potential of drama to boost young people's language learning through digital storytelling. Drama, in the same way as digital storytelling, is seen as a communal art form requiring participation and co-operation to take place (Winston & Tandy 2001).

Drama also captures tension, contradictory realities, and shifting emotions. Neelands (2009) interrogates the notion of togetherness in drama with its inherent contradictions: 'it is the art of togetherness even if much of its content and form is about representing un-togetherness' (p. 9). Lambert (2018) talks about digital storytelling in a similar way, noticing that digital stories cannot 'simplify the messiness of living' (p. 13) and 'story is essentially an exercise in controlled ambiguity' (p. 13). I analyse these ideas in the digital stories presented in this chapter and how students grapple with shifting perspectives and viewpoints on controversial social issues such as migration. Lambert (2018) describes a shared story as a symphony, and in our project, the digital storytellers learn to collaborate effectively, bringing together disparate elements into a meaningful film. The transformative orientation of drama allows young people to 'live inside an imagined context' (Gallagher 2010, p. 43) to see what they can learn together. In our research, we argue that 'the imaginary as if worlds we create in theatre, a necessary precondition for drama to happen, give room for alternative narratives to be built and the imagining of different ways of being' (Stavrou et al. 2019, p. 103).

Conceptualising drama as transformative pedagogy in practice is holding onto these alternative narratives and creating classroom environments where young people have the freedom to imagine otherwise. During the digital storytelling process, the young filmmakers move in and out of role, learning to play with and juxtapose different perspectives and 'fictionalise life as they experience it and alternatively, to make the imaginary world tangible and real' (Stavrou et al. 2019, p. 103). These ideas build on a view of digital storytelling as an applied theatre praxis through which young people '(re)construct complex notions of (their) identity, culture and community' (Alrutz 2013, p. 45).

Enhancing learning English and all languages

The challenge in this chapter is to examine how drama within digital storytelling can enhance learning English and all languages. The challenge for language education, in general, is to develop an approach that is translingual and transcultural in orientation. In our CC work and research, we argue that this means recognising the part that learners' backgrounds and life experiences play in interactions with another language and culture. It means understanding subjective and symbolic meanings and deeper cultural significances of the ways we use language. In our digital storytelling work, it requires integrated, critical and creative use of digital media for local and global communication and developing 'Knowledge About Language (KAL) by highlighting connections between languages, uncovering the origins of words and word relationships as well as how meanings are expressed differently in different languages' (Anderson & Macleroy 2021, p. 175). In combining drama with digital storytelling and language learning, I look at how young people become agentive in these spaces and seek out new language and forms of expression. This relates closely to Craft's (2011) research on learning in digital spaces and the concept of 'possibility thinking', which involves a shift from the given to the possible and 'posing in multiple ways the question "What if?"' (2011, p. 51). I explore how combining the dramatic 'what if?' question with digital storytelling can enable young people to develop fluency and confidence in drawing on their multilingual repertoires.

In recent research on digital storytelling as translanguaging, Linville and Vinogradova (2024) explore how digital storytelling with translanguaging can 'improve language learning, develop MLs' [multilingual learners] critical language awareness, build community in the classroom and beyond, and promote linguistic social justice' (p. 19). Building on research in the field, including our findings on digital storytelling being useful for language development and digital literacy development (Anderson et al. 2018), these researchers examine the pedagogical implications. They argue that in the past decade, 'the field of language education, especially English language education, has shifted from a monolingual focus to a multilingual focus' (Linville & Vinogradova 2024, p. 18). In our multilingual digital storytelling work, we start with the multilingual dimension and make young people aware that this filmmaking process is about exploring critical connections between languages and how their languages and cultures can be represented in their digital stories. Composing multilingual digital stories provides a rich context for dynamic translation at each stage of the filmmaking process, including storytelling, storyboarding, rehearsing, performing, subtitling and presenting digital stories. Learning English in this way enables multilingual learners to expand and utilise their full linguistic repertoire, as 'each step of the digital storytelling process engages MLs in understanding and improving their translanguaging skills' (Linville & Vinogradova 2024, p. 149). In rethinking the education of multilingual learners, Cummins (2021) cites our project as inspirational pedagogy, highlighting its strong multilingual processes and concrete outcomes:

> students' active engagement with the MDST activities, enthusiasm for using the full range of their plurilingual skills, willingness to employ translanguaging as a scaffold to support task completion, affirmation of the identities of students.
>
> (p. 364)

In the next sections, I analyse our pedagogical approach in context.

Research context for multilingual digital storytelling

The multilingual digital stories presented here were created with young people (11–17 years old) learning English and other languages in schools across four countries. Research data was collected from field notes; conversations with lead teachers and students; online team meetings; filmmaking, comics making, and creative writing workshops; storyboards, scripts, rehearsals, and performances; photographs, poetry, artwork, film posters, Padlet, and digital stories; and online webinars, research posters, and reflections (2023–2024). The four lead project schools are all co-educational secondary schools. Fengshan Senior High School (FSHS) in Taiwan is a mixed 16–18-year-old school that has been a lead project school since 2012; Europa School (ES) in the UK is a mainstream bilingual school (English with French, German, and Spanish) in Oxfordshire that has been part of the project since 2015; K'sirs International School (KS) in southern India and Herz-Jesu Institut (HJI) in northern Italy became part of the CC project in 2021.

In this chapter, I present research data from these four countries to demonstrate how drama has become an integral part of our pedagogical approach in multilingual digital storytelling. The CC project has an overarching theme each year to connect the digital stories across countries and languages. In 2023–2024, the theme for the project was 'Care, Community and Hope', and I was awarded additional funding to work closely with forty adolescents in four lead project schools. These adolescents explored well-being, pain, resilience, and hope through multilingual digital storytelling in different global educational settings. The forty students received physical copies of the graphic novel *Sunshine* (Krosoczka 2023) to read in English (first/additional/foreign language for students in Italy, India, Taiwan, and the UK). The Re-imagining Adolescent Well-Being (RAW) project became known as the 'Sunshine (RAW) Project'. I focus on the following digital stories (3–5 minutes) in the Sunshine (RAW) project:

1 *Face It – Stay Strong – Not Alone* 2024, Herz-Jesu Institut Italy [English, Albanian, German dialect, Standard German, Italian, Ladin]: https://vimeo.com/995117571
2 *Lost In the Mirror* 2024, Europa School UK [English, German]: https://vimeo.com/1007267245
3 *Echoes of Solitude* 2024, K'sirs International School India [English, Tamil]: https://vimeo.com/950563014
4 *Encounter, Conflict, Understanding: The Migrant Worker* 2024, Fengshan Senior High School, Taiwan [English, Indonesian, Mandarin, Taiwanese]: https://vimeo.com/1007447593

Analysing the digital stories across the key stages in multilingual digital storytelling

I use these four key stages of the filmmaking process (pre-production, production, post-production, final multilingual digital story) to analyse how drama is utilised in the digital storytelling process to boost the learning of English and other languages (Figure 8.1).

The role of drama in the pre-production stage of digital storytelling

An experimental and innovative feature of the Sunshine (RAW) project was that schools across four different countries were reading the same graphic novel, *Sunshine*, in English. This text connects intimately with the way stories are told within digital storytelling projects. *Sunshine* is a graphic memoir, a true story about the author volunteering at a summer camp for children with cancer and their families. Krosoczka (2023) tells his personal story through a first-person perspective as a 16-year-old, 'time and chance had plucked me up and placed

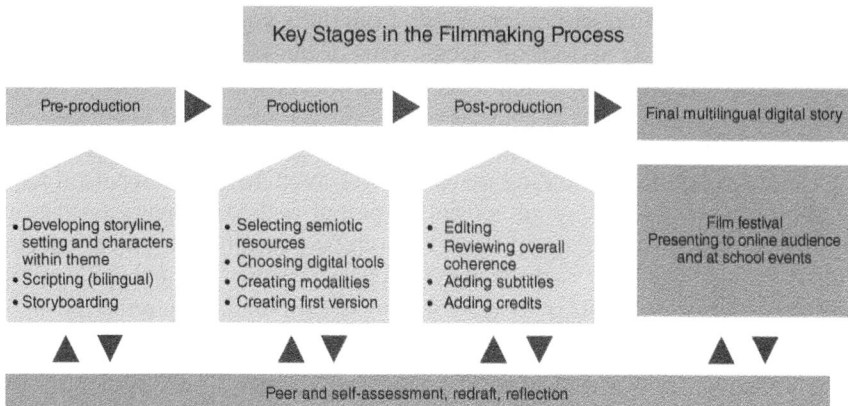

Figure 8.1 Key stages in the filmmaking process in the Critical Connections project.

me here' (9), and how this experience altered the trajectory of his life. In a similar way to digital stories, this graphic memoir uses photographs, artwork, sketches, songs, motifs and strong character development to tell a powerful story about hope, where 'the kids I met weren't dying – they were living. Living life to its fullest' (Krosoczka 2023, p. 3).

The young people in the project responded to the graphic novel through a comics making online workshop devised and led by Helen Jones (doctoral researcher in comics making at Goldsmiths). They actively explored how emotions are expressed through drawings with the idea of 'amplification through simplification' (McCloud 1994, p. 30) and compared emotions in comics across the world (France, UK, Japan). Inspired by *Sunshine*, they developed characters (connected a song with their character) and thought about colour, motifs and patterns as well as objects and animals (dreams and reality) across the story. Comics making became part of the drama process where students experimented with different ways of scripting, subtitling, writing dialogue and creating characters. Students started to understand how to utilise storyboarding in more effective ways, capturing shifting emotions across panels and leaving space for the imagination in gutters between panels (or frames). Students were then able to capture these shifts in characters' feelings and emotions in short dramatic dialogue and dynamic language usage.

A further innovative and creative feature of the Sunshine (RAW) project was a focus on creative writing to support scripting and character development in the digital storytelling process. All the young people were asked to watch the short 10-minute animation film, *WiNDUP* (Unity 2019), ahead of an online creative writing workshop and think about a journey they did not want to make or made them nervous. This animation has no words and focuses on the fragile nature of life, fear of loss, resilience, and hope. The online workshop was led by Harry Oulton (doctoral researcher in YA creative writing at Goldsmiths and award-winning script editor and drama producer), with students translanguaging, listening in English to others, and writing across their different languages. These young digital storytellers experimented with how to script a digital story through charting the changing emotions, identifying the main obstacle(s), and finding a way forward across a narrative arc. They learnt how to identify the turning point in a narrative and explore different ways of representing shifting emotions, including characters' gestures and interactions with others, the environment, and personal objects (e.g., the musical box). The turning point in the animation is when the musical box breaks, and the father starts singing the tune. Creative writing became an integral part of the drama process, providing students with the tools and skills to present hard emotions through moving images and script a meaningful story.

Drama teacher and lead project educator at Herz-Jesu Institut, Elfi Troi, recognised how the project gave students a 'voice and a platform to share their narratives to highlight the importance of empathy, support and resilience. Creating the comics and digital stories made learning more engaging and interactive' (HJI Teacher). Her students (11–12 years old) created three interconnected short films, *Face it – Stay Strong – Not Alone*, on 'anxiety, loneliness, bullying and feeling different as well as acceptance, kindness, care and friendship as a healing power which makes people feel happy' (HJI Student Film Booklet). I focus on the central film, *Stay Strong*, which exposes bullying between students because one girl is wearing shoes that are different. The shoes are a trigger for conflict and online bullying, as the other girls use social media to create #uglyshoes. The opening frame of the storyboard for *Stay Strong* depicts a character hunched up in the corner of a room alone, looking deeply upset with tears drawn on her cheeks (Figure 8.2). Students creating this

Figure 8.2 Storyboard for *Stay Strong* 2024.

storyboard were thinking very carefully about the scenarios for their digital story: gestures and interactions between the characters, building of tension, and turning point when the girl with different shoes is seen in a new light.

In the Europa School, the lead English teacher worked in collaboration with the International Baccalaureate project teachers and two groups of Year 9 students (13–14 years old) in the French and German school strands. The second digital story, *Lost in the Mirror*, was created in German and English and centres on a girl who imagines her friends turning away from her, but then she finds a mirror in the bathroom:

> When plotting our short film, we wanted to have it revolve around belonging, fitting in and changing yourself for others. It was very important to us that it was relatable to teens nowadays. That is why we made the story of a normal schoolgirl trying to fit in.
>
> (ES Student Research Poster)

The creative writing and scripting workshop supported these students in thinking about how to tell their story in speculative and imaginative ways. Personal objects became significant in the scripting and performing of their digital stories. In *Lost in the Mirror*, the mirror is the trigger for the main character's transformation: 'it symbolizes how she overly judges herself and becomes extremely self-aware' (ES Student Research Poster). These young filmmakers come up with a dramatic image to represent changes in character, shifting emotions, and building tension. Instead of a cracked mirror, cracks start to appear on the film screen itself to 'show how she is coping inside with pretending to be something she's not. They reflect her mental state' (ES Student Research Poster). In speculating in this way, these students have clearly utilised the dramatic 'what if?' question (Craft 2011).

In K'sirs International School, the lead project teachers worked with students across the school (13–17 years old) in two groups. The students presented different stories on a plan board and selected this storyboard for its convincing plot. The third film, *Echoes of Solitude*, demonstrates the effectiveness of carefully crafted storyboards for scripting and dramatic realisation of the digital story. In presenting her storyboard online to other schools, the student author/illustrator talked about the main character: 'He feels odd. He feels left out. He loses his sense of belonging in society' (Figure 8.3). *Echoes of Solitude* demonstrates the value of the creative writing workshop for scripting and imagining changes and shifts in emotion across the narrative arc. These young digital storytellers describe their story as a 'heart-warming tale' that 'follows the journey of a young boy named Aadhitiya as he navigates the challenges of a learning disability and the loneliness it brings' (KS Student Film Booklet).

In Fengshan Senior High School, the lead English teacher, Peter Luo, guided ten students (16–17 years old) in producing two digital stories telling

Multilingual Digital Storytelling 121

Figure 8.3 Storyboard for *Echoes of Solitude* 2024.

the same story, *Encounter, Conflict, Understanding*, but the first from the employer's perspective and the second from the migrant worker's perspective. I focus on analysing *Encounter, Conflict, Understanding: The Migrant Worker* and how students shifted perspectives and experimented with a plurality of personae and multiple selves (Craft 2011). The comics making and storyboarding were valuable processes in students finding ways to represent conflicts, misunderstandings and character development. The creative writing and scripting work was apparent in how these students used a personal object, a watch, in imaginative ways to build dramatic tension, shifts in emotion, and physical confrontation. The young digital storytellers used the broken watch to symbolise broken trust, fractured family ties, and lost memories. There are two identical watches, and the watch for the migrant worker is a gift from her mother, a symbolic object and a central motif (Figure 8.4).

In these digital stories, the role of drama was crucial in the pre-production stage as the young digital storytellers became skilled in transferring meaning across modes (linguistic, visual, spatial, auditory, and gestural) and enhancing their translanguaging skills (Linville & Vinogradova, 2024).

The role of drama in the production stage of digital storytelling

I now turn to examine how these young digital storytellers moved from storyboarding, scripting, and developing characters and scenarios to utilising drama to bring their stories to the screen. This transition is supported through a guided activity where students actively view a series of digital

Figure 8.4 Storyboard for *encounter, conflict, understanding: The Migrant Worker* 2024.

stories and analyse language, culture, genre, mise-en-scène, cinematography, and audience. Lead educators use ideas, resources and production tasks from the CC online workshops to support students during the production stage, including selecting film locations, preparing props, directing the filming, and acting as camera operators, actors, changing objects, and timekeepers. All the young people decided to use moving images to tell their stories and convey a meaningful message about conflict and hope to multilingual audiences across the world.

In the first digital story, *Stay Strong*, these four young filmmakers were given one day to act out and shoot all the film clips for the first version of their story. They wanted to experiment with different camera angles and shots to capture the journey of the main character and shifts in emotion across the digital story. Their detailed storyboard and scripting facilitated the production stage and how to build the dramatic tension between the characters and depict the main character's isolation and loneliness. *Stay Strong* was shot in and around the school, and the young filmmakers used doors for barriers (entrances and exits), toilets as places to hide, and open spaces for shifts in action. The protagonist was filmed entering the school alone, and the action shifts to a high-angle shot of her feet as she slowly puts on her indoor yellow shoes. The students were learning how to build dramatic tension between characters, show the main protagonist from her back as she was trapped by the bullies in the corridor, and use large gestures to demonstrate her anger and despair. These young filmmakers utilised dramatic dialogue to understand the power of language to hurt and humiliate and movements and gestures to bring this to the screen with the discarded rucksack and slammed doors. Students used a mobile phone to create #uglyshoes, which the main character views on her phone, deeply upset. These filmmakers took the action outside to capture the dramatic turning point in their film when the bully falls down some stairs (adapted from their storyboard where she falls into a river), and the main character shows kindness. The students created a mood of reconciliation in the last scene, filming the characters sitting on the floor in a circle and the words, 'Yes! Finally, friends'.

In the second digital story, *Lost in the Mirror*, the five filmmakers captured the story of the main teenage character using different locations, props, costumes, and special effects. Their story is brought to life through these dramatic techniques that are utilised to build peer pressure and represent the confusion and contradictions in the main character's actions. The students filmed most scenes in their school using outside spaces, bathrooms, classrooms and corridors, but also some scenes were shot at home. The film starts with the main character waking and then shifts to her walking alone towards the closed school doors with headphones on, listening to music. The main character is becoming isolated from her peers, and the filmmakers use film locations well to capture the shifting moods and gathering tension. She meets with her friend under a tree, and the discussion of makeup is casual and friendly, but then the camera cuts to three friends putting on false eyelashes, lipstick and mascara, and then cuts back to the main character walking through a school corridor, and when she greets two friends, they immediately stop talking and look down and away from her. Finding the small compact mirror discarded in the bathroom becomes the catalyst for the main character's shift in emotions: 'Maybe I should change something!' It is at this point that the first crack appears on the main screen. It is through the integral use of drama techniques (changing appearance, altering character, shifting emotions, character conflict, turning point, resolution) that the students are able to tell their truth and create a story that matters to them (Bramley & Rowsell, 2024).

In the third digital story, *Echoes of Solitude*, the filmmakers think carefully about the different locations to represent the character's journey and the growing feelings of isolation and disconnection. The increase in tension is internalised by the main character, and the conflicts are described as silent battles. The film starts with the main character outside in the street, slowly walking to school alone. The filmmakers use dramatic techniques (character interaction, mockery and laughter, chatting and exclusion, silence, and bodily posture) to create empathy and a shift in perspective to understanding the main character's silence. Collaborating with adults to take roles as teacher and parents, the filmmakers further built the dramatic tension and truth of the story. The main character is unable to express how he feels or the contradictory emotions of needing to be alone but feeling isolated. These students faced the challenge of finding a dog to take the leading role in the resolution of the story. They talked about the production stage being quite challenging, as they had high expectations for the film.

> We did not give up even though we were disappointed by the outcomes of certain scenes and continued to experiment until we got them right. Our commitment to realise on screen what we had imagined initially kept our spirits high throughout the filming process.
>
> (KS Student Introduction)

In the fourth digital story, *Encounter, Conflict, Understanding: The Migrant Worker*, the students shifted the genre of the digital story from documentary to a fictionalised story inspired by real-life encounters between employers and migrant workers. This shift to a narrative drama was key to students using language in more imaginative ways, having more creative freedom when acting in role, developing greater empathy when stepping into the shoes of the characters, and opening up more aesthetic choices. The narrative drama still maintained qualities of documentary realism through situating the personal experiences of the migrant worker within the wider social and political context of intercultural conflict. An innovative aspect of this narrative drama was that the filmmakers gained access to a real factory to film their drama on location. They wanted to get to know what it was like to work in a factory in Taiwan and commented that 'to get close to the life of our main character is a really important part, and bringing our video to another level, enhancing realism' (FSHS Student). These young filmmakers recognised the power of acting in role with close-up shots of factory tools and machinery to capture the truth and powerful message in their story.

Drama was integral in the production stage for these young filmmakers as they utilised role play, drama techniques, character conflict, dramatic tension, and resolution to decide exactly what truth they wanted to tell.

The role of drama in the post-production stage of digital storytelling

The post-production stage of the digital storytelling process is challenging and demanding and requires perseverance but also creativity and vision. These students are learning how to capture the affordances of different modes in their digital stories as well as working across English and other languages. Young people learn many skills in the post-production process, including ways to make their digital story dramatic through shifts in emotions, mood and tempo; aesthetically engaging through colour, lighting, and location; and meaningful through creative subtitling and a strong script. Students are thinking carefully about the dramatic effect of their digital stories on a global audience. They are learning to become adept at translating, adding subtitles, soundtracks, animation and special effects to their 3–5-minute digital stories. The Sunshine (RAW) project was the first time young people had used comics making in their digital stories to represent dramatic moments: 'the images present the exterior, what we see on the outside, while the words provide the interior, what the characters are thinking and feeling on the inside' (Hughes & King 2010, p. 71). These young filmmakers used comics making to represent characters' inner fears and uncertainty and animated objects to shift perspectives and tell their story from a different angle.

In the first digital story, *Stay Strong*, the young filmmakers experimented with the dramatic effect of using different languages for the voice-over of the animated shoes. The action starts with animated shoes of the three main characters (on a shoe rack in the entrance of the school), and the yellow shoes (of the character who is bullied) are the only shoes that speak in English. The other shoes taunt the yellow shoes in other languages because of colour and difference (subtitles – What colour is that! It's so ugly!), and the yellow shoes respond in English with, 'why are you so mean?' The filmmakers use their languages to create dramatic tension in the narrative and show how the main character is bullied and made to feel ugly, unwanted and odd. Repetition is used dramatically to increase the tension, and the same dialogue is repeated in the girls' encounter in the corridor with the English subtitle: 'They are so ugly!' The main character is reaching her lowest point in the narrative arc of the drama, and the students used comic-making to capture the intensity of feeling and show her tears. They also experimented with subtitling by including the German subtitles in a speech bubble with the main character speaking in English, 'Nobody likes me. I'm so ugly' (Figure 8.5).

In the digital story, *Lost in the Mirror*, the young film editors use music in the opening sequence to create dramatic tension and ambiguity around the main character and highlight pressures on teenagers to fit in. The main character is

Figure 8.5 Comics making in digital storytelling.

listening to Demi Lovato's 'La La Land' on headphones and the lyrics, 'Who said I can't wear my converse with my dress? ... I have to go out and mingle ... I won't change anything of my life, I'm staying myself tonight'. The film switches into German with English subtitles, and these bilingual students are translating and thinking across their languages to capture meaning and create new connections. They experimented with special effects and film language to heighten the dramatic effect in their digital story. As the emotional tension builds in the character, they reflected on how they 'made the colour fade slightly during the scene where everyone stopped talking when she walked past to show how that is how she is seeing it and that's not really what happened' (ES Student Research Poster). These students are capturing ambiguity in their digital story and increasing inner conflict in the main character. Their editorial decision to slowly bring in cracks on the main film screen is striking as a metaphor for the main character becoming lost. The dramatic moment when the cracks fill the screen is a powerful message about communication and adolescent well-being (Figure 8.6).

In the digital story, *Echoes of Solitude*, the editors incorporated traditional Tamil music into their soundtrack as 'an emotional way of sharing our culture and our tradition into the movie' (KS Student, Team Meeting). The editors capture the hopeful mood of the film with the upbeat music playing at the start, which contrasts with the sadness and loneliness of the main character. These young filmmakers made an imaginative and creative decision to tell the story through the perspective of a main character who never speaks in the film. The editors draw the audience in through the actions and interactions of his movements, gestures, and facial expressions. The soundtrack switches from upbeat music to the very loud noise of chattering students as the main

Figure 8.6 Special effects in digital storytelling.

character enters the classroom and feels out of place. The film editors reveal the main character is dyslexic through the dialogue of the teacher who complains, 'are you done? what is taking you so long? read out what you have written!' The camera pans to the main character's notebook with the title of the lesson (with some letters backwards). The editors increase the tension in the film, as the action shifts to home where the parents try to connect with the main character in Tamil, but he walks away. It is the main character's connection with a stray dog that finally brings hope and a smile to his face.

In the digital story, *Encounter, Conflict, Understanding: The Migrant Worker*, the young film editors created a sense of contrasting perspectives and viewpoints. This digital story shifted the perspective from the employer to the migrant worker and imagined these conflicting realities. The editors draw us into the viewpoint of the migrant worker as she walks through the airport and imagines her future in a new country. The editors shift the action to the factory and create an upbeat mood where the migrant worker is praised for her skilled work by the employer: 'the size is perfect. That's great! Good! Keep going!' The misunderstanding over the watch is carefully orchestrated, and, at the moment of conflict, the migrant worker and employer scream in their first languages, 'This is mine! Give it back!' with subtitles in English, including 'fighting ...'. English is used by the migrant worker to talk to friends, but she feels powerless to act. These young film editors bring in comics making at this point with thought bubbles capturing her lack of agency and the text, 'I don't want to go to work!' (Figure 8.7). The film editors carefully show how this misunderstanding impacts

Figure 8.7 Comics language in digital storytelling.

the employer and migrant worker, and their miscommunication is finally resolved with the support of a translator.

In the post-production stage across these four digital stories, the young film editors learn how to develop dramatic tension through shifting character emotions and mood; changing colours, images and special effects; and experimenting with comics making, languages, and music.

Conclusion

The research and work from the CC project clearly demonstrate how drama can be utilised in multilingual digital storytelling to capture young people's responses to texts and scaffold their production of imaginative digital stories in English and other languages. Our CC pedagogical approach to learning English and other languages is vital at a time when young people's reading enjoyment is at its lowest in 20 years, and findings indicate they would benefit from 'reading being aligned with personal interests and other media that children and young people already recognise as part of their cultural life' (NLT 2025, n.p.). Our creative integration of graphic novels and comics making into storyboarding, scripting and performing digital stories contributes to research findings that comics reading improves comprehension and understanding, as well as motivation, and 'young people who read comics were more engaged with reading' (NLT 2023, n.p.). Many young people on the Sunshine (RAW) project were reading a novel in English (additional/foreign language) for the first time and reflected: 'In *Sunshine*, which is the first English novel I have read, I learnt a lot from it ... everyone has their own advantages ... if we don't look at them critically they are also our friends, part of society' (FSHS Student, Webinar 2024). Drama was used effectively at each stage of the digital storytelling process to enhance students' learning of English and other languages. The digital stories are a powerful testament to young people's dramatic skills and their vision for more collaborative and caring friendships within local and global communities. A lead teacher on the project commented that truth is not always evident at first glance: 'it's through respect and care that we can connect with unfamiliar people and create a community that embodies hope and hospitality' (FSHS Teacher Reflection).

In the final stage of the digital storytelling process, the young people in the Sunshine (RAW) project presented research posters on their digital storytelling work at an international conference on children's and young adult literature and at the 'Care, Community and Hope Festival 2024'. These young digital storytellers had gained the confidence and dramatic skills to stand up and present their digital stories to a global audience.

> I was amazed by the stories presented during the film festival and extremely proud of my students for bravely speaking in English in front of peers and experts during the event. The head teacher remarked that after this

experience, they gained significant confidence and self-esteem they can rely on. They can now believe in their abilities and know they can achieve their goals and fulfil their dreams.

(HJI Teacher)

Drama played a key role in the young people's transformation and courage to share their stories in English and other languages.

Acknowledgements

Critical Connections website: https://goldsmithsmdst.com/

My sincere thanks are due to all who have participated in the Critical Connections project from the UK and across the world. This research project has ethical approval from the university ethics board and signed consent from all participants that their digital stories, photographs, interviews and film footage can be used for educational purposes. Publicly exhibited and shared data, such as posters and digital stories, remain a lasting legacy of the project.

References

Alexandra, D. (2017). Reconceptualising digital storytelling: Thinking through audiovisual inquiry. In M. Dunford & T. Jenkins, eds., *Digital Storytelling: Form and Content*, London: Palgrave Macmillan, pp. 167–182.

Alrutz, M. (2013). Sites of possibility: Applied theatre and digital storytelling with youth, *Research in Drama Education. The Journal of Applied Theatre and Performance*, 18(1), 44–57. https://doi.org/10.1080/13569783.2012.756169

Anderson, J., Chung, Y. C., & Macleroy, V. (2018). Creative and critical approaches to language learning and digital technology: Findings from a multilingual digital storytelling project. *Language and Education*, 32(3), 195–211. https://doi.org/10.1080/09500782.2018.1430151

Anderson, J., & Macleroy, V. (2021). What is a multilingualism activist? Multilingual moves: Changing the mindset of teachers and policy makers. In A. de Medeiros & D. Kelly, eds., *Language Debates*, London: John Murray Learning, pp. 173–184.

Bramley, R., & Rowsell, J. (2024). What sits, what sticks: moving into lived, disruptive, co-produced filmmaking practices in literacy classrooms. *Education*, 3-13, 52(7), 1019–1032. https://doi.org/10.1080/03004279.2024.2357056

Brecht, B. (1935). *Writing the Truth: Five Difficulties*, 11 June. Retrieved from https://revolutionary-socialism.com/wp-content/uploads/2015/03/brecht_fivedifficulties1.pdf

Craft, A. (2011). *Creativity and Education Futures: Learning in a Digital Age*, Stoke on Trent: Trentham.

Cummins, J. (2000). *Language, Power and Pedagogy: Bilingual Children in the Crossfire*, Clevedon: Multilingual Matters.

Cummins, J. (2021). *Rethinking the Education of Multilingual Learners: A Critical Analysis of Multilingual Learners*, Bristol: Multilingual Matters.

Gallagher, K. (2010). Improvisation and education: Learning through? *Canadian Theatre Review*, 143, 42–46. https://doi.org/10.3138/ctr.143.42

Hughes, J., & King, A. (2010). Dual pathways to expression and understanding: Canadian coming-of-age graphic novels. *Children's Literature in Education*, 41(1), 64–84. https://doi.org/10.1007/s10583-009-9098-8

Krosoczka, J. (2023). *Sunshine*, New York: Scholastic.

Lambert, J. (2013). *Digital Storytelling: Capturing Lives, Creating Community*, New York: Routledge.

Lambert, J. (2017). The central role of practice in digital storytelling. In M. Dunford and T. Jenkins, eds., *Digital Storytelling: Form and Content*, London: Palgrave Macmillan, pp. 22–26.

Lambert, J. (5th ed. with Brooke Hessler) (2018). *Digital Storytelling: Capturing Lives, Creating Community*, New York: Routledge.

Linville, H. A., & Vinogradova, P. (2024). *Digital Storytelling as Translanguaging. A Practical Guide for Language Educators*, New York: Routledge.

Macleroy, V. (2024). Drama, English and digital storytelling: Using drama to create digital stories across languages and cultures. *NATE Teaching English*, 35, 68–74.

Macleroy, V. (2025). How can young people's multilingual digital storytelling foster intercultural responsibility and an ethics of care? In E. Bauer, N. Haring & R. Maierhofer, eds., *Mediating Social Challenges: Art, Storytelling and Critical Pedagogies*, Bielefeld University Press, pp. 131–153.

Macleroy, V., Anderson, J., & Chung, Y. C. (2023). Grassroots policymaking in practice: including heritage languages in the critical connections project through agency, activism, and alternative voices. *Current Issues in Language Planning*, 25(5), 590–611. https://doi.org/10.1080/14664208.2023.2221151

Macleroy, V., & Chung, Y. C. (2023). How can digital storytelling open up spaces for activist citizenship where young children create stories of hope and resilience across the world? *IJEC* 55, 441–461. https://doi.org/10.1007/s13158-023-00371-0

McCloud, S. (1994). *Understanding Comics*, New York: Harper Perennial.

National Literacy Trust (2023). Children and young people's engagement with comics in 2023. 11 June. Retrieved from https://literacytrust.org.uk/research-services/research-reports/children-and-young-peoples-engagement-with-comics-in-2023/

National Literacy Trust (2025). Children and young people's reading in 2025. 11 June. Retrieved from https://literacytrust.org.uk/research-services/research-reports/children-and-young-peoples-reading-in-2025/

Neelands, J. (2009). The art of togetherness: Reflections on some essential artistic and pedagogic qualities of drama curricula. *NJ Drama Australia*, 33(1), 9–18. https://doi.org/10.1080/14452294.2009.12089351

Stavrou, S., Charalambous, C., & Macleroy, V. (2019). Translanguaging through the lens of drama and digital storytelling: shaping new language pedagogies in the classroom. *Pedagogy, Culture & Society*, 29(1), 99–118. https://doi.org/10.1080/14681366.2019.1692058

Unity (2019). *WiNDUP*. 11 June. Retrieved from https://www.youtube.com/watch?v=efGqe1j3RNk

Willox, A, Harper, S., & Edge, V. (2012). Storytelling in a digital age: digital storytelling as an emerging narrative method for preserving and promoting indigenous oral wisdom. *Qualitative Research*, 13(2) 127–147. https://doi.org/10.1177/1468794112446105

Winston, J., & Tandy, M. (2001). *Beginning Drama 4–11*, London: David Fulton Publishers.

Chapter 9

Teaching English under Occupation
Classroom Fictions and the World Outside

Raja' Farah, Ghoson Orouq and Maggie Hulson

Introduction

> Story-time is different from clock-time. Clock time, however punctual it may purport to be is distorted and too deceptive. It runs under the illusion that everything is moving steadily forward and the future, therefore, will always be better than the past. Storytime understands the fragility of peace, the fickleness of circumstances, the dangers lurking in the night, but also appreciates small acts of kindness. That's why minorities do not live in clock time. They live in story-time.
>
> Elif Shafak (2024, p. 255)

Shafak's words are those of a consummate storyteller who, once upon a time, learnt English as a foreign language. Her stories are both epic and personal; they tell of now and of then, and they ripple with humanity.

And isn't that what each of us, we teachers, wish for our students? To be able to embrace English as something to swim freely in, to find fluidity between their own personal/cultural history and that of the English context, to form thoughts and share new understandings? This search for enrichment and deep learning is what drives the work described below.

This chapter arises out of a collaboration between educators in Palestine and England and examines the transformative use of 'process drama' and 'Mantle of the Expert' (MoE) in English teaching. In the first section, we lay the ground by discussing the relationship between historical and current Palestinian curricula, still tethered to the vestiges of British colonialism. An emphasis on teacher-centred instruction and discipline, rote learning and summative assessment fails not only to meet modern Palestinian needs but continues to tie teachers to a rationale and ethics not of their own. Furthermore, worsening political instability creates conditions which continually challenge ordinary citizens' lives, including the work of schools.

The development of pedagogical links between drama practitioners in Palestine and England has served to provide a counterpoint to these impositions. In this chapter, we describe examples of classroom practice in two Palestinian schools, supported by an outline of the theoretical approaches employed. We show how carefully structured lessons enhance language learning as students make live connections between classroom fiction and their lived reality. In the first example, Ghoson describes her early endeavours in planning an MoE project with seven-year-olds. As her work develops, she adopts process drama strategies and is surprised by the positive impact on the progress of her class. The second case is a detailed account of an MoE scheme taught by Raja', an experienced secondary English teacher. We demonstrate how a restrictive curriculum can be imaginatively and creatively adapted to meet the needs of students, and through the two practical examples, we reveal how the work provides safe spaces for emotional expression and empowerment.

Finally, we reflect on the power of this pedagogy as students develop English language skills while processing their experiences of displacement, occupation, and resilience. Drama education's potential is highlighted as both a survival strategy and a pedagogical innovation in challenging contexts. This reflexive process is vital for educators seeking liberational approaches to language teaching that honour students' lived experiences while expanding their communicative possibilities.

Our desire to collaborate continues to survive, even thrive, against the odds.

Background: education in Palestine

Palestinian education has been a pillar of Palestinian resilience under occupation, embodying empowerment and resistance amidst persistent challenges. For more than two decades, English gained prominence in Palestine[1] during the British Mandate (1920–1948) as a language of power, becoming a popular second language in schools. The British Mandate effectively ended when the State of Israel was established on Palestinian lands[2] in 1948, based on the British Balfour Promise dated 2 November 1917. The resulting displacement of Palestinians led to the establishment of the United Nations Relief and Works Agency (UNRWA),[3] and fragmented education under Israeli occupation. Gaza was obliged to adopt the Egyptian curriculum for English, while Jordan supplied the West Bank's English curriculum.

The impact of that was to perpetuate curriculum content and teaching methods not necessarily aligned with the needs of Palestinians. However, following the 1993 Oslo Peace Accords[4], Palestinians were granted limited autonomy and administration of Gaza and the West Bank. This allowed for an independent Palestinian curriculum, with English regaining importance for international communication and higher education (Bianchi and Hussein-Abdel Razeq 2017).

Despite ongoing political instability, the Palestinian Ministry of Higher Education collaborated with Macmillan Education to develop the *English for Palestine*[5] textbook series in 2000, introducing English from the first grade (age six). This resulted in a curriculum based on widely accepted principles of second/foreign language pedagogy gradually being implemented for the Occupied

Palestinian Territory (OPT) between 2000 and 2006. The curriculum sought to align with modern ESOL (English for Speakers of Other Languages) trends, promoting English as a vehicle for cultural values and critical thinking as well as for effective communication. However, as noted by Dajani and McLaughlin (2009), the textbook often falls short when it comes to putting these objectives into practice, not helped by the cancellation of a crucial teacher-education programme during the 2000 Intifada.[6] This left Palestinian English teachers and supervisors lacking relevant experience and without the necessary skills to effectively implement new textbook materials. Since then, 'any teacher-training programmes which do offer a course on English Language Teaching (ELT) methods are, unfortunately, focused on theory rather than feasible ideas for practical application in the classroom' (Dajani and McLaughlin 2009, p. 35).

The instability of the Palestinian situation also affects teachers' ability to plan effectively. Plans might be interrupted at any moment and for an uncertain amount of time, forcing educators to adapt hastily, adversely affecting the quality of education they can provide. As Qaimari (2016) explains, living and working in a war zone creates immense stress, self-doubt, and guilt. These intense emotions can undermine positive values, beliefs and attitudes fundamental to shaping a teacher's professional identity. The heavy reliance teacher education has tended to place on traditional didactic teaching methods can leave teachers underprepared and struggling in these extremely testing circumstances.

Even though English is taught from kindergarten to the twelfth grade (aged eighteen) and at university level, according to Zayed and Hussein-Abdel Razeq (2021, p. 7), 'Palestinian students' English language proficiency needs great improvement'. Since English is rarely used by most people in daily life, students find themselves memorising vocabulary and abstract grammar rules; classroom interaction is heavily textbook-driven. Teacher-centred pedagogy, where only the teacher uses the target language, makes it worse. (Bianchi and Hussein-Abdel Razeq 2017). However, Palestinian students are aware of the necessity of English for future university learning and career development, resulting in instrumental motivation. Musleh's (2011) research indicates that the precise social and cultural contexts in which individual Palestinian students live greatly influence their attitude and motivation to study English.

More recently, several initiatives have been introduced to improve the teaching of English. According to Zayed and Hussein-Abdel Razeq (2021, p. 7) these include 'improving teacher education preparation programmes, and cooperating with Nongovernmental Organizations, the British Council, for instance, in conducting professional development workshops for English teachers'. In this context, some educators have made a conscious effort to shift their teaching methods to meet the students' needs (Bianchi and Hussein-Abdel Razeq 2017). The Qattan Centre for Educational Research and Development (QCERD)[7] has been offering workshops and training across disciplines, focusing on aligning methodologies with learning styles, using drama, and fostering communicative teaching strategies. It has successfully equipped participating

English teachers with communicative methodologies for young learners, fostering their reflective and critical practice (Dajani and McLaughlin 2009).

The background to our collaboration

i The Summer School

The germination of our collaboration lies root and branch in the Qattan Foundation's Summer School, which took place in Jordan from 2007 to 2019. Wasim Kurdi, then of the Qattan Foundation based in Ramallah, Palestine, and David Davis, then Professor of Drama at Birmingham University in England, collaborated to write the Drama in Education Summer School programme.[8] Designed to run for two weeks every summer in Jordan,[9] it enabled Palestinian educators and others to study drama theory and practice in the classroom. The attendees came from diverse subject disciplines and educational phases, including teachers of English. Those who were able to complete three modules over three summers gained a Drama in Education Diploma. At the same time, both Kurdi and Davis had varying connections with the National Association for the Teaching of Drama (NATD), a UK-based professional association for Drama teachers. Maggie Hulson, a long-standing NATD member and author of a key drama in education textbook (2006), was therefore invited to be a tutor for several years (2012–2019) on the Summer School, forging productive links with Qattan Foundation tutors and developing an abiding respect for busy Palestinian teachers giving up summer holidays to co-develop progressive pedagogy.

ii Strengthening the links

The connections were further advanced when NATD sponsored Raja' to attend an international Drama conference in Aberdeen (October 2023). This sponsorship was matched by the Qattan Foundation's Cultural Centre in Ramallah, enabling their education specialist, Mutasem Atrash, to also attend the conference. Maggie, by then a member of the executive committee of NATD, was responsible for hosting the Palestinian delegates. We (Maggie, Raja', and others) planned to sustain and develop this contact by collaboratively designing an MoE scheme via email and video conferencing. We managed not only to maintain this contact but also to write it up, despite the latest Israel-Gaza conflict and the rise in settler violence on the West Bank (see Hulson, Farah, Bayley and Atrash 2024). In 2024, NATD repeated their sponsorship, hoping Ghoson would be able to attend two international Drama conferences in England. Unfortunately, because of the nature of the escalating occupation of Palestine, Ghoson was refused a visa. Nevertheless, both Ghoson and Raja' were able to contribute to each conference online.

The A.M. Qattan Foundation's Drama in Education programme served as a transformative experience for us all, a prompt to recognise drama as a powerful pedagogy that has the capacity to deepen learning, foster empathy and bring language to life. The collaboration between the three of us for this chapter stems from a shared commitment to pedagogical innovation; it reflects an ongoing and particular interest in exploring drama as a meaningful approach to English language teaching.

As teachers of English, we (Raja' and Ghoson) have been interested in planning and reflecting on each other's work. We also cooperate in planning new MoE schemes for our students and helping other trainee teachers to plan their own mantle schemes.

Imaginative enquiry: Mantle of the Expert

i Much more than role-play

Mantle of the Expert and process drama have much in common. Both employ fictional contexts and role-play; both are inquiry-based, rather than performance-orientated. Improvisation and responding in the moment within a given situation are also features of both. However, while process drama can focus more on character, 'issues', motivation and story development, MoE schemes address specific curricular demands. For instance, this could be a sequence of planned activities taking place within 'imaginary contexts to generate purposeful and engaging activities for learning'[10] that will require the use and application of the target language.

Created by renowned Drama pedagogue Dorothy Heathcote and developed by such pioneers as Luke Abbot and Tim Taylor[11], MoE is a thriving educational force. It exemplifies Taylor's maxim that 'a pedagogy is only as good as its utility in the classroom' (Taylor 2013). By taking the experience of the learner as its starting point, it enables the teacher to move beyond traditional methodology to a process involving the whole child as a social being.

The first stages of a scheme involve building a responsible team, introducing the fictional client and establishing their request (or 'commission'). For example, the teacher might begin by reading out a letter as if sent by 'National Heritage', inviting the class to map out and plan a leaflet describing a mansion-house tour for tourists whose first language is the target language. As they develop their responsible team, such as map makers or tour guides or graphic artists and so on, the class, alongside the teacher, will decide on tasks and on the roles needed to fulfil them. Crucially, the teacher's planning considers both the curriculum and the specific needs of the class. A first task might be to share their vision of the house, then collaboratively draw a plan of the iconic building. Next, as they begin working on the leaflet, discussion of possible visitors' needs edges students into taking on responsibility, supported by the teacher. At this moment, the teacher would have ready resources and prompts that would enable the class to apply the curricular learning required. Perhaps they must learn cardinal and intercardinal directions in the target language or the vocabulary for key transport needs and facilities. These could be applied to the leaflet in written descriptions or annotated maps, or vocal recordings linked by an (imagined) QR code. As the class works out how to achieve this, mediated activity enables decision-making and concrete plans. They begin to behave as if they are experts. At the same time, they know they are not really experts. Young people are adept at moving between modes, moving between the 'here and now' of the fiction and the 'there and then' of the world beyond. It is a creative facility we all have, practised first in the actions of infant imitation and developed in imaginative play. The imagination is a particular form of human consciousness that, as 'the basis of all creative activity, is an important component of absolutely all aspects of cultural life, enabling artistic, scientific, and technical creation alike' (Vygotsky 2004, p. 9). The fictional context of MoE and carefully sequenced challenges support and expand the developing imagination. At the same time, by the nature of the collaboration and the human-centred approach it provides, guidelines for the application of what is learnt are developed through negotiated decisions.

ii Metaxis

In addition, this pedagogy, this taking on of role responsibility and rising to the challenge, allows the teacher to remain alert to other possible learning areas and to consciously enable them. With the 'power of being in two worlds' (Davis 2014, p. 53), the teacher can offer connections through resonating events, descriptions or objects. The learning here is being guided by the teaching strategies employed and by the choice and unfolding of content.

For example, we could look at a discussion between children in a small group. Collaborative talk, dialogic reasoning and sorting of ideas and views are powerful learning processes where 'a child's ability to consider different points of view on the mental plane depends on actual arguments between children' (Kozulin 1998, p. 63). As the child hears and responds to the ideas of others, they are constructing their own understanding in a social interaction that has a motivating purpose and is both fluid and guided by the teacher. The world in which they live outside the classroom is in dialogue with the world being co-constructed in the classroom. In MoE, the motivating purpose is an imagined demand from the social world, be it designing a hospital garden or working as a team of journalists trying to report an injustice (as in Raja's classroom example that follows). Importantly, the imagined demand has a 'need' at its heart; it is humane and resonates truthfully. The examples of classroom practice we describe below show students rising to the challenge, committing fully to their role-based language learning in the fictional context, despite external disruptions to their schooling. Furthermore, when classwork is structured to enable respectful, validating discussion within the student-to-student-to-teacher triad, it leads to enriched and shared understandings. This kind of learning is measurable and observable, as is demonstrated by Dorothy Heathcote in a publication edited by Myra Barrs for the National Association for the Teaching of English (NATE). The primary school teachers involved in this drama-based project describe how they were 'fascinated at the depth of thought as children became aware of cause and effect, examining and refining their views against the background of other viewpoints and beliefs'. They report that 'Opportunities for organising ideas arose in ways which previously appeared only possible in written work' (Heathcote 1980, p. 23).

iii English as a second language and communicative language teaching

Communicative Language Teaching (CLT) is a pedagogical approach in which 'Language techniques are designed to engage learners in the pragmatic, authentic functional use of language for meaningful purpose' (Brown 2007, p. 241). Process drama and MoE provide a rich pedagogical foundation for applying CLT in the ESOL/EFL classroom. They encourage the natural use of language for communication, inquiry, and problem-solving by immersing the learners in different contexts. These contexts create emotionally engaging, purpose-driven interactions. Consequently, this reflects the goals of CLT, which emphasises authentic language use, student agency, and contextual learning (Richards 2006). Kao and O'Neill (1998) argue that process drama not only fosters fluency and communicative competence but also enhances learners' confidence and motivation by placing them at the centre of the learning process.

Engaging students through drama: classroom examples

i Ghoson's 'Happy Birthday' lesson sequence

I teach at a primary school in Jenin city, working with children aged six to nine. My students are very aware of the ongoing war in Gaza and the daily reality of living under occupation in the West Bank. Many have lost family members, friends, or their homes. They witness tanks and bulldozers tearing through our streets, and sometimes schools are forced to close due to curfews or military raids. They express frustration and a sense of futility about their studies, finding it increasingly difficult to sit in the classroom and simply listen to the teacher. When I witnessed how they were being affected, I felt impelled to implement new teaching strategies that could help them better understand their environment while remaining sensitive to their young age. Therefore, I decided to move away from traditional teaching methods and adopt a more dynamic approach that incorporates drama.

I selected a lesson from the second-grade *English for Palestine* textbook called 'Happy Birthday'. In this lesson, students, aged seven, are expected to know how to tell their age, to ask people about their age, to say 'Happy Birthday', and to be able to express feelings. I decided to teach this lesson using process drama. I created a fictional context: a mother of a wounded boy from Gaza has contacted us to arrange a birthday party for her son, currently being treated in the USA.

Since my students are only aged seven, I found it essential to teach the necessary knowledge in advance: who we are, our location in the world, our language, who opposes us, and the role of the country where the fictional child receives treatment abroad. Some of this preparation included:

- displaying a world map, identifying the location of Palestine and some foreign countries, and focusing on the language of each country
- drawing a map of Palestine and marking the locations of Jenin and Gaza
- teaching 'getting to know you' in English with myself in the role of a foreign journalist

When my students were ready, we sat on the floor in a circle, and I showed the children an imaginary picture of Abdullah. I narrated his story in Arabic, explaining that he is an injured child who travelled with his mother to the USA for treatment. Despite the presence of foreign activists offering him support, he feels sad and lonely, especially with his birthday approaching. The children suggested contacting him and proposed a video call to get to know Abdullah, ask about his condition, and discuss organising a birthday party for him. I agreed with my students that we would imagine making a call with Abdullah, whom I would portray.

We agreed that as soon as I was seated on the chair, I was playing the role of Abdullah, and they would step into their roles as Palestinian children trying to convince him to celebrate his birthday. At one point during the call, one student called out (in Arabic), 'Your voice is breaking up. We can't hear you well', which took me by surprise. It showed how deeply immersed they were in the imagined situation. They asked Abdullah about his condition and expressed their wish to celebrate his birthday. At first, he refused, saying he felt too sad given the circumstances. However, the students gently encouraged him, and one of them suggested that the theme would be about Palestine and said, 'it won't be a regular party; we will make it about Palestine'. So, eventually, he agreed.

Unfortunately, because of a military raid by occupying forces in Jenin immediately after this lesson, schools were forced to close for over ten days. I was worried that by the time we returned, the children might have forgotten all about our project. To my surprise, they came back full of excitement. One of them told me, 'We were counting the days for the raid to end so we could return to school and finish what we started!' Hearing this filled me with relief. We got back to work immediately. The students discussed how they could cheer

Abdullah up, considering that we were in Palestine, he was in the USA, and his birthday was approaching soon. They decided it would be easiest to make a video for him. I didn't give them any instructions; they planned everything themselves. They chose to use balloons, cards, flags, and music in the video. Every single student participated. Some students wrote messages on the cards in English, and others drew pictures. One student grabbed a keffiyeh[12] and wore it; another brought in the Palestinian flag. They wrote 'Happy Birthday' in English and included the phrase 'Free Palestine'. Then, they asked me to film them. They sang 'Happy Birthday' in English to Abdullah while holding the cards, balloons, and, of course, the flag. They also chanted, 'Free Palestine!' Within this imaginative framework, we worked together to, as we Arabs often say, 'create joy out of nothing', finding hope and connection amid the harsh conditions of war.

This experience revealed the profound impact that drama can have on teaching English. By immersing my students in a meaningful and emotionally resonant context, they became more than passive learners. They transformed into active participants, eager to communicate and express themselves in English. This approach gave them a renewed sense of agency and purpose. I witnessed a remarkable shift: children who once struggled to stay engaged became enthusiastic, confident, and willing to speak English.

ii Raja's journalism and Civil Defence lesson sequence

The scheme of work that I describe below grew in part out of a collaboration with colleagues in England: Dr Rebecca Paterson at Manchester University and a secondary teacher, Harry Dixon (an arrangement facilitated by Maggie Hulson).

I had already begun work on a unit from the Palestinian curriculum for tenth graders (15-year-olds), Unit Four: 'Emergency'. I had identified that the team should be journalists investigating the wartime struggles of Civil Defence services. Following online meetings with Rebecca and Harry, I further developed an MoE scheme of work, identifying two more key components:

- (fictional) client: Tate Modern, in Britain
- commission: participating in making a short film to be presented in a virtual exhibition

With the first Unit Four lesson, we learnt new vocabulary about emergencies, Civil Defence services and firefighters in Canada and Britain, discussing the importance of Civil Defence personnel in saving people's lives, along with the names of their tools and equipment. We also read together a story of heroism from this unit, where a young woman is saved from a fire. We then considered the Palestinian context, thinking about the work of Civil Defence workers in the Gaza Strip, working in unprecedented circumstances. By discussing photos from Gaza of the struggle of the Civil Defence to save people's lives, comparing the actual capabilities of equipment with what it should be, and reading quotes about the pictures published on foreign news websites, I was able to extend the language experience for my students.

Using real-life online accounts of Civil Defence workers in Gaza (for example, from Al Jazeera's website) provided us with an opportunity to expand relevant language use even further. For example, one report described how Civil Defence workers in Gaza work around the clock with limited resources and no guarantee of their safety, witnessing horrors. This was an opportunity to learn the language by reading and translating. The following are some quotes from first-hand accounts on that webpage: 'The hardest thing I've seen is the torn bodies of children, the children under the rubble who we can't reach'; 'It drives me crazy that we can't save these people'; 'I've had to tell people that we cannot rescue them. I could see them, but there was no way to reach them. Imagine waiting for death like this'; and 'The Civil Defence is sorely lacking in heavy machinery and equipment needed to move the rubble. Our vehicles are rusty, and if they don't break down from a mechanical problem, the damaged roads and shrapnel hinder their operations'.

To develop the fictional context, we adopted the viewpoint of fictitious foreign journalists and wrote moving sentences (in Arabic and English) about Gazan Civil Defence workers. The students read and reflected on those sentences and agreed to translate any in Arabic into English later. As the students began to take on the role of Civil Defence workers in Gaza, we listened to their planned dialogue in Arabic. The dialogue revolved around what happens during their work and the importance of the media and journalism (they could agree or disagree with each other), followed by a reflection on feelings as I scribed their comments for them to see. We also discussed the importance of the media from their point of view.

This developed into a moment of drama between a foreign journalist who belongs to a team that writes supportively about the victims of war, played by one of the students, and one of the Civil Defence workers in Gaza, played by me. The journalist explored ideas to write about, quoting the people of Gaza, and tried to convince the Palestinian firefighter of the important role of journalism in publishing what is possible to change the painful reality.

To build their in-role teamwork and expertise, the students drew equipment used by the journalists, such as cameras, microphones and cables. Then, each portrayed in a still image what they thought the journalist would be doing. The stills and the equipment were discussed, and ideas were developed through further still images. In this way, each member of the class was building and sharing information about the role of the journalist they were taking on. They then went on to create still images of events reported in previous articles, moving between the perspective of a journalist and the perspective of those they were reporting on. After contemplating the still images, they talked about the meaning of each image and event and deduced the principles and values of the team. Meanwhile, I helped to crystallise the meanings that the students came up with, such as accuracy, objectivity, credibility, integrity, social responsibility, respect for privacy, empathy, and humanity.

The process of naming the team and designing its logo was highly collaborative. The students initially brainstormed numerous words, thinking in both languages, Arabic and English. In English, they came up with and collectively agreed on 'humanity' from the word 'human', but another suggestion, 'echo', was translated from Arabic to English. Some who were more confident in their use of English suggested words like 'lens, lightening, reality, humanity, rescue, future', and others offered Arabic words, translating into English with their group. As a teacher, I accepted and wrote on the board every student's suggested words, even in Arabic, because they needed to feel that their ideas were respected and understood. Finally, they looked at the English words that had been recorded on the board and chose from them to create the logo. After a respectful discussion of further suggestions, 'echo' was chosen, forming 'The Echo of Humanity'. It was impressive. I felt from their discussions that they were capturing the core aim of their role as journalists in the bad days that Palestinians are going through. Teams then collaboratively designed various logos on large sheets of paper. Following a group presentation and discussion of each design, a new, creatively merged logo was drawn, ultimately created via Canva, shared, and displayed in their fictional team workspace. We hung the logo on the wall in an imagined location representing the team's workplace.

The next step was to introduce the client and the commission. I was shifting between 'being in and out of role'[13] to achieve that aim. I had prepared an email, and before playing the role, I made it clear to the students that I was now going to be one of the team members in role: 'We are now going to work as journalists, and I will be a colleague of yours'. In role, I explained: 'I invite you to look at this email and discuss it. We will need then to respond to it'. The email was presented as though sent from the Tate Modern, and a decision was needed before a reply. In role, I presented the email in English and distributed printed copies to contemplate and try to discover what it meant. Then, out of that role, I helped the students understand the email and the required task. It became clear that what was required was to participate in a virtual art exhibition highlighting the suffering of victims of war and humanitarian disasters. We stepped into the role again and agreed as a team on the possible participation, but the students had some conditions. For example, they suggested we request the artists (in reality, Harry Dixon's class in England working on drama presentations for the same fictional exhibition at the Tate Modern) send their artistic work to the journalists to agree on it or not. We also discussed how the task was going to be done. Then, out of role, we wrote the reply email, including the students' ideas and conditions, and agreed to imagine that we had sent it.

At that phase of the collaboration with colleagues in England, we were planning a virtual drama-based learning experience for both my students and Harry's in England, with the Tate Gallery as the 'client' and the students as 'experts' tasked with designing compelling narratives that explore topics such as firefighting in Gaza, displacement, resistance, and care in crisis, to create a new virtual exhibition on the theme of global solidarity and humanitarian courage. Rebecca Patterson played the role of the museum curator. She created audio material and a video to talk about the museum's vision – a meaningful opportunity to extend my students' repertoire of English. The students first listened for meaning and then discussed their understanding together to conclude what was said about the museum and its vision. One of them explained her understanding to the others in Arabic: 'This kind of art could be very relevant to our written stories' messages. Our participation is an opportunity to help people learn about the suffering of others and talk about it while sharing thoughts and feelings'. Soon, the students were preparing written pieces on the agreed-upon topics, as the final task was to create short films weaving together journalistic narrative and dramatic storytelling. We planned to schedule a video conference between the two groups of our students as a simulated Tate Modern briefing, but unfortunately, we were not able to achieve that. We were disrupted by the situation in Ramallah, which had significantly deteriorated since we had first met as a group online, and by the inevitable time constraints in both the Palestinian and UK school and university systems.

However, my students created some stories as if they were written by the journalists and sent them to our online messenger group. The following are some examples of the students' real stories and messages shaped by their role as journalists:

> She filmed the war until it swallowed her. Her camera outlived her but not her truth. Fatima didn't just show Gaza. She became its lens.

> Ali saved others until no one could save him. The fire took him while he was trying to put it out.

> Where cameras were crushed, let your paintbrushes roll. Where pens were snapped, let colours bleed truth. Let your art scream where voices were muted—where pens were crushed and ambulances became coffins.

We stopped there, but it is an open-ended activity in that it may leave many students reflecting on what they have been doing in that MoE experience.

Conclusions

In this chapter, we have discussed how a drama-based pedagogical approach not only enhances the students' engagement and their proficiency in English but also cultivates critical thinking, empathy, and a sense of agency. We have experienced first-hand how drama offers an engaging context for authentic language use, employing the universally innate capacity for 'play' that pre-exists in humans and enabling communication in ways that mirror real-life situations (Bessadet 2022). We have demonstrated how, rather than simply memorising vocabulary or grammar rules, students have actively participated in meaningful exchanges as they develop both fluency and accuracy in speech (Dawoud, Hasim, and Saad 2023). Our experience has shown us that incorporating dramatic activities enhances not only language skills but also emotional, cognitive, and social development. We have seen how role-playing and performance help learners overcome anxiety, build confidence, and tap into their creativity (Shorna and Suchona 2023). Our own classroom work echoes others' accounts in showing that drama-based techniques increase motivation and bring authenticity to classroom interactions, fostering a more dynamic and student-centred learning environment (Ali and Kani 2024). Moreover, along with other scholars, we propose that drama promotes cultural awareness, encouraging learners to explore diverse perspectives and worldviews (Angélianawati 2019). Consequently, a drama-based pedagogy enhances linguistic competence by supporting holistic learner growth.

A key argument of ours has been that traditional techniques, such as rote memorisation of grammar rules, repetitive drill-based exercises and the exclusive use of decontextualised dialogues, foster a disconnect between students' needs and the curriculum, leaving them questioning the relevance of learning English. This gap between the curriculum and the students' experience of the world outside school not only undermines meaningful engagement but also highlights a pressing need for a more authentic and dynamic learning environment that connects language skills to real-world applications, as Dajani and McLaughlin (2009) conclude. The potential of drama as a pedagogical tool should be more widely heeded, and we continue to develop our own teacher education with the A.M. Qattan Foundation by working closely with other teachers in Palestine and internationally to facilitate the application of drama-based pedagogy.

Notes

1. Here we use the term Palestine to refer to the historical Palestine (pre-1948), which largely corresponds to the present-day territory of the state of Israel along with the Gaza Strip and the West Bank and East Jerusalem.
2. In 1948 Israel was established on most of Mandatory Palestine with the exception of the central hilly part, known as the West Bank of Jordan (which was annexed to Jordan), and a small enclave to the South adjoining Egypt, known as the Gaza Strip, which was administered by Egypt.
3. The 1948 creation of Israel led to a major refugee crisis, displacing roughly 750,000 Palestinian Arabs. In response, the UN established UNRWA to assist these refugees, subsequently opening schools in camps across the region starting in the 1960s (UNRWA 2013). These UNRWA schools now comprise nearly a quarter of all schools in the Occupied Palestinian Territories (Dajani & McLaughlin 2009).
4. The first Intifada (1987–1993) was a popular, peaceful uprising of Palestinians in the West Bank and Gaza Strip aimed at ending Israel's occupation of those territories and creating an independent Palestinian state. The first Intifada ended with the signing of the first Oslo Accords, which provided a framework for peace negotiations between Israel and the Palestinians.

5 We use the term Palestine here to refer to the West Bank including West Jerusalem and the Gaza Strip.
6 The Second Palestinian Intifada began on September 28, 2000, after Ariel Sharon's controversial visit to Al-Aqsa Mosque ignited clashes. This uprising was marked by intensified military confrontations, widespread incursions, and extensive destruction in the West Bank and Gaza, including the Jenin camp invasion, resulting in 4,412 Palestinian deaths. In 2002, Israel also began constructing the separation wall.
7 The A.M. Qattan Foundation is independent, developmental and not-for-profit, serving culture and education in Palestine and the Arab world, with a focus on children, teachers, and young talents. The Foundation was established and registered in 1993 in the United Kingdom and began its operations in Palestine in 1998. Today, the Foundation works through its cultural centres in Ramallah, Gaza, and the Mosaic Room in the United Kingdom. See: https://qattanfoundation.org
8 An account of this will be published in *The Journal for Drama in Education*, scheduled for Autumn 2025.
9 Under Israeli occupation travel between the Palestinian territories is restricted, therefore it was more straightforward for Palestinians to obtain travel permits for Jordan than for other parts of their own country.
10 See https://www.mantleoftheexpert.com, introductory page.
11 Luke Abbot studied for his MA under Dorothy Heathcote in 1980. He later initiated the Mantle of the Expert network then joined by Tim Taylor as the network became mantleoftheexpert.com (mantleoftheexpert.com), a rich resource offering far-reaching articles, advice and examples.
12 A keffiyeh is a traditional Palestinian scarf.
13 'One of the most distinctive features of Dorothy Heathcote's approach is the way the teacher moves between the world of the fiction and the classroom, stepping in and out of role. Heathcote's approach is distinctive because the teacher continually shifts roles, a fluidity [that] mirrors children's imaginative play'. Tim Taylor, paper for NATD Conference June 2025.

References

Ali, N., & Kani, Z. G. (2024). Using drama in English Language Teaching: Primary and secondary school teachers' perspectives and practices. *Novitas-ROYAL*, 18(2), 183–203. https://files.eric.ed.gov/fulltext/EJ1446810.pdf

Angélianawati, L. (2019). Using drama in the EFL classroom. *Journal of English Teaching*, 5(2), 125–133.

Bessadet, L. (2022). Drama-based approaches in English Language Teaching. *Arab World English Journal*, 13(1), 525–533.

Bianchi, R., & Hussein-Abdel Razeq, A. (2017). The English language teaching situation in Palestine. In R. Kirkpatrick, ed., *English Language Education Policy in the Middle East and North Africa*. Cham, Switzerland: Springer, pp. 147–169.

Brown, H. (2007). *Principles of Language Learning and Teaching*. Englewood Cliffs, NJ: Prentice Hall.

Dajani, D., & McLaughlin, S. (2009). Implementing the first Palestinian English Language curriculum: A need for teacher empowerment. *Mediterranean Journal of Educational Studies*, 14(2), 27–47.

Davis, D. (2014). *Imagining the Real: Towards a New Theory of Drama in Education*. London: IoE Press/Trentham Books.

Dawoud, L., Hasim, Z., & Saad, M. R. M. (2023). Effect of drama techniques on EFL speaking fluency and accuracy. *Journal of Southwest Jiaotong University*. https://scite.ai/reports/effect-of-drama-techniques-on-9O1OR5jb

Heathcote, D. (1980). Drama as context for talking and writing: The Ozymandias saga at Broadwood Junior School. In M. Barrs, ed., *Drama as Context: NATE Papers in Education*. Aberdeen: NATE in association with Aberdeen University Press, 4–24.

Hulson, M. (2006). *Schemes for Classroom Drama*. Stoke on Trent: Trentham Books.

Hulson, M., Farah, R., Bayley, A., & Atrash, M. (2024). The Grit – catching the mantle. *The Journal for Drama in Education*, 38(2), 15–32.

Kao, S.-M., & O'Neill, C. (1998). *Words into Worlds: Learning a Second Language Through Process Drama*. Santa Barbara, CA: Greenwood Publishing.

Kozulin, A. (1998). *Psychological Tools: A Sociocultural Approach to Education*. Cambridge, MA: Harvard University Press.

Musleh, R. Y. (2011). *Language Learning Motivation: The Palestinian Context. Attitudes, Motivation, and Orientations*. PhD, University of Barcelona.

Qaimari, B. (2016). Exploring teachers' professional identity in the context of war zone: A case study from Palestine. *American Journal of Educational Research*, 4(2A), 15–24.

Richards, J. C. (2006). *Communicative Language Teaching Today*. Cambridge: Cambridge University Press.

Shafak, E. (2024). *There Are Rivers in the Sky*. New York: Viking.

Shorna, S. A., & Suchona, I. J. (2023). Incorporating drama in English Language Teaching: A case study at a private university in Bangladesh, *International Journal of Research and Innovation in Social Science*, 7(9), 1284–1290.

Taylor, T. (2013). *Why Lev Vygotsky Keeps Me Awake at Night*. Retrieved from: https://www.mantleoftheexpert.com

UNRWA (2013). *The Harmonized Results Report*. Retrieved from: https://www.unrwa.org/system/files/2013_harmonised_results_report.pdf

Vygotsky, L. S. (2004) Imagination and creativity in childhood. *Journal of Russian and East European Psychology*, 42(1), 7–97.

Zayed, N., & Hussein-Abdel Razeq, A. (2021). Palestinian high school students' attitudes towards studying English language and culture. *International Journal of Arabic-English Studies*, 21(2), 7. https://doi.org/10.33806/ijaes2000.21.2.1

Index

Pages in *italics* refer to figures and pages followed by 'n' refer to notes.

access 43, 46n1, 59, 84, 104, 124; accessible 52, 67, 88; inaccessible 97; linguistic access 68
'active Shakespeare' 8, 49–52, 54, 57, 60; *see also* rehearsal room pedagogy
activist citizenship 11, 112
adaptation 19, 22–26, 30–31, 45, 51; literary adaptation 7, 18, 20, 31, 52; *see also* transmedia
affective 99; affective engagement 9
agency 21, 26, 28, 51, 114, 127, 139, 142; learner agency 3, 5, 111; student agency 12–13, 71, 137; teacher agency 91
A Level 25, 65, 73n2
All-Party Parliamentary Group (APPG) 3–4, 31n3
assessment 4, 10–11, 23, 25, 31, 36, 40, 44–46, 51, 96–97, 131; peer and self-assessment *118*; spoken language assessment 32n5; *see also* Curriculum & Assessment Review; examinations
attitude 40, 53, 56, 68, 73, 133; authorial attitude 24, 34; colonial attitude 38; to reading 4; to texts 65; to writing 8
Atwood, M.: *The Handmaid's Tale* 100
audience 18, 21, 23, 25, 55–56, 60, 66, 72, 101, 103, *118*, 122, 126; global 124, 128; imagined 102; spectators 36, 70; theatre 29, 33
autonomy 44; independence 53; professional autonomy 3

Barrs, M. 2, 5, 9, 63, 66, 69, 99, 101, 104, 106, 137; drama in the head 7, 99, 107; drama on paper 63, 66, 71, 99

Beowulf 7, 9–10, 66–73, 73n3
bilingual: note-taking 89; students 126; *see also* multilingual
Black Lives Matter 35
Bolton, G.: metaxis 78; reflection 77
Brecht, B.: gestus 69; writing the truth 113
Bryer, T., Pitfield, M., & Coles, J. *Drama at the Heart of English* 2, 8, 64, 101

canonical knowledge 4, 96; classic texts 7, 34; literature 34; texts 24, 67; understanding 7, 95
collaboration 10, 14n3, 23–24, 49, 55, 60, 85, 90–91, 120; approaches 8, 13; collaborative analysis 77, 80–81, 84; discussion 42; exploration 76; filmmaking 111; friendships 128; international 1, 5, 11, 131, 134–136, 139, 141; knowledge 77; process 23; reading 6; research 76; space 43, 49, 51; talk 10, 12, 136; team 2; *see also* ensemble
colonialism 36–43, 131; Anglocentric 7, 97; coloniality 34–39, 42; colonial legacy 33, 42; Eurocentric 40, 98; Eurocentrism 41, 44; Western-centric 38
Common English Forum 3–4
communication 126, 133, 142; communicative modes 2; global 115; international 132; language for communication 137; miscommunication 128
Communicative Language Teaching (CLT) 5, 137

Index   147

confidence: academic confidence 79; communicative 97, 107, 137; examination 12, 105; lack of 25, 37; multilingual 115; student confidence 9, 11, 40, 51, 53, 102–108, 128–129; teacher confidence 28, 37
constraints 49, 52, 96; exam 102; of occupation 11; time 142
Covid-19/Covid 35, 49, 52–53, 60; restrictions 3; socially distanced 49, 52, 60
creativity 2, 5, 31, 34, 39, 55, 65, 99, 103, 108, 124; creative approaches 22, 49, 51–53; creative-critical 12, 64, 113–114; creative endeavour 23; creative-expressive 7, 40; engagement 50, 54; facility 136; freedom 124; intellectual creativity 14; of learners 6, 12, 45, 56, 104, 143; learning 20, 89; playful creativity 14; practitioners 28; process 24, 31, 70; re-creation 24; response 1; skills 18; spaces 79; storytelling 111; subject 3; of teachers 3; thinking 45; translanguaging 77; *see also* writing
critical appreciation 52; awareness 62; distance 69; imagination 98–99; insights 65; language awareness 113, 115; literacy 43–44, 113; practice 134; response 64, 68, 100; thinking 113, 142
Critical Connections 5, 12, 111–112, 116, *118*, 129; *see also* multilingual digital storytelling
criticality 36, 40, 43, 73; in relation to creativity 5–6, 34, 65, 99
culture 6, 24, 40, 51, 122, 126; Arabic culture 144n7; artefacts 45, 113; authority 22; awareness 143; centre 134, 144n7; contexts 133; cultural activism 112; culturally distant 50; culture and identity 79; cultures and languages 88, 114–116; different cultures 34, 78; diverse 96; folk culture 112; hegemony 96–97; history 131; imperialism 35–36; intercultural conflict 124; knowledge 71; Korean culture 12; life 136; lives of learners 12; norms 97; responsive 10, 77, 91; wars 4; *see also* multicultural
curriculum 3–5, 13, 24, 33, 35–37, 40, 43–44, 51, 80, 90, 135; English/Language Arts 1–2, 6–8, 34, 49, 52, 95–97, 108; ESOL 133, 143; in Gaza 132; 'knowledge rich' 4; Palestinian 139; in Singapore 14n3; in West Bank 132
Curriculum & Assessment Review 3, 19, 33, 40

decolonising/decolonial 36, 40; assessment 44; education 36–37, 43; literature teaching 4; method 40, 42; pedagogy 4, 10, 34, 40, 45; research 37; strategy 33, *41*; teaching 34, 44
deficit 102; deficit narratives 103; linguistic deficit 38, 79, 91; professional deficit 25
democracy 112; democratic process 21
de Waal, K.: *My Name is Leon* 19, 26–27, 30
dialogic methods 42; pedagogy 10, 41; practices 8; reasoning 136; space 49, 54; teaching 51
dialogue 18, 29, 58, 90, 118, 122, 125, 127, 136; classroom dialogue 10, 63, 83, 89, 140, 143; professional dialogue 76–77
Dickens, C.: *Great Expectations* 7, 19, 21, 23, 25–26, 29–30
digital media 1, 6, 11, 62, 115; digital devices 56; Digital Transformations 73n3; filmmaking 12; landscape 11; moving-image 11, 119, 122; realm 59; storytelling 11, 111–129; technologies 5, 55; *see also* video
diversification 34–36
Drama (as discrete subject) 5–6, 18–20, 31, 34, 46n3, 62, 72, 99, 134–135
drama approaches: antiphonal reading 57; choral reading/speaking 51, 57; collective voice 57–58; freeze-frame 5; hot-seating 5, 25, 29; improvisation 30, 52, 72, 81, 99, 135; inquiry-based 5, 135; 'Mantle of the Expert' (MoE) 3, 5, 131–142, 144n11; mime 3, 6, 10, 12, 81–91; playscripts 20, 30; 'process drama' 2, 5, 52, 54, 131, 135, 137–138; Readers' Theatre 6, 57; scripting/script writing 6, 21, 23, 27, 116, 118, 120–122, 128; still-image 5, 63, 140; tableaux 26, 52; *see also* embodiment; role
drama concepts: 'drama in the head' 7, 99, 107; drama in the heart 9;

'drama on paper' 63, 66, 71, 99; 'dual affect' 85; enactment 6–8, 28, 42, 45, 60, 66, 69, 73, 105; framing 71–72, 105; inside out/from the inside 7, 9, 50, 85, 98–99, 101, 104, 125; learning through 114; in the moment/immediate 9, 18, 42, 66, 85–86, 100, 102, 135; *see also* educational drama
'drama-in-English' 1–2, 5–7, 13, 22, 34, 36, 40–41, 43, 46, 62, 72, 98–99, 103; drama-inflected 3, 5–6, 9, 12, 41, 96, 107; 'reading through drama' 44
drawing 8, 12, 50, 54, 86, 90, 118, 138

educational drama 52
embodiment 2, 6, 8, 12, 34, 59, 69, 73, 77, 82, 86–89, 107; composition 106; 'bodiliness' 5; bodily 69, 73, 102; embodied 28, 66, 68, 73, 76, 80, 82, 91; embodied approaches 12, 95–109; embodied/disembodied space 59; experience 83, 85–86, 88–90; learning 77, 84, 91; potential 56
empathy 99–100, 119, 123–124, 135, 141–142
empowerment 132; 'Empowered English' 9, 99, 108
engaged pedagogy 3, 98; disengagement 7, 24, 88, 95
English for Speakers of Other Languages (ESOL) 133, 137; English as an Additional Language (EAL) 90; second language acquisition 81, 90; *see also* bilingual; language proficiency
English language 80, 116, 133; English Language exam 1, 96–97
English Language Teaching (ELT) 11, 133, 135
English Mastery 38, 46n7
enjoyment 6, 13, 26, 51, 101; fun 55, 95; reading enjoyment 4, 20, 31n1, 128; teacher enjoyment 14; wit 14, 100; witty 12, 55, 59; *see also* pleasure
ensemble 10, 24, 31
epistemology 39; epistemological diversity 43–45; epistemological hierarchy 39–41; *see also* knowledge
examinations 73n2, 96, 109n2; exam prep 95–99, 102, 108; exams 31n2, 40, 45, 50, 96, 109n1

feature-spotting 97; technique-spotting 102
filmmaking 11–12, 111, 113, 116–117, *118*; cinematography 122; *see also* digital media
frame/framing *see* drama concepts

Garcia Lorca, F.: *The House of Bernarda Alba* 43
gaze 2, 39, 67
Gibson, R. 8, 20–21, 24, 50–52, 54, 96; learner-centredness 57; *see also* 'active Shakespeare'
Globe Theatre 50
gothic 9, 72

Hansberry, L.: *A Raisin in the Sun* 33, 45
Heathcote, D. 2, 10, 52, 63–64, 66, 69–71, 73, 77, 101, 135, 137, 144n11, 13; 'press for language' 10, 64; selective signing 71; *see also* role
hooks, b. 3, 44, 96, 98–99; hooksian 100, 103; *see also* embodied approaches
Hourd, M. 63
humane 136; English as a humane subject 1, 101

identity 19, 30, 35, 41, 68, 78–79, 111, 115; multicultural identity 35; professional identity 133
imagination 2, 22, 50, 52, 59, 66–67, 70, 77, 90, 98–99, 103–108, 111, 118, 136; make-believing 62; 'what if?' 2, 13, 116, 120; as if world 115; *see also* play; role
improvisation *see* drama approaches
inclusive pedagogy 2; approaches 10, 43, 76; curriculum 33; environment 28; spaces 91
inspection 4, 25; *see also* Ofsted

Jackson, S.: *The Haunting of Hill House* 100, 102, 108

Kneehigh Theatre Company 23
knowledge 3, 10–11, 39–44, 46, 59, 77, 138; academic 36; acquisition 35; canonical 4, 96; cultural 71; funds of 79; gaps 38, 90; knowledge for writing 76, 81, 84; knowledge-rich 4, 38, 96; language 89, 116; literary 22; professional 2; real world 5; subject 37, 80, 85–86, 88

Language Arts *see* curriculum
language proficiency 79–80, 88, 90, 133; languaging (process) 8, 90; linguistic repertoires 76, 78, 84, 89; *see also* translanguaging
learner-centred 5, 8, 12, 49–50, 58; learner-centeredness 57
Lee, H.: *To Kill a Mockingbird* 26, 36, 65
lighting *29*, 45, 83–84, 124
Lit Circles 43; play circles 43–44; story circle 113
literacy 2, 9, 11–13, 46n7, 63–64, 76–77, 80–87, 91, 111; critical literacy 43–44, 113; digital 116; multilingual 114; National Literacy Trust 4, 20, 95; PIRLS 4, 7, 14n2; racial 34
literary adaptation 18, 20
literature *see named authors*
Lit in Colour 33, 97

Mantle of the Expert *see* drama approaches
'metaxis' 6, 78–79, 85, 87, 91, 136; *see also* drama concepts
mood: of a character 128; of a scene *29*, 54–56, 123–124, 126–127
Morpurgo, M.: *War Horse* 18, 20–21, 31
multicultural 35, 50–51
multilingual: activism 114; audiences 122; digital storytelling 111–129; knowledge 84; learners 3, 5–6, 8, 11, 77, 79–81, 85, 88–91, 115–116; literacy 114; meaning-making 76, 87; plurilingual 116; practices 91; repertoires 115; resources 79, 84; stories 12
multimodal: approaches to learning 11; aspects of lesson 90; entry points to language 80; expression 76, 84; intervention 66; multisensory 77; representation 86; space 82; storytelling 1; techniques 77
music *29*, 30, 33, 54–56, 125–126, 128, 139; *see also* sound

narrator 67–68, 101; first-person 68, 117; teacher-as-narrator 101
National Association for the Teaching of Drama (NATD) 134
National Association for the Teaching of English (NATE) 137
National Education Union 36

National Literacy Trust *see* literacy
National Theatre 18, 21, 28, 31
neoliberal 3

observing *see* visualisation
OECD (Organisation for Economic Co-operation and Development) 4
Ofsted 4
O'Neill, C. 62; fictional worlds 65; process drama 2; teacher-in-role 66; writing-in-role 71

pace 55–56, 101
Palestine 111, 131, 134, 138–139; education in 132, 143; history of 143n1–143n2, 144n5, 144n7; location of 138; occupation of 134, 139
pandemic *see* Covid-19
performance 6, 11, 134; assessment of 45; examination performance 96; measuring schools' performance 4; *The Merchant of Venice* 52, 57–60; online 45; performance-based activities 45, 50; skills 45; texts 56; theatrical performance 25; *see also* adaptation; enactment; theatre roles
personal development 20; experiences 124; freedom 100; history 131, 143; impact 27; interests 128; personal connection 43–44; personally meaningful 7; personal objects 113, 119–120; reflection 53; story 117; storytelling 5
perspectival learning 65
physical 12; decolonisation 35; demonstration 84; energy 98; environment 49, 52, 56, 60, 107; movement 2, *29*, 45, 57, 84; responses 68–69; restrictions 57; physical activities 21, 28, 50, 69; physicalise 5, 72; physicality 21; physically active 2, 22; physically interact 49, 107; *see also* embodiment; enactment
play 5, 23, 103, 107, 136, 142; creativity 14; dramatic play 5, 99; embodied play 99; embodiment 8; exploration 29; play circles 43; player 50; playful activity 6, 13; playfulness 8, 13–14, 20–21, 23, 30, 49, 55; playwright 25, 30, 113; role-play *see* role; adaptation; enjoyment

pleasure 13, 98; pleasure in reading 7, 22, 46n7, 96, 108; pleasure in writing 13, 96, 108; *see also* enjoyment
Priestley, J. B.: *An Inspector Calls* 25
Progress in International Reading Study (PIRLS) *see* literacy
progressive practice 8, 63, 134
Project-Based Language Learning (PBLL) 12, 112
props 12, 25, 45, 57–59, 63, 113, 122–123

Qattan Centre for Educational Research and Development 133; Qattan Foundation 134–135, 143; summer school 134

Raciolinguistics 38
reader response theory 1, 62; textual gaps 65; *see also* Rosenblatt, L.
reading: achievement 7; aloud 20, 30, 44; analytical 99; antiphonal 57; assessment 7; attitudes 4; choral 57; close 56; collaborative 6; comics 128; curriculum 2, 6; diversifying reading 34–35; drama in the head *see* drama-in-English; drama in the heart *see* drama-in-English; dramatised reading 44, 56, 58–59, 102; embodied reading *see* embodiment; experience of reading 101; habits 4; immersive reading 99; 'from the inside out' 7; literary reading 1, 22, 34, 62, 95, 107; for pleasure 4, 7, 13, 20, 22, 96, 128; process of 66, 101; reading extracts 101; reading impact 95; response to 9; *see also* drama approaches; reader response theory
reflection 64; critical 44; language reflection 85–86; reflection on feelings 140; student reflection 72, 86, 111, 114, 116; teacher 53, 128; written 65, 81, 86–89
reflexivity 9, 44; reflective dialogue 78; reflexive process 132
rehearsal room pedagogy 2, 7, 18, 20–21, 25, 28, 30–31; techniques 10, 18, 50, 58
representation 12, 26, 45; embodied 82; multimodal 86; self-representation 71; symbolic 77; visual 86, 88
risk 34, 79
role 2, 5–7; facilitator role 27; narrator role 67; role-play 2–9, 42, 52, 57, 64–66, 113, 135; role responsibility 136; shadowy role 67; spectator role 64; teacher-in-role 9, 66–69, 71, 101, 138, 141; teamwork in role 140; theatre roles 29; whole-class role-play 14; writing-in-role 7, 9–10, 51–52, 62–67, 70–71, 99, 104–105; *see also* drama approaches
Rosenblatt, L. 2
Royal Shakespeare Company (RSC) 20, 24–25, 31, 50; *see also* rehearsal room pedagogy

scaffold 45; scaffolding learning 12, 88, 114–116, 128; writing frames 9, 97, 102; *see also* Vygotsky
school systems 3; accountability 3–4, 40; assessment-driven curriculum 8, 96–97; collaborative practices 8, 11, 49, 53, 90, 96, 120, 131; didactic pedagogies 96, 108, 133
script 6, 19, 21–27, 50–52, 57–59, 116–126; playscripts 20, 30
semiotic 8, 26, 63, 84; resonating objects 112–113, 118–120, 125, 136; semiotic repertoires 79, 91; *see also* sign
Shakespeare: academic study of 20; *King Lear* 65; *The Merchant of Venice* 6, 8, 10, 14, 49–56; perceptions of 50; productions 20; *see also* 'active Shakespeare'; Gibson, R.
Shelley, M.: *Frankenstein* 7, 9–10, 65–66, 72
Shelley, P.: *Ozymandias* 63–64, 66
sign 63; bodily sign 71; signifying absence 58; signifying status 58; visual 63; vocal 71
social: activity of the classroom 8, 14, 49–51, 53–54, 85; approaches 13; context 133; development 143; media 119
social constructivism 2; *see also* Vygotsky
social justice 13, 35, 44, 96, 112, 116
socio-cultural processes 18, 123, 126, 139; contexts 101, 112, 125; perspective 14; resources 100; understandings 12
sound: design 29; effects 113; music 29, 54–56, 119, 123–126, 128, 139; soundscape 30; soundtrack 12, 28, 54–56, 59, 124, 126; 'Soundtrack This Scene' 54, 56
Soyinka, W.: *The Lion and the Jewel* 43

spaces 11; aesthetic 76, 90; creative 79, 118; dialogic 49, 54, 113; digital 115; inclusive 91; intellectual 2; learning 49; liminal 85; multimodal 82; online 49, 54, 56–57, 59–60; opening up space 11, 43, 112; pedagogical 2; physical 21, 42, 60, 63, 67, 69, 82–83; protected 79; public 35; safe 78, 80, 132; space to write 105, 108; symbolic use of 84; transformative 84, 91; translanguaging 77–79, 84
speaking and listening (S&L) 6, 10; oracy 20, 23, 27, 29–30; Oracy Education Commission 10, 41; spoken language 1, 29, 32n5; talk-rich 10, 44
spectator 36, 64, 70, 78, 85; *see also* metaxis
Stevenson, R. L.: *Strange Case of Dr. Jekyll and Mr. Hyde* 42–43
story 21–23, 106–107; co-creation 107; crafting 108; story-based pedagogy 113; storyboarding 116, 118–123, 128; storyline 97; story theatre 24; *see also* storytelling
storytelling 5, 40–41, 46, 67, 111–112; digital storytelling process 115–117; dramatic storytelling 142; multilingual digital storytelling 1, 11, 111–113, 116–117, 128; story circle 113; storytelling spaces 112
student ownership 8, 21, 51, 73, 85, 114
student-teachers 9, 62; *Beowulf* project 67–70, 72; *Frankenstein* 72–73; trainee teachers 37, 135; *see also* teacher education
symbol 84, 97, 117; costumes 58; interpretation 8; literary symbolism 43; meanings 115; narrative 36; object 121; props 12, 59; representation 77; symbolic action 69; symbolic use of space 84; *see also* Brecht, B.

teacher education: initial teacher education in England 36; Postgraduate Certificate in Education (PGCE) 4, 62, 72, 73n1, 73n3; by the Quattan Foundation 143; teacher education in Palestine 133
tension: dramatic tension 9, 65, 71, 114, 120–128; professional tensions 36
theatrical: adaptation 21; interpretation 18; performance 24; theatricality 6, 18

transformative pedagogy 2, 113; drama as 12, 111–115
translanguaging 76–77, 115; drama-rich translanguaging 76, 91; embodied 82; learning environments 79; pedagogies 80–81; translanguaging aesthetic spaces 90
transmedia 62, 67; transmedia adaptation 67

United Nations Relief and Works Agency (UNRWA) 132, 143n3

video 55, 81–82, 84, 90, 104, 124, 139; call 138; clips 52, 56; conferencing 134; recording 57, 81
virtual: spaces 11, 54, 60, 139, 141–142
visualisation 62, 65–66, 72; of drama 62, 64; visual depiction 86, 88; visual dimension of texts 8, 62, 67; representation 86–88; stimuli 84; of writing 9
voice: collective voice 57–58; diversity of voices 79, 103, 142; dominating voices 33, 35–36; lack of voice 34, 40, 65; reader's voice 57, 102; student voice 12, 28, 41, 53, 96, 102–106, 111, 119; tone of voice 45; voices of activism 35; voice-over 125
Vygotsky, L. 3, 5, 70, 103, 136; *see also* imagination; social constructivism

well-being 12, 53, 103–107, 126; Well-Being (RAW) project 117
White Saviour Trope 36
Williams, R. 2; 'dramatized society' 2
writing: analytical writing 96, 99; creative 62–63, 65, 96–98, 103, 105–108, 116, 118–121; creative writing workshop 116–118, 120; in the curriculum 6; developing students' writing 8; drama on paper 66; embodied composition 106; essay writing 101; examination writing 97, 103; explanation texs 81; formulaic writing 102; linguistic knowledge for writing 81–82; for pleasure 13; prompt for writing 66, 97; translanguaging writing strategies 89; writing dialogue 118; writing-in-role 27, 51–52, 62–67, 73, 99, 105; *see also* scaffold; script

Zoom 2, 12, 49, 52, 54, 56–59; zoom in 106

For Product Safety Concerns and Information please contact our EU representative GPSR@taylorandfrancis.com Taylor & Francis Verlag GmbH, Kaufingerstraße 24, 80331 München, Germany

Printed and bound by CPI Group (UK) Ltd, Croydon, CR0 4YY

14/04/2026

02089737-0020